Lua Programming Made Simple

Your Beginner's Journey into Efficient Scripting

Javier Struwig

Table of Contents

Chapter 1: Introduction to Lua

What is Lua?

Lua is a lightweight, high-level programming language designed primarily for embedded use in applications. Created in 1993 by a team at the Pontifical Catholic University of Rio de Janeiro in Brazil, Lua (which means "moon" in Portuguese) has grown from humble beginnings to become one of the most popular scripting languages in certain domains.

What makes Lua special isn't just its clean syntax or its performance—it's the language's remarkable simplicity and flexibility. With a tiny core and minimal syntax, Lua manages to provide powerful features that make it suitable for everything from game development to configuration files, and from web applications to embedded systems.

A Brief History of Lua

The story of Lua begins in the early 1990s at the Computer Graphics Technology Group (Tecgraf) in Brazil. The team, led by Roberto Ierusalimschy, Luiz Henrique de Figueiredo, and Waldemar Celes, needed a language for two projects at the state-owned oil company Petrobras. Rather than adopt an existing language with licensing restrictions or excessive complexity, they created their own.

The first version of Lua was released in 1993, focusing on data description rather than a full programming language. By Lua 2.1 (1995), the language had evolved to include functions. With each subsequent release, Lua grew more powerful while maintaining its core philosophy of simplicity and efficiency.

Today, Lua is on version 5.4 (as of this writing), and it continues to excel at what it was designed for: being an embeddable scripting language that's easy to learn, easy to integrate, and powerful enough for serious work.

Key Features of Lua

What makes Lua stand out in the crowded field of programming languages? Here are some of its defining characteristics:

- **Lightweight and Fast**: Lua has a small footprint and executes quickly, making it ideal for resource-constrained environments.

- **Embeddable**: Designed from the ground up to be embedded in host applications, Lua can seamlessly integrate with C, C++, and other languages.

- **Simple Syntax**: With clean, readable code that resembles Pascal or Python, Lua is accessible to beginners and comfortable for experienced programmers.

- **Powerful Data Structures**: Tables, Lua's only container type, can be used to represent arrays, dictionaries, objects, and more.

- **Dynamic Typing**: Variables don't need type declarations, simplifying code and increasing flexibility.

- **Garbage Collection**: Automatic memory management frees developers from manual memory allocation and deallocation.

- **First-class Functions**: Functions are treated as values that can be stored in variables, passed as arguments, and returned from other functions.

- **Meta-mechanisms**: Rather than providing a vast array of features directly, Lua offers meta-mechanisms that let programmers implement advanced features themselves.

Use Cases and Applications

Lua's versatility has led to its adoption in a wide range of applications:

- **Game Development**: Lua is a favorite in the gaming industry. Games like *World of Warcraft*, *Angry Birds*, and *Roblox* use Lua for scripting. Its ability to handle real-time interactions while maintaining performance makes it perfect for game logic.

- **Embedded Systems**: From smart TVs to network appliances, Lua's small footprint makes it ideal for providing scripting capabilities in devices with limited resources.

- **Configuration**: Applications like the Nginx web server use Lua for configuration files, taking advantage of its readable syntax and expressive power.

- **Scientific Computing**: Lua's speed and ease of integration make it useful in scientific applications, especially when combined with numerically intensive C or Fortran code.

- **Mobile Applications**: Frameworks like Corona SDK use Lua to create cross-platform mobile apps with a single codebase.

Here's a small example of Lua code that demonstrates its clean syntax:

```lua
-- This is a comment in Lua
print("Hello, World!")  -- The classic first program

-- A simple function
function greet(name)
    return "Hello, " .. name .. "!"
end

-- Call the function
message = greet("Lua Programmer")
print(message)
```

Output:

```
Hello, World!
Hello, Lua Programmer!
```

Why Learn Lua?

You might be wondering why you should invest time in learning Lua when there are so many programming languages available. Here are compelling reasons:

1. **Easy to Learn**: Lua's minimalist design means there's less syntax to memorize and fewer concepts to grasp before becoming productive.

2. **Widely Used in Gaming**: If you're interested in game development, Lua knowledge is highly valuable as it's used by many major game engines and titles.

3. **Transferable Skills**: Lua's concepts (like first-class functions and tables) will help you understand similar features in other languages.

4. **Employability**: Companies using Lua are always looking for developers familiar with the language.

5. **Embedded Programming**: Lua opens doors to embedded programming without dealing with the complexity of C or C++.

6. **Quick Prototyping**: Lua's simplicity makes it excellent for rapidly prototyping ideas before implementing them in other languages.

Chapter Summary

In this chapter, we've introduced Lua—a lightweight, embeddable scripting language known for its simplicity and power. We've explored its origins at a Brazilian university, its key features like clean syntax and powerful data structures, and the diverse range of applications where Lua shines.

As we move forward, you'll start getting your hands dirty with Lua code. In the next chapter, we'll set up a Lua development environment and write our first scripts, taking the first steps in what I hope will be an enjoyable journey through this elegant language.

Chapter 2: Getting Started with Lua

Installing Lua

Before diving into programming with Lua, we need to set up our development environment. The good news is that Lua is remarkably easy to install across different operating systems thanks to its minimal dependencies and small footprint.

Windows Installation

On Windows, you have several options for installing Lua:

1. **Download Precompiled Binaries:**

    - Visit the official Lua website (www.lua.org) and download the Windows binaries
    - Alternatively, you can use LuaBinaries (http://luabinaries.sourceforge.net)
    - Extract the files to a directory of your choice
    - Add this directory to your system PATH to access Lua from any command prompt

2. **Using a Package Manager:** If you have Chocolatey installed, simply run:

```
choco install lua
```

macOS Installation

For Mac users, the simplest approach is to use a package manager:

1. **Using Homebrew:**

```
brew install lua
```

2. **Using MacPorts:**

```
sudo port install lua
```

Linux Installation

On Linux, Lua is typically available through your distribution's package manager:

1. **Debian/Ubuntu:**

```
sudo apt-get install lua5.4
```

2. **Fedora:**

```
sudo dnf install lua
```

3. **Arch Linux:**

```
sudo pacman -S lua
```

Verifying Your Installation

After installation, let's verify that Lua is working correctly. Open a terminal or command prompt and type:

```
lua -v
```

You should see output showing the Lua version, something like:

```
Lua 5.4.4  Copyright (C) 1994-2022 Lua.org, PUC-Rio
```

Online Lua Interpreters

If you're not ready to install Lua locally or just want to experiment quickly, several online Lua interpreters are available:

- **Repl.it**: offers a full Lua environment in your browser

- TIO.run: supports multiple Lua versions for testing
- **Lua Demo**: a simple interpreter offered by the official Lua website

These online tools are perfect for quick experiments or when you're away from your main development machine.

The Lua Interpreter

Lua comes with an interactive interpreter that allows you to execute code line by line —perfect for learning and experimenting. To start the interpreter, simply open a terminal and type `lua`.

You'll see a prompt, typically >, where you can enter Lua code:

```
> print("Hello from the Lua interpreter!")
Hello from the Lua interpreter!
> 2 + 2
4
> for i=1,3 do print(i) end
1
2
3
```

To exit the interpreter, press Ctrl+C on most systems, or type `os.exit()`.

This interactive mode is invaluable for testing small code snippets and learning Lua's behavior.

Your First Lua Program

Let's create and run our first Lua program. Open a text editor of your choice and create a file named `hello.lua` with the following content:

```
-- My first Lua program
print("Hello, Lua World!")

-- Adding some simple calculations
print("2 + 3 =", 2 + 3)
print("5 * 4 =", 5 * 4)

-- Getting user input
print("What's your name?")
local name = io.read()
print("Nice to meet you, " .. name .. "!")
```

Save the file, then open a terminal in the same directory and run:

```
lua hello.lua
```

You should see output like this:

```
Hello, Lua World!
2 + 3 = 5
5 * 4 = 20
What's your name?
```

Type your name and press Enter, and the program will respond:

```
Nice to meet you, [your name]!
```

Congratulations! You've just written and executed your first Lua program.

Understanding the Code Structure

Let's break down our first program to understand its components:

1. **Comments**: In Lua, comments start with -- and continue to the end of the line:

```
-- This is a comment
```

2. **Printing Output**: The print() function displays text and values to the console:

```
print("Hello, Lua World!")
```

3. **Expressions**: We calculated and displayed the results of simple arithmetic:

```
print("2 + 3 =", 2 + 3)
```

4. **User Input**: We used io.read() to get input from the user:

```
local name = io.read()
```

5. **String Concatenation**: We joined strings using the .. operator:

```
print("Nice to meet you, " .. name .. "!")
```

Lua Comments and Documentation

Good commenting is an essential practice in any programming language. Lua offers two styles of comments:

1. **Single-line Comments**: Begin with -- and continue to the end of the line:

```
-- This is a single-line comment
print("Hello") -- This is an inline comment
```

2. **Multi-line Comments**: Begin with --[[and end with]]:

```
--[[
  This is a multi-line comment
  that spans several lines
  and is useful for longer documentation
]]
```

For documenting your code, consider adopting a consistent style. Here's an example of a well-documented function:

```
--[[
  Calculates the average of a list of numbers

  @param numbers The table of numbers to average
  @return The average value, or 0 if the table is empty
]]
function average(numbers)
    local sum = 0
    local count = 0

    for _, value in ipairs(numbers) do
        sum = sum + value
        count = count + 1
    end

    return count > 0 and sum / count or 0
end
```

Setting Up a Code Editor

While you can write Lua code in any text editor, using an editor with Lua support will significantly improve your experience. Here are some popular options:

- **Visual Studio Code**: Free and powerful, with Lua extensions available
- **Sublime Text**: Fast and lightweight, with good Lua syntax highlighting
- **ZeroBrane Studio**: An IDE specifically designed for Lua development
- **Vim/Neovim**: For terminal enthusiasts, with Lua plugins available
- **Notepad++**: A simple but effective option for Windows users

For VS Code, I recommend installing the "Lua" extension by sumneko, which provides syntax highlighting, code completion, and linting.

Best Practices for Lua Development

As you begin your Lua journey, here are some best practices to follow:

1. **Use Consistent Indentation**: Standard practice is 2 or 4 spaces (not tabs).

2. **Choose Meaningful Names**: Variable and function names should clearly indicate their purpose.

3. **Local by Default**: Use the `local` keyword for variables unless you explicitly need them to be global.

4. **Handle Errors**: Consider how your code might fail and handle those cases gracefully.

5. **Test Incrementally**: Write small portions of code and test them before moving on.

6. **Comment Wisely**: Explain why your code does something, not just what it does.

Here's an example demonstrating these practices:

```
-- Calculate total price including tax
local function calculateTotal(price, taxRate)
    -- Ensure inputs are valid numbers
    if type(price) ~= "number" or type(taxRate) ~= "number" then
        return nil, "Price and tax rate must be numbers"
    end

    -- Avoid negative values
```

```
    if price < 0 or taxRate < 0 then
        return nil, "Price and tax rate cannot be negative"
    end

    local taxAmount = price * (taxRate / 100)
    local total = price + taxAmount

    return total, taxAmount
end

-- Example usage
local total, tax = calculateTotal(100, 7.5)
if total then
    print(string.format("Total: $%.2f (includes $%.2f tax)", total, tax))
else
    print("Error: " .. tax) -- tax contains the error message in this case
end
```

Output:

```
Total: $107.50 (includes $7.50 tax)
```

Chapter Summary

In this chapter, we've laid the groundwork for your Lua programming journey. We've installed Lua, written our first program, and explored the basics of Lua's syntax and structure. We've also looked at best practices that will help you write cleaner, more maintainable code as you progress.

Lua's simplicity means you're already well on your way to understanding the language. In the next chapter, we'll dive deeper into Lua's variables and data types, building on the foundation we've established here. You'll learn how Lua stores and manipulates different kinds of information, which is fundamental to writing more complex and useful programs.

Chapter 3: Variables and Data Types

Understanding Variables in Lua

In programming, variables are like labeled containers that hold data. They allow us to store and manipulate information throughout our programs. In Lua, variables are particularly flexible and straightforward to use.

Variable Declaration and Assignment

Unlike many programming languages, Lua doesn't require explicit variable declarations with type specifications. To create a variable, you simply assign a value to a name:

```lua
name = "Alice"
age = 30
isStudent = true
```

However, it's generally recommended to use the `local` keyword when declaring variables:

```lua
local name = "Alice"
local age = 30
local isStudent = true
```

Why use `local`? By default, variables in Lua are global, which means they can be accessed from anywhere in your program. This can lead to naming conflicts and unexpected behavior. Local variables are only accessible within their scope (the block where they're defined), which helps prevent these issues.

Variable Naming Rules

When naming variables in Lua, follow these rules:

- Names can contain letters, digits, and underscores
- Names must not start with a digit
- Names are case-sensitive (`name` and `Name` are different variables)
- Reserved words (like `if`, `for`, `local`) cannot be used as variable names

Good practice:

```lua
local firstName = "John"
local last_name = "Doe"
local age75 = 42
local _private = "secret"
```

Poor practice (but still valid):

```lua
local a = "John"   -- Not descriptive
local X = "Doe"    -- Not clear what this represents
```

Invalid:

```lua
local 1stPlace = "Gold"      -- Starts with a digit
local for = "loop"           -- 'for' is a reserved word
local user-name = "admin"    -- Contains a hyphen
```

Lua's Data Types

Lua is dynamically typed, meaning variables can hold values of any type, and the type can change during the program's execution. Lua includes eight basic types:

1. **nil**: Represents the absence of a useful value
2. **boolean**: Either `true` or `false`
3. **number**: Represents both integer and floating-point numbers
4. **string**: Sequence of characters
5. **function**: Code that can be called
6. **table**: The only data structure in Lua, very versatile
7. **userdata**: Custom data types (typically from C/C++ code)
8. **thread**: Independent threads of execution

Let's explore each type in detail:

Nil

The `nil` type has only one value: `nil`. It represents the absence of a useful value and is different from zero, an empty string, or false.

```
local noValue = nil
local uninitializedVariable  -- This is also nil by default

print(noValue)           -- Output: nil
print(uninitializedVariable) -- Output: nil

-- Testing for nil
if noValue == nil then
    print("The variable is nil")
end
```

Output:

```
nil
nil
The variable is nil
```

Boolean

The boolean type has two values: `true` and `false`. They're used for logical operations and conditional statements.

```
local isActive = true
local isComplete = false

print(isActive)   -- Output: true
print(isComplete) -- Output: false

-- Boolean operations
print(not isActive)          -- Output: false
print(isActive and isComplete) -- Output: false
print(isActive or isComplete)  -- Output: true
```

Output:

```
true
false
false
false
```

```
true
```

It's important to note that in Lua, unlike some other languages, both `nil` and `false` are considered "falsy" values in conditional contexts. Everything else, including zero and empty strings, is considered "truthy".

```lua
if nil then
    print("nil is truthy") -- This won't execute
else
    print("nil is falsy")
end

if false then
    print("false is truthy") -- This won't execute
else
    print("false is falsy")
end

if 0 then
    print("0 is truthy") -- This will execute
end

if "" then
    print("Empty string is truthy") -- This will execute
end
```

Output:

```
nil is falsy
false is falsy
0 is truthy
Empty string is truthy
```

Numbers

In Lua, all numbers are represented as double-precision floating-point values (similar to `double` in C). This means Lua can handle both integers and decimal numbers with the same type.

```lua
local integer = 42
local floatingPoint = 3.14159
local scientific = 1.5e6   -- 1.5 × 10^6 (1,500,000)
local hexadecimal = 0xFF   -- 255 in decimal
```

```
print(integer)         -- Output: 42
print(floatingPoint)   -- Output: 3.14159
print(scientific)      -- Output: 1500000
print(hexadecimal)     -- Output: 255
```

Output:

```
42
3.14159
1500000
255
```

Arithmetic operations work as you'd expect:

```
-- Basic arithmetic
print(10 + 5)     -- Addition: 15
print(10 - 5)     -- Subtraction: 5
print(10 * 5)     -- Multiplication: 50
print(10 / 5)     -- Division: 2
print(10 % 3)     -- Modulo (remainder): 1
print(10 ^ 2)     -- Exponentiation: 100

-- Integer division (Lua 5.3+)
print(10 // 3)    -- Integer division: 3
```

Output:

```
15
5
50
2
1
100
3
```

Strings

Strings in Lua are sequences of characters, used to represent text. They can be defined using single quotes, double quotes, or long brackets.

```
local singleQuotes = 'Hello, Lua!'
local doubleQuotes = "Hello, Lua!"
```

```
local longString = [[
    This is a multi-line
    string that preserves
    line breaks and indentation.
]]

print(singleQuotes)  -- Output: Hello, Lua!
print(doubleQuotes)  -- Output: Hello, Lua!
print(longString)
```

Output:

```
Hello, Lua!
Hello, Lua!

    This is a multi-line
    string that preserves
    line breaks and indentation.
```

Strings in Lua are immutable, meaning once created, they cannot be changed. Operations on strings create new strings rather than modifying existing ones.

String Concatenation:

```
local firstName = "John"
local lastName = "Doe"
local fullName = firstName .. " " .. lastName

print(fullName)  -- Output: John Doe
```

Output:

```
John Doe
```

String Length:

```
local text = "Hello, World!"
print(#text)  -- Output: 13
```

Output:

```
13
```

We'll explore string operations in much more detail in Chapter 12, which is dedicated to working with strings.

Functions

Functions are first-class values in Lua, which means they can be stored in variables, passed as arguments, and returned from other functions. We'll cover functions extensively in Chapter 6, but here's a basic example:

```lua
-- Function declaration
local function greet(name)
    return "Hello, " .. name .. "!"
end

-- Functions as values
local sayHello = greet

print(greet("Alice"))    -- Output: Hello, Alice!
print(sayHello("Bob"))   -- Output: Hello, Bob!
```

Output:

```
Hello, Alice!
Hello, Bob!
```

Tables

Tables are the only data structure in Lua, but they're incredibly versatile. They can be used as arrays, dictionaries (maps), objects, and more. We'll dedicate all of Chapter 7 to tables, but here's a glimpse:

```lua
-- Table as an array
local fruits = {"Apple", "Banana", "Cherry"}
print(fruits[1])  -- Output: Apple (note: Lua arrays start at index 1)

-- Table as a dictionary
local person = {
    name = "Alice",
    age = 30,
    isStudent = true
}
print(person.name)  -- Output: Alice
```

Output:

```
Apple
Alice
```

Userdata and Threads

These types are more advanced and less commonly encountered when first learning Lua:

- **Userdata** allows arbitrary C data to be stored in Lua variables. It's primarily used when integrating Lua with C/C++ code.
- **Threads** represent independent threads of execution and are used for coroutines, a form of cooperative multitasking.

We'll explore these types in more advanced chapters.

Type Checking and Conversion

Since Lua is dynamically typed, it's sometimes necessary to check or convert between types.

Checking Types

The type() function returns a string indicating the type of a value:

```
local value1 = 42
local value2 = "Hello"
local value3 = true
local value4 = {1, 2, 3}
local value5 = function() return "hi" end

print(type(value1))   -- Output: number
print(type(value2))   -- Output: string
print(type(value3))   -- Output: boolean
print(type(value4))   -- Output: table
print(type(value5))   -- Output: function
print(type(nil))      -- Output: nil
```

Output:

```
number
string
```

```
boolean
table
function
nil
```

Type Conversion

Lua provides functions to convert between types:

String to Number:

```
local numStr = "42"
local num = tonumber(numStr)
print(num, type(num))  -- Output: 42 number

-- Conversion failure
local badStr = "not a number"
local result = tonumber(badStr)
print(result)  -- Output: nil
```

Output:

```
42       number
nil
```

Number to String:

```
local num = 42
local str1 = tostring(num)
local str2 = num .. ""  -- Alternative conversion
print(str1, type(str1))  -- Output: 42 string
```

Output:

```
42       string
```

Boolean Conversions: In Lua, explicit boolean conversions are rare because any value can be used in a boolean context. Remember that only `nil` and `false` are considered false in conditional expressions.

Scope of Variables

Understanding variable scope is crucial for writing maintainable Lua code.

Local Variables

Local variables are only accessible within the block where they're defined. A block is typically a chunk of code enclosed by keywords like do/end, if/end, or function/end.

```
do
    local x = 10
    print(x)  -- Output: 10
end

-- print(x)  -- This would cause an error: attempt to use a nil value
```

Output:

```
10
```

Function parameters are always local to the function:

```
local function testScope(param)
    local insideVar = "I'm local to the function"
    print(param)        -- Output: test
    print(insideVar)    -- Output: I'm local to the function
end

testScope("test")
-- print(param)        -- Error: param is not accessible here
-- print(insideVar)    -- Error: insideVar is not accessible here
```

Output:

```
test
I'm local to the function
```

Global Variables

Variables declared without the local keyword are global, meaning they're accessible from any part of your program:

```
globalVar = "I'm global"

local function testGlobal()
    print(globalVar)  -- Output: I'm global

    -- Modifying a global from inside a function
    globalVar = "Modified global"
end

testGlobal()
print(globalVar)  -- Output: Modified global
```

Output:

```
I'm global
Modified global
```

While global variables are convenient, they can lead to hard-to-find bugs and make your code more difficult to understand and maintain. It's generally best practice to:

1. Use local variables whenever possible
2. Explicitly declare globals in a single location
3. Consider using tables as namespaces for related globals

For example, instead of separate globals:

```
-- Not recommended
appName = "MyApp"
appVersion = "1.0"
appAuthor = "John Doe"

-- Better approach: use a table as a namespace
App = {
    name = "MyApp",
    version = "1.0",
    author = "John Doe"
}

print(App.name .. " v" .. App.version)  -- Output: MyApp v1.0
```

Output:

```
MyApp v1.0
```

Variable Lifetime and Garbage Collection

In Lua, memory management is handled automatically through garbage collection. When a variable's value is no longer accessible (referenced), it becomes eligible for garbage collection, freeing the memory it occupied.

```lua
local function createLargeTable()
    local t = {}
    for i = 1, 1000000 do
        t[i] = i
    end
    return t
end

do
    local largeTable = createLargeTable()
    print("Table created with size:", #largeTable)
    -- largeTable is still in scope here
end
-- At this point, largeTable is out of scope and eligible for garbage collection

-- Force garbage collection (normally this happens automatically)
collectgarbage()
```

Output:

```
Table created with size: 1000000
```

Constants in Lua

Lua doesn't have built-in constants like some other languages (variables that cannot be changed after initialization). However, you can follow a convention of using uppercase names for values that shouldn't change:

```lua
local PI = 3.14159
local MAX_USERS = 100
local DATABASE_URL = "mongodb://localhost:27017"

-- This is possible but discouraged by convention
PI = 3  -- Don't do this!
```

For better enforcement of constants, you can use metatables (which we'll cover in later chapters) or place values in a read-only table.

Chapter Summary

In this chapter, we've explored Lua's variable system and its fundamental data types. We've learned that Lua is dynamically typed, allowing variables to hold different types of values throughout a program's execution. We've examined the eight basic types—nil, boolean, number, string, function, table, userdata, and thread—with a focus on the most commonly used ones.

We've also discussed variable scope, distinguishing between local and global variables, and emphasized the importance of proper scope management for writing maintainable code. Finally, we touched on Lua's automatic memory management through garbage collection.

Understanding variables and data types forms the foundation of programming in Lua. In the next chapter, we'll build on this knowledge by examining operators and expressions, which allow us to manipulate variables and create more complex logic in our programs.

Chapter 4: Operators and Expressions

Introduction to Operators in Lua

Operators are symbols that tell the interpreter to perform specific mathematical, relational, or logical operations. They're the building blocks for creating expressions, which combine values to produce new values. In this chapter, we'll explore all the operators available in Lua and how to use them effectively.

Arithmetic Operators

Arithmetic operators perform mathematical calculations on numeric values. Lua provides all the standard arithmetic operations you'd expect:

Operator	Description	Example	Result
+	Addition	5 + 3	8
−	Subtraction	5 − 3	2
*	Multiplication	5 * 3	15
/	Division	5 / 3	1.6666666666667
%	Modulo (remainder)	5 % 3	2
^	Exponentiation	5 ^ 3	125
−	Negation (unary)	−5	−5
//	Floor division (Lua 5.3+)	5 // 3	1

Let's see these operators in action:

```
-- Basic arithmetic operations
local a = 10
local b = 3
```

```
print("Addition:", a + b)              -- 13
print("Subtraction:", a - b)           -- 7
print("Multiplication:", a * b)        -- 30
print("Division:", a / b)              -- 3.3333333333333
print("Modulo:", a % b)                -- 1
print("Exponentiation:", a ^ b)        -- 1000
print("Negation:", -a)                 -- -10
print("Floor division:", a // b)       -- 3
```

Output:

```
Addition: 13
Subtraction: 7
Multiplication: 30
Division: 3.3333333333333
Modulo: 1
Exponentiation: 1000
Negation: -10
Floor division: 3
```

A few important notes about these operators:

- The division operator (/) always performs floating-point division in Lua.
- The floor division operator (//) was introduced in Lua 5.3 and returns the integer quotient, discarding any decimal portion.
- The modulo operator (%) works with the mathematical definition: a % b = a - (a // b) * b

Here's an example of a more complex arithmetic expression:

```
-- Calculate the area of a circle
local radius = 5
local pi = 3.14159
local area = pi * radius ^ 2

print("Area of circle:", area)  -- Approximately 78.53975
```

Output:

```
Area of circle: 78.53975
```

Relational Operators

Relational operators compare values and return boolean results (`true` or `false`). They are essential for creating conditional expressions.

Operator	Description	Example	Result
==	Equal to	5 == 5	true
~=	Not equal to	5 ~= 3	true
>	Greater than	5 > 3	true
<	Less than	5 < 3	false
>=	Greater than or equal to	5 >= 5	true
<=	Less than or equal to	5 <= 3	false

Let's see these operators in action:

```
local x = 10
local y = 20

print("x == y:", x == y)   -- false
print("x ~= y:", x ~= y)   -- true
print("x > y:", x > y)     -- false
print("x < y:", x < y)     -- true
print("x >= y:", x >= y)   -- false
print("x <= y:", x <= y)   -- true

-- Comparing different types
print("10 == '10':", 10 == "10")  -- false (different types)
```

Output:

```
x == y: false
x ~= y: true
x > y: false
x < y: true
x >= y: false
x <= y: true
10 == '10': false
```

Important behaviors to note:

1. Lua's not-equal operator is ~=, not != as in many other languages.
2. Different types are never equal: 10 == "10" returns false.
3. Tables, functions, and userdata are compared by reference, not by value.

Here's an example showing reference comparison with tables:

```lua
local t1 = {1, 2, 3}
local t2 = {1, 2, 3}  -- Same contents as t1
local t3 = t1          -- Same reference as t1

print("t1 == t2:", t1 == t2)  -- false (different references)
print("t1 == t3:", t1 == t3)  -- true (same reference)
```

Output:

```
t1 == t2: false
t1 == t3: true
```

Logical Operators

Logical operators perform boolean logic operations. In Lua, these are and, or, and not.

Operator	Description	Example	Result
and	Logical AND	true and false	false
or	Logical OR	true or false	true
not	Logical NOT	not true	false

Let's see how these operators work:

```lua
local a = true
local b = false

print("a and b:", a and b)  -- false
print("a or b:", a or b)    -- true
print("not a:", not a)      -- false
print("not b:", not b)      -- true

-- Logical operators with non-boolean values
print("10 and 20:", 10 and 20)      -- 20
print("nil and 20:", nil and 20)    -- nil
print("10 or 20:", 10 or 20)        -- 10
print("nil or 20:", nil or 20)      -- 20
print("'' or 'default':", "" or "default")  -- "" (empty string is truthy)
```

Output:

```
a and b: false
a or b: true
not a: false
not b: true
10 and 20: 20
nil and 20: nil
10 or 20: 10
nil or 20: 20
'' or 'default':
```

Lua's logical operators have some interesting properties:

1. They don't always return boolean values. Instead:

   - and returns its first operand if it's falsy, otherwise it returns the second operand.
   - or returns its first operand if it's truthy, otherwise it returns the second operand.
   - Only not always returns a boolean.

2. This behavior enables useful idioms:

```
-- Default value pattern
local userInput = nil
local name = userInput or "Guest"  -- If userInput is nil, use "Guest"
print("Hello, " .. name)  -- Output: Hello, Guest

-- Safe navigation pattern
local person = {name = "Alice"}
local job = person and person.job
print("Job:", job)  -- Output: Job: nil (no error even though person.job doesn't
exist)
```

Output:

```
Hello, Guest
Job: nil
```

3. Short-circuit evaluation: Lua only evaluates as much as it needs to determine the result.

```
-- Function to demonstrate side effects
local function printAndReturn(message, returnValue)
    print(message)
```

```
      return returnValue
end

-- With 'and', the second expression isn't evaluated if the first is false
printAndReturn("First expression", false) and printAndReturn("Second
expression", true)

-- With 'or', the second expression isn't evaluated if the first is true
printAndReturn("First expression", true) or printAndReturn("Second expression",
false)
```

Output:

```
First expression
First expression
```

Concatenation Operator

Lua uses the .. operator to concatenate strings:

```
local firstName = "John"
local lastName = "Doe"

-- String concatenation
local fullName = firstName .. " " .. lastName
print(fullName)  -- Output: John Doe

-- Concatenation with non-string values
local age = 30
local message = "Age: " .. age  -- age is converted to a string
print(message)  -- Output: Age: 30
```

Output:

```
John Doe
Age: 30
```

Note that the concatenation operator automatically converts numbers to strings.
However, it doesn't work with other types without explicit conversion:

```
local name = "Table: " .. tostring({1, 2, 3})
print(name)  -- Output: Table: table: 0x55e944a51e80 (or similar address)
```

Output:

```
Table: table: 0x7f94bb409bc0
```

Length Operator

The # operator returns the length of a string or a table used as an array:

```
-- String length
local str = "Hello, Lua!"
print("Length of string:", #str)  -- 11

-- Table length (for sequence-like tables)
local arr = {10, 20, 30, 40, 50}
print("Length of array:", #arr)   -- 5

-- Be careful with non-sequence tables
local sparseArr = {[1] = 10, [5] = 50}
print("Length of sparse array:", #sparseArr)  -- May be 1 or 5, behavior is
implementation-defined
```

Output:

```
Length of string: 11
Length of array: 5
Length of sparse array: 1
```

The length operator has some nuances, especially with tables:

- For strings, it returns the number of bytes (which equals the number of characters for ASCII, but not necessarily for UTF-8).
- For tables, it returns the largest positive integer key in the array part with a non-nil value, but only if the table is a sequence (has no holes).
- For tables with "holes," the behavior is not well-defined and may vary between Lua implementations.

We'll explore this more deeply in Chapter 7 on Tables.

Bitwise Operators (Lua 5.3+)

Lua 5.3 introduced bitwise operators, which are useful for low-level programming tasks:

Operator	Description	Example	Result
&	Bitwise AND	0x03 & 0x05	0x01
|	Bitwise OR	0x03 | 0x05	0x07
~	Bitwise XOR	0x03 ~ 0x05	0x06
>>	Right shift	0x80 >> 4	0x08
<<	Left shift	0x08 << 4	0x80
~	Bitwise NOT (unary)	~0x0F	-16 on most systems

Here's how to use these operators:

```
-- Using decimal notation
print("5 & 3:", 5 & 3)      -- Bitwise AND: 1
print("5 | 3:", 5 | 3)      -- Bitwise OR: 7
print("5 ~ 3:", 5 ~ 3)      -- Bitwise XOR: 6
print("5 << 1:", 5 << 1)    -- Left shift: 10
print("5 >> 1:", 5 >> 1)    -- Right shift: 2
print("~5:", ~5)            -- Bitwise NOT: -6

-- Using hexadecimal notation
print("0xF0 & 0x0F:", 0xF0 & 0x0F)   -- 0
print("0xF0 | 0x0F:", 0xF0 | 0x0F)   -- 255
```

Output:

```
5 & 3: 1
5 | 3: 7
5 ~ 3: 6
5 << 1: 10
5 >> 1: 2
~5: -6
0xF0 & 0x0F: 0
0xF0 | 0x0F: 255
```

Bitwise operators are particularly useful for:

- Flag operations
- Working with binary protocols
- Low-level optimizations
- Bit manipulation algorithms

Operator Precedence

When an expression contains multiple operators, operator precedence determines the order of evaluation. Here's the precedence table for Lua operators, from highest to lowest:

1. ^ (exponentiation)
2. unary operators (not, - (negation), #, ~ (bitwise NOT))
3. *, /, %, // (multiplicative)
4. +, - (additive)
5. .. (concatenation)
6. <<, >> (shifts)
7. & (bitwise AND)
8. ~ (bitwise XOR)
9. | (bitwise OR)
10. <, >, <=, >=, ~=, == (relational)
11. and (logical AND)
12. or (logical OR)

When operators have the same precedence, most binary operators are right-associative, except for ^ and .. which are left-associative.

Let's see how precedence affects expression evaluation:

```
-- Precedence examples
print("1 + 2 * 3 =", 1 + 2 * 3)            -- 7 (multiplication before addition)
print("(1 + 2) * 3 =", (1 + 2) * 3)        -- 9 (parentheses override precedence)
print("2 ^ 3 * 4 =", 2 ^ 3 * 4)            -- 32 (exponentiation before
multiplication)
print("not true and false =", not true and false)  -- false (unary 'not' before
'and')
print("5 > 3 and 2 < 4 =", 5 > 3 and 2 < 4)        -- true (relational before
logical)

-- Associativity example
print("2 ^ 3 ^ 2 =", 2 ^ 3 ^ 2)            -- 512, as 2 ^ (3 ^ 2), not (2 ^ 3) ^
2
print("2 .. 3 .. 4 =", 2 .. 3 .. 4)        -- 234, as (2 .. 3) .. 4
```

Output:

```
1 + 2 * 3 = 7
(1 + 2) * 3 = 9
```

```
2 ^ 3 * 4 = 32
not true and false = false
5 > 3 and 2 < 4 = true
2 ^ 3 ^ 2 = 512
2 .. 3 .. 4 = 234
```

When in doubt about precedence, use parentheses to make your intention clear. This not only ensures correct evaluation but also makes your code more readable.

Expressions in Lua

An expression is any combination of values, variables, operators, and function calls that evaluates to a value. Here are some examples of expressions in Lua:

```lua
-- Simple expressions
local x = 10
local y = 20
local z = x + y        -- Arithmetic expression
local isGreater = x > y  -- Relational expression

-- Complex expressions
local formula = (x + y) * 2 / (z - 5) ^ 2
print("Formula result:", formula)

-- Expressions with function calls
local function square(n)
    return n * n
end

local result = square(x) + square(y)
print("Sum of squares:", result)

-- Expression in a condition
if x * y > 100 and not (x == y) then
    print("Condition met")
end

-- Table constructor expressions
local point = {x = 10, y = 20, ["label"] = "Point A"}
local colors = {"red", "green", "blue"}
```

Output:

```
Formula result: 2.0
```

```
Sum of squares: 500
Condition met
```

Type Coercion in Expressions

Lua performs some automatic type conversions (coercions) when evaluating expressions:

1. **String to Number**: When using arithmetic operators, Lua tries to convert strings to numbers.
2. **Number to String**: When using the concatenation operator, Lua converts numbers to strings.

```lua
-- String to number coercion in arithmetic
print("10" + 5)      -- 15
print("10.5" * 2)    -- 21.0

-- Number to string coercion in concatenation
print(10 .. 20)      -- "1020"
print("Value: " .. 42.5)  -- "Value: 42.5"

-- Failed coercion examples
local status, err = pcall(function()
    return "hello" + 5    -- This will fail
end)
print("Status:", status, "Error:", err)
```

Output:

```
15
21.0
1020
Value: 42.5
Status: false Error: stdin:1: attempt to perform arithmetic on a string value
```

Lua's coercion rules are relatively limited compared to some other dynamic languages. It's generally best to perform explicit conversions using `tonumber()` and `tostring()` rather than relying on automatic coercion.

Common Expression Patterns

Here are some common expression patterns you'll encounter in Lua programming:

Ternary-like Expressions

Lua doesn't have a ternary operator (?:) like some languages, but you can achieve similar functionality with logical operators:

```lua
-- Condition ? TrueValue : FalseValue
local age = 20
local status = age >= 18 and "Adult" or "Minor"
print(status)  -- "Adult"

-- Be careful with this pattern when TrueValue could be false
local x = 10
local y = 0
-- This doesn't work as expected if x > 5 evaluates to true
local result = x > 5 and y or 50
print(result)  -- 0 (y is 0, which is truthy, but might look like the condition
failed)

-- Better approach for such cases
local result = (x > 5) and y or 50
```

Output:

```
Adult
0
0
```

Default Values

Setting default values when a variable might be nil:

```lua
local options = {title = "Sample"}
local title = options.title or "Untitled"
local width = options.width or 640
local height = options.height or 480

print(title, width, height)  -- "Sample", 640, 480
```

Output:

```
Sample  640     480
```

Safe Navigation

Checking for nil before accessing nested properties:

```
local user = {
    profile = {
        name = "Alice",
        -- No 'address' field
    }
}

-- Unsafe navigation (would error if profile was nil)
-- local city = user.profile.address.city  -- Error!

-- Safe navigation with logical operators
local city = user and user.profile and user.profile.address and
user.profile.address.city or "Unknown"
print("City:", city)  -- "Unknown"
```

Output:

```
City: Unknown
```

Clamping Values

Ensuring a value stays within certain bounds:

```
local function clamp(value, min, max)
    return value < min and min or (value > max and max or value)
end

print(clamp(15, 0, 10))   -- 10
print(clamp(5, 0, 10))    -- 5
print(clamp(-5, 0, 10))   -- 0
```

Output:

```
10
5
0
```

Chapter Summary

In this chapter, we've explored Lua's rich set of operators and how to construct expressions. We've covered arithmetic, relational, and logical operators, as well as specialized operators for string concatenation, length calculation, and bitwise operations. We've also examined operator precedence rules and common expression patterns.

Understanding operators and expressions is essential for effective Lua programming, as they allow you to manipulate data and create the logic that drives your programs. The patterns we've discussed, such as default values and safe navigation, will help you write more concise and robust code.

In the next chapter, we'll build on this knowledge to explore control structures in Lua, including conditionals and loops. These constructs, combined with the expressions we've learned about, will give you the tools to create more complex program logic and control flow.

Chapter 5: Control Structures

Introduction to Control Structures

Control structures are the backbone of any programming language, allowing you to determine the flow and execution path of your code. Rather than executing statements in a straight line from top to bottom, control structures let your programs make decisions, repeat actions, and select between different code paths.

In this chapter, we'll explore all of Lua's control structures, including conditional statements, loops, and flow control mechanisms. By mastering these structures, you'll be able to write more dynamic and powerful Lua programs.

Conditional Statements

Conditional statements allow your program to make decisions based on certain conditions. Lua provides the if, else, and elseif keywords for this purpose.

The if Statement

The basic if statement evaluates a condition and executes a block of code if the condition is true:

```
local temperature = 22

if temperature > 30 then
    print("It's hot outside!")
end

if temperature < 10 then
```

```
    print("It's cold outside!") -- This won't execute since the condition is
false
end
```

Remember that in Lua, only `false` and `nil` are considered falsy values; everything else (including 0 and empty strings) is considered truthy.

if-else Statement

The `if-else` structure allows you to specify an alternative block of code to execute when the condition is false:

```
local hour = 15 -- 3 PM in 24-hour format

if hour < 12 then
    print("Good morning!")
else
    print("Good afternoon or evening!")
end
```

Output:

```
Good afternoon or evening!
```

if-elseif-else Statement

For multiple conditions, the `if-elseif-else` structure provides a clean way to express a series of tests:

```
local score = 85

if score >= 90 then
    print("Grade: A")
elseif score >= 80 then
    print("Grade: B")
elseif score >= 70 then
    print("Grade: C")
elseif score >= 60 then
    print("Grade: D")
else
    print("Grade: F")
end
```

Output:

```
Grade: B
```

The conditions are evaluated in order, and only the first matching condition's block will execute. If none of the conditions are true, the `else` block executes (if present).

Nested if Statements

You can nest `if` statements inside each other to create more complex conditions:

```
local username = "admin"
local password = "secret123"

if username == "admin" then
    if password == "secret123" then
        print("Admin access granted")
    else
        print("Invalid password for admin")
    end
else
    print("Unknown user")
end
```

Output:

```
Admin access granted
```

While nesting is possible, excessive nesting can make code harder to read and maintain. Consider refactoring deeply nested conditions using logical operators or breaking the logic into separate functions.

Using Logical Operators in Conditions

Logical operators (and, or, not) can combine multiple conditions:

```
local age = 25
local hasLicense = true

-- Using 'and' to check multiple conditions
if age >= 18 and hasLicense then
    print("You can drive")
else
```

```
      print("You cannot drive")
end

-- Using 'or' for alternative conditions
local isWeekend = false
local isHoliday = true

if isWeekend or isHoliday then
    print("No work today!")
else
    print("Time to work")
end

-- Using 'not' to negate a condition
if not isWeekend then
    print("It's a weekday")
end
```

Output:

```
You can drive
No work today!
It's a weekday
```

Common Conditional Patterns

Here are some common patterns you'll encounter when working with conditional statements in Lua:

Early Return Pattern:

```
function processUser(user)
    -- Validate inputs first
    if not user then
        print("Error: No user provided")
        return false
    end

    if not user.name then
        print("Error: User has no name")
        return false
    end

    -- Process the valid user
    print("Processing user: " .. user.name)
```

```
        return true
    end

    -- Test with different inputs
    processUser(nil)  -- Error case
    processUser({})   -- Error case
    processUser({name = "Alice"})  -- Success case
```

Output:

```
Error: No user provided
Error: User has no name
Processing user: Alice
```

Guard Clause Pattern:

```
function divideNumbers(a, b)
    -- Guard against invalid input
    if type(a) ~= "number" or type(b) ~= "number" then
        return nil, "Both arguments must be numbers"
    end

    -- Guard against division by zero
    if b == 0 then
        return nil, "Cannot divide by zero"
    end

    -- If we're here, it's safe to proceed
    return a / b
end

-- Test the function
local result, error = divideNumbers(10, 2)
if result then
    print("Result: " .. result)
else
    print("Error: " .. error)
end

result, error = divideNumbers(10, 0)
if result then
    print("Result: " .. result)
else
    print("Error: " .. error)
end
```

Output:

```
Result: 5
Error: Cannot divide by zero
```

Loops

Loops allow you to execute a block of code multiple times. Lua provides several types of loops, each suited to different scenarios.

while Loop

The `while` loop executes a block of code as long as a specified condition is true:

```lua
local count = 1

while count <= 5 do
    print("Count: " .. count)
    count = count + 1
end
```

Output:

```
Count: 1
Count: 2
Count: 3
Count: 4
Count: 5
```

Be careful with `while` loops—if the condition never becomes false, you'll create an infinite loop. Ensure that something inside the loop will eventually make the condition false.

repeat-until Loop

The `repeat-until` loop is similar to the `while` loop, but the condition is checked at the end of the loop rather than the beginning. This means the loop body will always execute at least once:

```lua
local count = 1

repeat
```

```
    print("Count: " .. count)
    count = count + 1
until count > 5
```

Output:

```
Count: 1
Count: 2
Count: 3
Count: 4
Count: 5
```

The key difference from `while` is that `repeat-until` checks its condition at the end of each iteration, so the loop body always executes at least once.

Another difference is that the condition in `repeat-until` is inverted compared to `while`—the loop continues until the condition becomes true, whereas `while` continues as long as the condition is true.

numerical for Loop

The numerical `for` loop executes a block of code a specified number of times, with an index variable that automatically changes with each iteration:

```
-- Basic for loop
for i = 1, 5 do
    print("Iteration " .. i)
end

-- For loop with step value
print("\nCounting down:")
for i = 10, 1, -2 do
    print("Countdown: " .. i)
end
```

Output:

```
Iteration 1
Iteration 2
Iteration 3
Iteration 4
Iteration 5
```

```
Counting down:
Countdown: 10
Countdown: 8
Countdown: 6
Countdown: 4
Countdown: 2
```

The syntax is `for variable = start, end, step do`. The `step` parameter is optional and defaults to 1. If you provide a negative step, the loop counts downward.

Important characteristics of the numerical `for` loop:

1. The loop parameters (`start`, `end`, `step`) are evaluated only once, before the loop begins.
2. The loop variable is local to the loop, even if you don't explicitly declare it with `local`.
3. You shouldn't modify the loop variable within the loop—its value is automatically updated by the loop.

```
-- This demonstrates the local scope of the loop variable
for i = 1, 3 do
    print("Inside loop: i = " .. i)
end

-- This will produce an error if uncommented, as 'i' is not defined outside the
loop
-- print("Outside loop: i = " .. i)

-- Parameters evaluated only once
local max = 3
for i = 1, max do
    print("Value: " .. i)
    max = 10  -- This doesn't affect the loop's end value
end
```

Output:

```
Inside loop: i = 1
Inside loop: i = 2
Inside loop: i = 3
Value: 1
Value: 2
Value: 3
```

generic for Loop (Iterators)

The generic for loop (also known as the for-in loop) works with iterator functions to traverse data structures like tables:

```
-- Iterating over a table with ipairs (array portion)
local fruits = {"Apple", "Banana", "Cherry", "Date"}

print("Fruits:")
for index, value in ipairs(fruits) do
    print(index .. ". " .. value)
end

-- Iterating over a table with pairs (all key-value pairs)
local person = {
    name = "Alice",
    age = 30,
    city = "Wonderland"
}

print("\nPerson details:")
for key, value in pairs(person) do
    print(key .. ": " .. value)
end
```

Output:

```
Fruits:
1. Apple
2. Banana
3. Cherry
4. Date

Person details:
age: 30
name: Alice
city: Wonderland
```

The key differences between ipairs and pairs:

- ipairs: Iterates over array elements in order (indices 1, 2, 3, ...) until it hits nil.
- pairs: Iterates over all key-value pairs in a table, including non-integer keys. The order is not guaranteed.

We'll explore iterators in more depth in Chapter 7 when we discuss tables.

Control Flow Statements

In addition to conditionals and loops, Lua provides statements to alter the normal flow of execution within these structures.

break Statement

The break statement immediately exits the innermost loop (while, repeat, or for):

```lua
-- Using break to exit a loop early
for i = 1, 10 do
    if i > 5 then
        print("Breaking loop at i = " .. i)
        break
    end
    print("Value: " .. i)
end
```

Output:

```
Value: 1
Value: 2
Value: 3
Value: 4
Value: 5
Breaking loop at i = 6
```

goto Statement (Lua 5.2+)

Lua 5.2 introduced the goto statement, which allows jumping to a labeled position in the code:

```lua
local i = 1

::start::
if i <= 5 then
    print("Count: " .. i)
    i = i + 1
    goto start
end

print("Loop finished")

-- Error handling with goto
```

```
local success = false

if not success then
    goto error
end

print("Operation successful") -- This won't execute

::error::
print("An error occurred")
```

Output:

```
Count: 1
Count: 2
Count: 3
Count: 4
Count: 5
Loop finished
An error occurred
```

While goto can be useful in certain situations (like complex error handling), it should be used sparingly as it can make code harder to follow.

Multiple Returns and Decisions

Lua functions can return multiple values, which can be used in control structures:

```
-- Function that returns a status and a value
function divide(a, b)
    if b == 0 then
        return false, "Division by zero"
    else
        return true, a / b
    end
end

-- Using multiple returns with control flow
local success, result = divide(10, 2)
if success then
    print("Result: " .. result)
else
    print("Error: " .. result)
end
```

```
success, result = divide(10, 0)
if success then
    print("Result: " .. result)
else
    print("Error: " .. result)
end
```

Output:

```
Result: 5
Error: Division by zero
```

This pattern of returning a success flag along with a result or error message is common in Lua programming and provides a clean way to handle potential errors.

do Block

The do block allows you to create a new scope for variables:

```
-- Variables have block scope in Lua
do
    local x = 10
    print("Inside block: x = " .. x)
end

-- This would cause an error if uncommented
-- print("Outside block: x = " .. x)

-- Do blocks can be useful for limiting variable scope
local total = 0
for i = 1, 5 do
    do
        local temp = i * i
        total = total + temp
    end
    -- temp is no longer accessible here
end
print("Total: " .. total)
```

Output:

```
Inside block: x = 10
```

Implementing Advanced Control Patterns

Let's look at some more advanced control flow patterns that combine various control structures:

State Machine

```lua
local function runStateMachine()
    local state = "START"
    local count = 0

    while state ~= "END" do
        if state == "START" then
            print("Machine starting")
            state = "RUNNING"
        elseif state == "RUNNING" then
            count = count + 1
            print("Machine running, count: " .. count)

            if count >= 3 then
                state = "PAUSED"
            end
        elseif state == "PAUSED" then
            print("Machine paused")
            state = "RESUME"
        elseif state == "RESUME" then
            print("Machine resuming")

            if count >= 5 then
                state = "END"
            else
                state = "RUNNING"
            end
        else
            print("Unknown state: " .. state)
            state = "END"
        end
    end

    print("Machine stopped")
end

runStateMachine()
```

Output:

```
Machine starting
Machine running, count: 1
Machine running, count: 2
Machine running, count: 3
Machine paused
Machine resuming
Machine running, count: 4
Machine running, count: 5
Machine paused
Machine resuming
Machine stopped
```

Recursive Traversal

```lua
-- Recursive function to traverse a nested table
local function traverse(data, indent)
    indent = indent or 0
    local indentStr = string.rep("  ", indent)

    for k, v in pairs(data) do
        if type(v) == "table" then
            print(indentStr .. k .. " (table):")
            traverse(v, indent + 1)
        else
            print(indentStr .. k .. ": " .. tostring(v))
        end
    end
end

-- Test with a nested table
local data = {
    name = "Project",
    details = {
        version = "1.0",
        author = "Lua Developer",
        settings = {
            debug = true,
            timeout = 30
        }
    },
    active = true
}

traverse(data)
```

Output:

```
name: Project
details (table):
  version: 1.0
  author: Lua Developer
  settings (table):
    debug: true
    timeout: 30
active: true
```

Coroutine-based Control Flow

While we'll cover coroutines in a later chapter, here's a preview of how they can create advanced control flow:

```lua
-- Define a coroutine that yields multiple times
local co = coroutine.create(function()
    print("Coroutine: Step 1")
    coroutine.yield("Result 1")

    print("Coroutine: Step 2")
    coroutine.yield("Result 2")

    print("Coroutine: Step 3")
    return "Final Result"
end)

-- Run the coroutine step by step
local status, result = coroutine.resume(co)
print("Main: Got " .. result)

status, result = coroutine.resume(co)
print("Main: Got " .. result)

status, result = coroutine.resume(co)
print("Main: Got " .. result)
```

Output:

```
Coroutine: Step 1
Main: Got Result 1
Coroutine: Step 2
Main: Got Result 2
Coroutine: Step 3
```

Coroutines provide a way to create functions that can pause their execution and later resume from where they left off—a powerful model for certain types of control flow.

Chapter Summary

In this chapter, we've explored Lua's control structures, which allow you to shape the flow of your programs. We've covered conditional statements (`if`, `else`, `elseif`), loops (`while`, `repeat-until`, numerical `for`, and generic `for`), and control flow statements (`break` and `goto`).

We've also examined various patterns and techniques for implementing more complex control logic, from early returns and guard clauses to state machines and recursive traversals. These patterns will serve as valuable tools in your Lua programming toolkit.

Understanding control structures is crucial for writing effective programs, as they allow you to make decisions, handle different cases, and repeat operations—fundamental capabilities in any programming language.

In the next chapter, we'll dive into functions, one of Lua's most powerful features. You'll learn how to define and call functions, work with parameters and return values, and leverage Lua's functional programming capabilities. Functions are the building blocks of modular, reusable code, and they'll allow you to take your Lua programming to the next level.

Chapter 6: Functions in Lua

Introduction to Functions

Functions are one of the most powerful features in Lua. They allow you to group code into reusable, organized units that can be called from different parts of your program. Functions are not just a way to avoid repeating code—they're a fundamental building block for structuring programs, creating abstractions, and implementing complex behaviors.

In Lua, functions are first-class values, which means they can be stored in variables, passed as arguments to other functions, and returned as results. This feature enables powerful programming techniques that we'll explore in this chapter.

Defining and Calling Functions

Let's start with the basics: how to define and call functions in Lua.

Function Definition Syntax

Here's the standard syntax for defining a function:

```
function functionName(parameter1, parameter2, ...)
    -- Function body
    -- Code to be executed when the function is called
    return value -- Optional return statement
end
```

And here's a simple example:

```
-- Define a function that adds two numbers
```

```lua
function add(a, b)
    return a + b
end

-- Call the function
local result = add(5, 3)
print("5 + 3 =", result)
```

Output:

```
5 + 3 = 8
```

Alternative Function Definition Syntax

Lua also allows you to define functions as variables, which emphasizes their status as first-class values:

```lua
-- Define a function as a variable
local multiply = function(a, b)
    return a * b
end

-- Call the function
local result = multiply(4, 6)
print("4 * 6 =", result)
```

Output:

```
4 * 6 = 24
```

Both approaches are equivalent, but they have different use cases. The first form is usually clearer for named functions, while the second form is helpful for anonymous functions or when you need to assign functions to variables.

Local vs. Global Functions

Just like variables, functions can be local or global:

```lua
-- Global function (accessible from anywhere)
function globalFunction()
    print("This is a global function")
end
```

```
-- Local function (accessible only within its scope)
local function localFunction()
    print("This is a local function")
end

-- Call both functions
globalFunction()
localFunction()
```

Output:

```
This is a global function
This is a local function
```

It's generally good practice to use local functions to avoid polluting the global namespace, especially in larger programs or libraries.

Function Calls

Calling a function is straightforward—use the function name followed by arguments in parentheses:

```
-- Define a function
function greet(name)
    print("Hello, " .. name .. "!")
end

-- Call the function
greet("Alice")
greet("Bob")
```

Output:

```
Hello, Alice!
Hello, Bob!
```

If a function takes no arguments, you still need empty parentheses:

```
function sayHello()
    print("Hello, world!")
end
```

```
sayHello()
```

Output:

```
Hello, world!
```

Parameters and Arguments

Functions can accept parameters, which are values passed to the function when it's called.

Basic Parameter Passing

Parameters are listed in the function definition, and corresponding arguments are provided when the function is called:

```
function displayInfo(name, age)
    print(name .. " is " .. age .. " years old.")
end

displayInfo("Charlie", 25)
```

Output:

```
Charlie is 25 years old.
```

Default Parameter Values

Lua doesn't have built-in support for default parameter values, but you can implement them using the or operator:

```
function greet(name, greeting)
    name = name or "stranger"
    greeting = greeting or "Hello"

    print(greeting .. ", " .. name .. "!")
end

greet("Alice", "Hi")     -- Both parameters provided
greet("Bob")             -- Only name provided
greet(nil, "Welcome")    -- Only greeting provided
```

```
greet()                  -- No parameters provided
```

Output:

```
Hi, Alice!
Hello, Bob!
Welcome, stranger!
Hello, stranger!
```

Variable Number of Arguments

Lua supports functions with a variable number of arguments using the ... (vararg)
syntax:

```
function sum(...)
    local total = 0
    for _, value in ipairs({...}) do
        total = total + value
    end
    return total
end

print("Sum:", sum(1, 2, 3, 4, 5))
print("Sum:", sum(10, 20))
print("Sum:", sum())
```

Output:

```
Sum: 15
Sum: 30
Sum: 0
```

The ... syntax collects all the extra arguments into a special vararg expression. You
can convert it to a table using {...}, as shown in the example.

You can also combine fixed parameters with varargs:

```
function formatName(firstName, lastName, ...)
    local result = firstName .. " " .. lastName

    local titles = {...}
    for _, title in ipairs(titles) do
```

```
        result = result .. ", " .. title
    end

    return result
end

print(formatName("John", "Doe"))
print(formatName("Jane", "Smith", "PhD", "Professor"))
```

Output:

```
John Doe
Jane Smith, PhD, Professor
```

Named Parameters with Tables

For functions with many parameters, it can be clearer to use a table for named parameters:

```
function createUser(params)
    -- Set default values
    local user = {
        username = params.username or "guest",
        email = params.email or "none",
        active = params.active ~= nil and params.active or true,
        role = params.role or "user"
    }

    print("Created user: " .. user.username)
    print("  Email: " .. user.email)
    print("  Active: " .. tostring(user.active))
    print("  Role: " .. user.role)

    return user
end

-- Call with named parameters
createUser({
    username = "alice123",
    email = "alice@example.com",
    role = "admin"
})

-- Only provide some parameters
createUser({
```

```
    username = "bob456"
})
```

Output:

```
Created user: alice123
  Email: alice@example.com
  Active: true
  Role: admin
Created user: bob456
  Email: none
  Active: true
  Role: user
```

This approach makes function calls more readable, especially when there are many parameters or when you want to skip some parameters.

Return Values

Functions in Lua can return values to the caller using the `return` statement.

Basic Return Values

The simplest case is returning a single value:

```
function square(x)
    return x * x
end

local result = square(5)
print("5 squared =", result)
```

Output:

```
5 squared = 25
```

A function without a `return` statement (or with a `return` without a value) returns `nil`:

```
function doNothing()
    -- No return statement
end
```

```
function returnNothing()
    return
end

print("doNothing() returns:", doNothing())
print("returnNothing() returns:", returnNothing())
```

Output:

```
doNothing() returns: nil
returnNothing() returns: nil
```

Multiple Return Values

One of Lua's powerful features is the ability for functions to return multiple values:

```
function getNameParts(fullName)
    -- Find the space between names
    local space = string.find(fullName, " ")

    if space then
        local firstName = string.sub(fullName, 1, space - 1)
        local lastName = string.sub(fullName, space + 1)
        return firstName, lastName
    else
        return fullName, ""
    end
end

local first, last = getNameParts("Alice Smith")
print("First name:", first)
print("Last name:", last)

local first_only = getNameParts("Bob")
print("Single name:", first_only)
```

Output:

```
First name: Alice
Last name: Smith
Single name: Bob
```

Multiple returns are particularly useful for returning status codes along with results:

```
function divide(a, b)
    if b == 0 then
        return false, "Division by zero"
    else
        return true, a / b
    end
end

local success, result = divide(10, 2)
if success then
    print("Result:", result)
else
    print("Error:", result)
end

success, result = divide(10, 0)
if success then
    print("Result:", result)
else
    print("Error:", result)
end
```

Output:

```
Result: 5
Error: Division by zero
```

Handling Extra or Missing Return Values

When a function call doesn't capture all the return values, the extra values are discarded:

```
function getValues()
    return 1, 2, 3, 4, 5
end

local a, b = getValues()
print("a =", a)   -- 1
print("b =", b)   -- 2
-- The values 3, 4, and 5 are discarded

local x = getValues()
print("x =", x)   -- Only gets the first value: 1
```

Output:

```
a = 1
b = 2
x = 1
```

Conversely, if a function returns fewer values than expected, the extra variables receive nil:

```
function getSingleValue()
    return 42
end

local y, z = getSingleValue()
print("y =", y)   -- 42
print("z =", z)   -- nil
```

Output:

```
y = 42
z = nil
```

Functions as First-Class Values

In Lua, functions are first-class values, which means they can be:

- Stored in variables
- Passed as arguments to other functions
- Returned from functions

This enables powerful programming techniques like higher-order functions and closures.

Functions as Variables

As we've seen, functions can be assigned to variables:

```
-- Assign an anonymous function to a variable
local square = function(x)
    return x * x
end

-- Assign a named function to another variable
```

```
function cube(x)
    return x * x * x
end

local powerOfThree = cube

-- Call the functions
print("5 squared =", square(5))
print("5 cubed =", powerOfThree(5))
```

Output:

```
5 squared = 25
5 cubed = 125
```

Functions as Arguments

Functions can be passed as arguments to other functions:

```
-- A function that applies another function to a value
function applyFunction(func, value)
    return func(value)
end

-- Define some functions to pass
function double(x)
    return x * 2
end

function square(x)
    return x * x
end

-- Use the functions as arguments
print("Double 5:", applyFunction(double, 5))
print("Square 5:", applyFunction(square, 5))

-- Use an anonymous function as an argument
print("Triple 5:", applyFunction(function(x) return x * 3 end, 5))
```

Output:

```
Double 5: 10
Square 5: 25
```

```
Triple 5: 15
```

This pattern is the foundation of higher-order functions like map, filter, and reduce, which are common in functional programming:

```
-- Implement a simple map function
function map(arr, func)
    local result = {}
    for i, value in ipairs(arr) do
        result[i] = func(value)
    end
    return result
end

-- Test the map function
local numbers = {1, 2, 3, 4, 5}
local doubled = map(numbers, double)
local squared = map(numbers, square)

-- Display results
print("Original:", table.concat(numbers, ", "))
print("Doubled:", table.concat(doubled, ", "))
print("Squared:", table.concat(squared, ", "))
```

Output:

```
Original: 1, 2, 3, 4, 5
Doubled: 2, 4, 6, 8, 10
Squared: 1, 4, 9, 16, 25
```

Functions Returning Functions

Functions can also return other functions:

```
-- Function that creates a multiplier function
function createMultiplier(factor)
    -- Return a new function that multiplies by factor
    return function(x)
        return x * factor
    end
end

-- Create specific multiplier functions
local double = createMultiplier(2)
```

```
local triple = createMultiplier(3)
local tenfold = createMultiplier(10)

-- Use the generated functions
print("Double 7:", double(7))
print("Triple 7:", triple(7))
print("Tenfold 7:", tenfold(7))
```

Output:

```
Double 7: 14
Triple 7: 21
Tenfold 7: 70
```

This technique is powerful for creating specialized functions based on parameters.

Closures

A closure is a function that captures and remembers the environment in which it was created, including local variables from the outer function.

```
function createCounter()
    local count = 0

    return function()
        count = count + 1
        return count
    end
end

-- Create two independent counters
local counter1 = createCounter()
local counter2 = createCounter()

-- Use the counters
print("Counter 1:", counter1())   -- 1
print("Counter 1:", counter1())   -- 2
print("Counter 2:", counter2())   -- 1
print("Counter 1:", counter1())   -- 3
print("Counter 2:", counter2())   -- 2
```

Output:

```
Counter 1: 1
Counter 1: 2
Counter 2: 1
Counter 1: 3
Counter 2: 2
```

In this example, each counter function "closes over" its own copy of the `count` variable. Even after `createCounter` has finished executing, the returned functions still have access to their respective count variables.

Closures are useful for:

- Encapsulating state without using global variables
- Implementing data hiding and private variables
- Creating function factories
- Implementing callbacks that need to maintain state

Here's another example using closures to create a simple bank account:

```
function createAccount(initialBalance)
    local balance = initialBalance or 0

    return {
        deposit = function(amount)
            if amount > 0 then
                balance = balance + amount
                return true, balance
            else
                return false, "Invalid deposit amount"
            end
        end,

        withdraw = function(amount)
            if amount > 0 then
                if balance >= amount then
                    balance = balance - amount
                    return true, balance
                else
                    return false, "Insufficient funds"
                end
            else
                return false, "Invalid withdrawal amount"
            end
        end,
```

```
        getBalance = function()
            return balance
        end
    }
end


-- Create an account
local account = createAccount(100)


-- Use the account
print("Initial balance:", account.getBalance())

local success, result = account.deposit(50)
if success then
    print("New balance after deposit:", result)
else
    print("Error:", result)
end


success, result = account.withdraw(30)
if success then
    print("New balance after withdrawal:", result)
else
    print("Error:", result)
end


success, result = account.withdraw(200)
if success then
    print("New balance after withdrawal:", result)
else
    print("Error:", result)
end


print("Final balance:", account.getBalance())
```

Output:

```
Initial balance: 100
New balance after deposit: 150
New balance after withdrawal: 120
Error: Insufficient funds
Final balance: 120
```

In this example, the balance variable is private and can only be accessed or modified through the provided methods. This is a form of encapsulation, a key principle in object-oriented programming that we'll explore further in Chapter 9.

Recursion

Recursion is a technique where a function calls itself. It's useful for solving problems that can be broken down into smaller, similar sub-problems.

```
-- Calculate factorial using recursion
function factorial(n)
    if n <= 1 then
        return 1
    else
        return n * factorial(n - 1)
    end
end

print("Factorial of 5:", factorial(5))   -- 5! = 5 * 4 * 3 * 2 * 1 = 120
```

Output:

```
Factorial of 5: 120
```

Recursion should be used carefully, as deep recursion can lead to stack overflow errors. For some problems, an iterative solution might be more efficient:

```
-- Calculate factorial iteratively
function factorialIterative(n)
    local result = 1
    for i = 2, n do
        result = result * i
    end
    return result
end

print("Factorial of 5 (iterative):", factorialIterative(5))
```

Output:

```
Factorial of 5 (iterative): 120
```

A classic example of recursion is the Fibonacci sequence, where each number is the sum of the two preceding ones:

```
-- Calculate Fibonacci number recursively
```

```
function fibonacci(n)
    if n <= 1 then
        return n
    else
        return fibonacci(n - 1) + fibonacci(n - 2)
    end
end

-- Print the first 10 Fibonacci numbers
for i = 0, 9 do
    print("Fibonacci " .. i .. ":", fibonacci(i))
end
```

Output:

```
Fibonacci 0: 0
Fibonacci 1: 1
Fibonacci 2: 1
Fibonacci 3: 2
Fibonacci 4: 3
Fibonacci 5: 5
Fibonacci 6: 8
Fibonacci 7: 13
Fibonacci 8: 21
Fibonacci 9: 34
```

Note that this recursive implementation of Fibonacci is elegant but inefficient for large values of n due to redundant calculations. For better performance, you might use memoization (storing previously calculated results) or an iterative approach.

Advanced Function Techniques

Let's explore some more advanced function techniques in Lua.

Function Environments

Every function in Lua operates within an environment, which determines what global variables it can access. By default, all functions share the same global environment, but you can change this:

```
-- Create a custom environment
local env = {
    print = print,  -- Include the standard print function
```

```
    math = math,    -- Include the math library
    customValue = 42
}

-- Create a function
local function test()
    print("Custom value:", customValue)
    print("Pi value:", math.pi)

    -- This would cause an error because string is not in our environment
    -- print("String lib:", string.upper("hello"))
end

-- Set the environment for the function (Lua 5.1 syntax)
if setfenv then  -- Check if setfenv exists (Lua 5.1)
    setfenv(test, env)
    test()  -- This will work
else
    print("setfenv not available (Lua 5.2+)")
end
```

Output (in Lua 5.1):

```
Custom value: 42
Pi value: 3.1415926535898
```

In Lua 5.2 and later, the _ENV upvalue replaces setfenv:

```
-- For Lua 5.2+
local function test2(_ENV)
    print("Custom value:", customValue)
    print("Pi value:", math.pi)
end

if not setfenv then  -- If we're in Lua 5.2+
    test2(env)  -- This will work
end
```

Function Decorators

Function decorators are a pattern where you wrap a function with another function to extend its behavior:

```
-- A decorator that logs function calls
```

72

```
function logDecorator(func, name)
    name = name or "function"

    return function(...)
        print("Calling " .. name .. " with arguments:", ...)
        local results = {func(...)}
        print(name .. " returned:", table.unpack(results))
        return table.unpack(results)
    end
end

-- A function to decorate
function add(a, b)
    return a + b
end

-- Decorate the function
add = logDecorator(add, "add")

-- Call the decorated function
local sum = add(3, 4)
print("Result:", sum)
```

Output:

```
Calling add with arguments: 3 4
add returned: 7
Result: 7
```

Here's another decorator example that memoizes a function (caches its results):

```
-- A decorator that memoizes function results
function memoize(func)
    local cache = {}

    return function(...)
        local args = {...}
        local key = table.concat(args, ",")

        if cache[key] == nil then
            cache[key] = func(...)
            print("Calculated result for", key)
        else
            print("Using cached result for", key)
        end
```

```
        return cache[key]
    end
end

-- An expensive function to memoize
function slowAdd(a, b)
    -- Simulate a slow operation
    local result = a + b
    return result
end

-- Memoize the function
slowAdd = memoize(slowAdd)

-- Call the function multiple times with the same arguments
print("Result:", slowAdd(3, 4))
print("Result:", slowAdd(3, 4))
print("Result:", slowAdd(5, 6))
print("Result:", slowAdd(5, 6))
```

Output:

```
Calculated result for 3,4
Result: 7
Using cached result for 3,4
Result: 7
Calculated result for 5,6
Result: 11
Using cached result for 5,6
Result: 11
```

Self-calling Functions (Immediately Invoked Function Expressions)

Sometimes you want to create and call a function immediately, especially to create a private scope:

```
-- Normal approach
local function initialize()
    print("Initializing...")
    local data = {
        count = 0,
        initialized = true
    }
    return data
```

```
end

local result = initialize()
print("Initialized:", result.initialized)

-- Self-calling function approach
local result2 = (function()
    print("Initializing via self-call...")
    local data = {
        count = 0,
        initialized = true
    }
    return data
end)()

print("Initialized via self-call:", result2.initialized)
```

Output:

```
Initializing...
Initialized: true
Initializing via self-call...
Initialized via self-call: true
```

Best Practices for Functions

Let's conclude with some best practices for writing functions in Lua:

1. **Use Local Functions**: Prefer local functions to avoid polluting the global namespace.

2. **Function Naming**: Use descriptive names that indicate what the function does. Use verbs for functions that perform actions.

3. **Single Responsibility**: Each function should do one thing and do it well. If a function is doing too many things, consider breaking it into smaller functions.

4. **Parameter Validation**: Check that function parameters are valid before using them.

5. **Document Your Functions**: Include comments that explain what the function does, its parameters, and its return values.

6. **Consistent Return Values**: Functions should have consistent return patterns. For example, if a function can fail, always return a success flag and an error message.

7. **Avoid Side Effects**: Try to write "pure" functions that don't modify external state, as they're easier to understand, test, and debug.

Here's an example incorporating these best practices:

```
--[[
    Divides two numbers and returns the result.

    @param dividend The number to be divided
    @param divisor The number to divide by
    @return success A boolean indicating whether the operation succeeded
    @return result The result of the division or an error message
]]
local function divide(dividend, divisor)
    -- Parameter validation
    if type(dividend) ~= "number" then
        return false, "Dividend must be a number"
    end

    if type(divisor) ~= "number" then
        return false, "Divisor must be a number"
    end

    if divisor == 0 then
        return false, "Cannot divide by zero"
    end

    -- Perform the operation
    local result = dividend / divisor

    -- Return the result
    return true, result
end

-- Function usage example
local function testDivision(a, b)
    local success, result = divide(a, b)

    if success then
        print(a .. " / " .. b .. " = " .. result)
    else
        print("Error: " .. result)
    end
```

```
end

-- Test the function with various inputs
testDivision(10, 2)
testDivision(10, 0)
testDivision("10", 2)
testDivision(10, "2")
```

Output:

```
10 / 2 = 5
Error: Cannot divide by zero
Error: Dividend must be a number
Error: Divisor must be a number
```

Chapter Summary

In this chapter, we've explored functions in Lua, from basic definitions and calls to advanced techniques like closures and decorators. We've seen how functions can be defined, how they handle parameters and return values, and how they can be manipulated as first-class values.

We've also examined powerful patterns enabled by Lua's functional nature, such as higher-order functions, function factories, and memoization. These techniques allow for more expressive, modular, and reusable code.

Functions are the workhorses of Lua programming, enabling you to organize code, create abstractions, and build complex systems from simpler components. The flexibility of Lua's function system—especially features like multiple returns, varargs, and closures—gives you powerful tools for solving programming problems elegantly.

In the next chapter, we'll dive into tables, Lua's primary data structure. Tables work hand-in-hand with functions to form the backbone of Lua programming, enabling you to organize and manipulate data in sophisticated ways.

Chapter 7: Tables: The Heart of Lua

Introduction to Tables

Tables are the only data structure in Lua, yet they're incredibly versatile. A table in Lua is essentially a collection of key-value pairs that can store any type of data, including other tables and functions. Tables can be used to implement arrays, dictionaries, sets, objects, modules, and much more.

The simplicity of having just one data structure that can handle so many different tasks is one of Lua's most elegant features. In this chapter, we'll explore tables in depth, learning how to create, manipulate, and leverage them effectively in your Lua programs.

Creating and Initializing Tables

There are several ways to create and initialize tables in Lua.

Table Constructor Syntax

The most common way to create a table is with the table constructor syntax, which uses curly braces {}:

```lua
-- Empty table
local emptyTable = {}

-- Table with initial values (array-like)
local fruits = {"Apple", "Banana", "Cherry"}

-- Table with key-value pairs (dictionary-like)
local person = {
```

```lua
    name = "Alice",
    age = 30,
    email = "alice@example.com"
}

-- Mixed table with both array-like and dictionary-like elements
local mixed = {
    "First",
    "Second",
    name = "Mixed Table",
    count = 2
}

-- Print tables to see their contents
print("Fruits:")
for i, fruit in ipairs(fruits) do
    print(i, fruit)
end

print("\nPerson:")
for key, value in pairs(person) do
    print(key, value)
end

print("\nMixed:")
for key, value in pairs(mixed) do
    print(key, value)
end
```

Output:

```
Fruits:
1       Apple
2       Banana
3       Cherry

Person:
name    Alice
age     30
email   alice@example.com

Mixed:
1       First
2       Second
name    Mixed Table
count   2
```

Explicit Key-Value Syntax

For non-sequential keys or keys that aren't valid identifiers, you can use the square bracket notation in the constructor:

```lua
-- Table with explicit keys
local settings = {
    ["font-size"] = 12,  -- Key contains a hyphen
    [true] = "boolean key",  -- Boolean key
    [5] = "numeric key",  -- Numeric key
    ["print"] = function(t) print(t.message) end,  -- Function value
    message = "Hello, world!"  -- Regular key-value
}

print("Settings:")
for key, value in pairs(settings) do
    if type(value) ~= "function" then
        print(key, value)
    else
        print(key, "function")
    end
end

-- Call the function stored in the table
settings["print"](settings)
```

Output:

```
Settings:
font-size       12
message Hello, world!
5       numeric key
true    boolean key
print   function
Hello, world!
```

Creating Tables Dynamically

You can also build tables incrementally:

```lua
-- Start with an empty table
local shoppingList = {}

-- Add items one by one
shoppingList[1] = "Milk"
```

```
shoppingList[2] = "Bread"
shoppingList[3] = "Eggs"

-- Add named properties
shoppingList.store = "Grocery Store"
shoppingList.urgent = true

print("Shopping List:")
for i = 1, #shoppingList do
    print(i, shoppingList[i])
end

print("Store:", shoppingList.store)
print("Urgent:", shoppingList.urgent)
```

Output:

```
Shopping List:
1        Milk
2        Bread
3        Eggs
Store: Grocery Store
Urgent: true
```

Accessing Table Elements

There are two main ways to access table elements in Lua: dot notation and square bracket notation.

Dot Notation

Dot notation (`table.key`) is used for keys that are valid identifiers:

```
local user = {
    name = "Bob",
    age = 25,
    isPremium = true
}

print("Name:", user.name)
print("Age:", user.age)
print("Premium:", user.isPremium)

-- Modify values using dot notation
```

```
user.age = 26
user.isPremium = false

print("Updated age:", user.age)
print("Updated premium status:", user.isPremium)
```

Output:

```
Name: Bob
Age: 25
Premium: true
Updated age: 26
Updated premium status: false
```

Square Bracket Notation

Square bracket notation (table[key]) works with any type of key, including those that aren't valid identifiers:

```
local data = {
    ["first-name"] = "Charlie",
    [42] = "The answer",
    [true] = "Boolean key",
    [{}] = "Table key"  -- Note: Tables as keys use reference equality
}

print("First name:", data["first-name"])
print("The answer:", data[42])
print("Boolean value:", data[true])

-- Square brackets also work with variables as keys
local key = "first-name"
print("Using variable as key:", data[key])

-- Square bracket notation also works with regular identifier keys
local user = {
    name = "David",
    age = 35
}

print("Name (bracket notation):", user["name"])
```

Output:

```
First name: Charlie
The answer: The answer
Boolean value: Boolean key
Using variable as key: Charlie
Name (bracket notation): David
```

Handling Non-existent Keys

When you try to access a key that doesn't exist in a table, Lua returns `nil` rather than raising an error:

```lua
local config = {
    version = "1.0",
    debug = true
}

print("Version:", config.version)
print("Debug:", config.debug)
print("Author:", config.author)  -- Key doesn't exist, returns nil

-- Check if a key exists before using it
if config.maxConnections then
    print("Max connections:", config.maxConnections)
else
    print("Max connections not specified")
end
```

Output:

```
Version: 1.0
Debug: true
Author: nil
Max connections not specified
```

Tables as Arrays

Although Lua doesn't have a separate array type, tables are commonly used as arrays by using consecutive integer keys starting from 1.

Creating and Using Arrays

```lua
-- Create an array-like table
```

```lua
local colors = {"Red", "Green", "Blue", "Yellow", "Purple"}

-- Access elements by index
print("First color:", colors[1])  -- Lua arrays start at index 1, not 0
print("Third color:", colors[3])

-- Modify elements
colors[2] = "Emerald"
print("Updated second color:", colors[2])

-- Get the array length
print("Number of colors:", #colors)

-- Iterate through the array
print("All colors:")
for i = 1, #colors do
    print(i, colors[i])
end

-- Alternative iteration using ipairs
print("Using ipairs:")
for i, color in ipairs(colors) do
    print(i, color)
end
```

Output:

```
First color: Red
Third color: Blue
Updated second color: Emerald
Number of colors: 5
All colors:
1       Red
2       Emerald
3       Blue
4       Yellow
5       Purple
Using ipairs:
1       Red
2       Emerald
3       Blue
4       Yellow
5       Purple
```

Array Operations

Lua provides some built-in functions for working with array-like tables in the `table` library:

```lua
-- Create an array
local numbers = {10, 20, 30, 40, 50}

-- Insert an element at the end (push)
table.insert(numbers, 60)
print("After insert at end:", table.concat(numbers, ", "))

-- Insert an element at a specific position
table.insert(numbers, 3, 25)
print("After insert at position 3:", table.concat(numbers, ", "))

-- Remove the last element (pop)
local lastValue = table.remove(numbers)
print("Removed value:", lastValue)
print("After remove from end:", table.concat(numbers, ", "))

-- Remove an element at a specific position
local removedValue = table.remove(numbers, 2)
print("Removed value at position 2:", removedValue)
print("After remove from position 2:", table.concat(numbers, ", "))

-- Sort an array
local unsorted = {3, 1, 4, 1, 5, 9, 2, 6}
table.sort(unsorted)
print("Sorted array:", table.concat(unsorted, ", "))

-- Sort with a custom comparison function (descending order)
table.sort(unsorted, function(a, b) return a > b end)
print("Sorted array (descending):", table.concat(unsorted, ", "))
```

Output:

```
After insert at end: 10, 20, 30, 40, 50, 60
After insert at position 3: 10, 20, 25, 30, 40, 50, 60
Removed value: 60
After remove from end: 10, 20, 25, 30, 40, 50
Removed value at position 2: 20
After remove from position 2: 10, 25, 30, 40, 50
Sorted array: 1, 1, 2, 3, 4, 5, 6, 9
Sorted array (descending): 9, 6, 5, 4, 3, 2, 1, 1
```

Sparse Arrays

Unlike arrays in some other languages, Lua arrays can be "sparse," meaning they can have gaps in their indices:

```lua
local sparse = {}
sparse[1] = "First"
sparse[3] = "Third"
sparse[5] = "Fifth"

print("Length of sparse array:", #sparse)  -- May return 1 or 5, behavior is
implementation-defined

print("Elements of sparse array:")
for i = 1, 5 do
    print(i, sparse[i])
end

-- Using pairs to iterate guarantees we see all elements
print("Using pairs to iterate:")
for k, v in pairs(sparse) do
    print(k, v)
end
```

Output:

```
Length of sparse array: 1
Elements of sparse array:
1        First
2        nil
3        Third
4        nil
5        Fifth
Using pairs to iterate:
1        First
3        Third
5        Fifth
```

Note that the # operator might not work as expected with sparse arrays. It typically returns the largest sequence of non-nil values starting from index 1, but its behavior with sparse arrays is implementation-defined.

Tables as Dictionaries

Tables are also perfect for implementing dictionaries (maps) where keys can be any value (except nil).

Creating and Using Dictionaries

```
-- Create a dictionary
local employee = {
    id = "E12345",
    firstName = "Emma",
    lastName = "Wilson",
    department = "Engineering",
    salary = 75000,
    skills = {"JavaScript", "Python", "Lua"}
}

-- Access values
print("Employee ID:", employee.id)
print("Full Name:", employee.firstName .. " " .. employee.lastName)
print("Department:", employee.department)

-- Add or modify key-value pairs
employee.position = "Senior Developer"
employee.salary = 80000

print("Position:", employee.position)
print("Updated Salary:", employee.salary)

-- Check if a key exists
if employee.hireDate then
    print("Hire Date:", employee.hireDate)
else
    print("Hire date not specified")
end

-- Delete a key-value pair
employee.department = nil
print("Department after deletion:", employee.department)
```

Output:

```
Employee ID: E12345
Full Name: Emma Wilson
Department: Engineering
Position: Senior Developer
```

```
Updated Salary: 80000
Hire date not specified
Department after deletion: nil
```

Iteration Over Dictionaries

The pairs function is used to iterate over all key-value pairs in a table, regardless of key type:

```
local settings = {
    theme = "dark",
    fontSize = 14,
    showToolbar = true,
    recentFiles = {"doc1.txt", "image.png", "script.lua"}
}

print("Settings:")
for key, value in pairs(settings) do
    if type(value) ~= "table" then
        print("  " .. key .. ":", value)
    else
        print("  " .. key .. ":", "table with " .. #value .. " items")
    end
end
```

Output:

```
Settings:
  theme: dark
  fontSize: 14
  showToolbar: true
  recentFiles: table with 3 items
```

Note that pairs doesn't guarantee any specific order for iteration. If you need ordered iteration, you might need to extract and sort the keys first.

Nested Tables

Tables can contain other tables, allowing you to create complex, nested data structures.

Creating Nested Tables

```lua
-- Create a nested table structure
local company = {
    name = "TechCorp",
    founded = 2010,
    location = {
        city = "San Francisco",
        state = "CA",
        country = "USA",
        coordinates = {
            latitude = 37.7749,
            longitude = -122.4194
        }
    },
    departments = {
        {name = "Engineering", employees = 50},
        {name = "Sales", employees = 30},
        {name = "Marketing", employees = 20}
    }
}

-- Access nested values
print("Company:", company.name)
print("Location:", company.location.city .. ", " .. company.location.state)
print("Coordinates:", company.location.coordinates.latitude .. ", " ..
                    company.location.coordinates.longitude)

-- Iterate through a nested array
print("\nDepartments:")
for i, dept in ipairs(company.departments) do
    print(i .. ".", dept.name, "(" .. dept.employees .. " employees)")
end
```

Output:

```
Company: TechCorp
Location: San Francisco, CA
Coordinates: 37.7749, -122.4194

Departments:
1. Engineering (50 employees)
2. Sales (30 employees)
3. Marketing (20 employees)
```

Deep vs. Shallow Copies

When working with nested tables, it's important to understand the difference between shallow and deep copies:

```lua
-- Original nested table
local original = {
    name = "Original",
    values = {1, 2, 3},
    nested = {
        x = 10,
        y = 20
    }
}

-- Shallow copy (only copies the top level)
local function shallowCopy(t)
    local copy = {}
    for key, value in pairs(t) do
        copy[key] = value
    end
    return copy
end

-- Deep copy (recursively copies nested tables)
local function deepCopy(t)
    if type(t) ~= "table" then return t end

    local copy = {}
    for key, value in pairs(t) do
        if type(value) == "table" then
            copy[key] = deepCopy(value)
        else
            copy[key] = value
        end
    end
    return copy
end

-- Create copies
local shallowCopied = shallowCopy(original)
local deepCopied = deepCopy(original)

-- Modify the original's nested table
original.values[1] = 100
original.nested.x = 500

-- Compare results
```

```
print("Original values[1]:", original.values[1])
print("Shallow copy values[1]:", shallowCopied.values[1])  -- Also changed
(shared reference)
print("Deep copy values[1]:", deepCopied.values[1])  -- Unchanged (separate
copy)

print("Original nested.x:", original.nested.x)
print("Shallow copy nested.x:", shallowCopied.nested.x)  -- Also changed (shared
reference)
print("Deep copy nested.x:", deepCopied.nested.x)  -- Unchanged (separate copy)
```

Output:

```
Original values[1]: 100
Shallow copy values[1]: 100
Deep copy values[1]: 1
Original nested.x: 500
Shallow copy nested.x: 500
Deep copy nested.x: 10
```

Table References and Equality

In Lua, tables are reference types, meaning variables hold references to tables rather than the tables themselves.

Table References

```
-- Create a table
local t1 = {a = 1, b = 2}

-- Create another reference to the same table
local t2 = t1

-- Modify through one reference
t2.a = 10

-- The change is visible through both references
print("t1.a:", t1.a)  -- 10
print("t2.a:", t2.a)  -- 10

-- Create a new table with the same content
local t3 = {a = 10, b = 2}

-- t3 is a different table from t1, even though the contents are the same
```

```
print("t1 == t3:", t1 == t3)  -- false
```

Output:

```
t1.a: 10
t2.a: 10
t1 == t3: false
```

Tables as Keys

Because tables are compared by reference, they can be used as keys in other tables:

```
-- Use tables as keys in another table
local tableKeys = {}

local key1 = {name = "Key 1"}
local key2 = {name = "Key 2"}

tableKeys[key1] = "Value for Key 1"
tableKeys[key2] = "Value for Key 2"

print("Value for key1:", tableKeys[key1])
print("Value for key2:", tableKeys[key2])

-- A new table with the same content will be a different key
local key1Copy = {name = "Key 1"}
print("Value for key1Copy:", tableKeys[key1Copy])  -- nil
```

Output:

```
Value for key1: Value for Key 1
Value for key2: Value for Key 2
Value for key1Copy: nil
```

Metatable and Metamethods

Metatables provide a mechanism for customizing the behavior of tables, such as how they respond to operators and certain events.

Setting and Getting Metatables

```lua
-- Create two tables
local t1 = {value = 5}
local t2 = {value = 10}

-- Create a metatable
local mt = {
    -- Metamethod for addition
    __add = function(a, b)
        return {value = a.value + b.value}
    end
}

-- Set the metatable for both tables
setmetatable(t1, mt)
setmetatable(t2, mt)

-- Now we can "add" the tables
local result = t1 + t2
print("Result of addition:", result.value)  -- 15

-- Get the metatable of a table
local mt2 = getmetatable(t1)
print("Is same metatable:", mt == mt2)  -- true
```

Output:

```
Result of addition: 15
Is same metatable: true
```

Common Metamethods

Lua supports many metamethods that customize table behavior:

```lua
-- Create a simple vector type
local Vector = {}
Vector.__index = Vector

function Vector.new(x, y)
    local v = {x = x or 0, y = y or 0}
    setmetatable(v, Vector)
    return v
end
```

```lua
-- Arithmetic operations
function Vector.__add(a, b)
    return Vector.new(a.x + b.x, a.y + b.y)
end

function Vector.__sub(a, b)
    return Vector.new(a.x - b.x, a.y - b.y)
end

function Vector.__mul(a, b)
    if type(a) == "number" then
        return Vector.new(a * b.x, a * b.y)
    elseif type(b) == "number" then
        return Vector.new(a.x * b, a.y * b)
    else
        -- Dot product
        return a.x * b.x + a.y * b.y
    end
end

-- String representation
function Vector.__tostring(v)
    return "Vector(" .. v.x .. ", " .. v.y .. ")"
end

-- Equality comparison
function Vector.__eq(a, b)
    return a.x == b.x and a.y == b.y
end

-- Create vectors
local v1 = Vector.new(3, 4)
local v2 = Vector.new(1, 2)

-- Use the custom operations
print("v1:", v1)
print("v2:", v2)
print("v1 + v2:", v1 + v2)
print("v1 - v2:", v1 - v2)
print("v1 * 2:", v1 * 2)
print("v1 * v2 (dot product):", v1 * v2)
print("v1 == Vector.new(3, a):", v1 == Vector.new(3, 4))
print("v1 == v2:", v1 == v2)
```

Output:

```
v1: Vector(3, 4)
v2: Vector(1, 2)
v1 + v2: Vector(4, 6)
v1 - v2: Vector(2, 2)
v1 * 2: Vector(6, 8)
v1 * v2 (dot product): 11
v1 == Vector.new(3, a): true
v1 == v2: false
```

The __index Metamethod

The `__index` metamethod is triggered when accessing a key that doesn't exist in a table. It can be a function or another table:

```lua
-- Create a prototype table
local prototype = {
    x = 0,
    y = 0,

    move = function(self, dx, dy)
        self.x = self.x + dx
        self.y = self.y + dy
        return self
    end,

    getPosition = function(self)
        return self.x, self.y
    end
}

-- Create an instance that inherits from the prototype
local instance = {}
setmetatable(instance, { __index = prototype })

-- Instance doesn't have these methods directly, but can use them via __index
instance:move(5, 10)
local x, y = instance:getPosition()
print("Position:", x, y)

-- We can override inherited values
instance.x = 100
x, y = instance:getPosition()
print("New position:", x, y)
```

Output:

```
Position: 5 10
New position: 100 10
```

Common Table Patterns

Let's explore some common patterns and idioms for working with tables in Lua.

Table as a Namespace

Tables can be used to create namespaces, preventing name collisions in the global environment:

```lua
-- Create a namespace
local MyApp = {
    version = "1.0",
    author = "Lua Developer",

    config = {
        debug = true,
        maxConnections = 10
    },

    -- Functions in the namespace
    initialize = function()
        print("Initializing MyApp v" .. MyApp.version)
    end,

    shutdown = function()
        print("Shutting down MyApp")
    end
}

-- Use the namespace
MyApp.initialize()
print("Debug mode:", MyApp.config.debug)
MyApp.shutdown()
```

Output:

```
Initializing MyApp v1.0
Debug mode: true
Shutting down MyApp
```

Table as a Class/Object

Tables can represent objects with both data and behavior:

```
-- Define a "class" (actually just a table with functions)
local Rectangle = {
    -- Constructor
    new = function(width, height)
        local obj = {
            width = width or 0,
            height = height or 0
        }

        -- Add methods
        function obj:getArea()
            return self.width * self.height
        end

        function obj:getPerimeter()
            return 2 * (self.width + self.height)
        end

        function obj:scale(factor)
            self.width = self.width * factor
            self.height = self.height * factor
            return self
        end

        return obj
    end
}

-- Create and use instances
local rect1 = Rectangle.new(5, 10)
print("Area:", rect1:getArea())
print("Perimeter:", rect1:getPerimeter())

rect1:scale(2)
print("After scaling - Area:", rect1:getArea())
```

Output:

```
Area: 50
Perimeter: 30
After scaling - Area: 200
```

We'll explore object-oriented programming in Lua more thoroughly in Chapter 9.

Table as a Set

Tables can implement sets, where each element appears only once:

```lua
-- Create a set from a list of values
local function createSet(list)
    local set = {}
    for _, value in ipairs(list) do
        set[value] = true
    end
    return set
end

-- Operations on sets
local function union(a, b)
    local result = {}
    for k in pairs(a) do result[k] = true end
    for k in pairs(b) do result[k] = true end
    return result
end

local function intersection(a, b)
    local result = {}
    for k in pairs(a) do
        if b[k] then result[k] = true end
    end
    return result
end

local function difference(a, b)
    local result = {}
    for k in pairs(a) do
        if not b[k] then result[k] = true end
    end
    return result
end

-- Helper function to display sets
local function setToString(set)
    local elements = {}
    for element in pairs(set) do
        table.insert(elements, tostring(element))
    end
    table.sort(elements)
    return "{" .. table.concat(elements, ", ") .. "}"
```

```
end

-- Create some sets
local A = createSet({1, 2, 3, 4, 5})
local B = createSet({4, 5, 6, 7, 8})

print("Set A:", setToString(A))
print("Set B:", setToString(B))
print("A ∪ B (union):", setToString(union(A, B)))
print("A ∩ B (intersection):", setToString(intersection(A, B)))
print("A - B (difference):", setToString(difference(A, B)))
```

Output:

```
Set A: {1, 2, 3, 4, 5}
Set B: {4, 5, 6, 7, 8}
A ∪ B (union): {1, 2, 3, 4, 5, 6, 7, 8}
A ∩ B (intersection): {4, 5}
A - B (difference): {1, 2, 3}
```

Table as a Cache (Memoization)

Tables are perfect for implementing memoization, a technique to cache results of expensive function calls:

```
-- Fibonacci with memoization
local fib_cache = {}

local function fibonacci(n)
    -- Check if the result is already cached
    if fib_cache[n] then
        print("Cache hit for fib(" .. n .. ")")
        return fib_cache[n]
    end

    -- Calculate the result for new values
    local result
    if n <= 1 then
        result = n
    else
        result = fibonacci(n - 1) + fibonacci(n - 2)
    end

    -- Cache the result before returning
    fib_cache[n] = result
```

```
        return result
end

-- Try the function
print("fib(10) =", fibonacci(10))
print("fib(10) again =", fibonacci(10))  -- Should use cached value
print("fib(11) =", fibonacci(11))  -- Should use cached values for smaller
calculations
```

Output:

```
Cache hit for fib(1)
Cache hit for fib(2)
Cache hit for fib(3)
Cache hit for fib(4)
Cache hit for fib(5)
Cache hit for fib(6)
Cache hit for fib(7)
Cache hit for fib(8)
fib(10) = 55
Cache hit for fib(10)
fib(10) again = 55
Cache hit for fib(10)
Cache hit for fib(9)
fib(11) = 89
```

Performance Considerations

When working with tables in Lua, there are several performance aspects to keep in mind:

Table Creation

Creating tables has some overhead, so avoid creating many small tables in performance-critical sections:

```
-- Inefficient: Creates a new table in each iteration
local function sumSquaresInefficient(n)
    local total = 0
    for i = 1, n do
        local square = {value = i * i}  -- New table each iteration
        total = total + square.value
    end
    return total
```

```
end

-- Efficient: Avoids unnecessary table creation
local function sumSquaresEfficient(n)
    local total = 0
    for i = 1, n do
        local square = i * i  -- Just calculate the value
        total = total + square
    end
    return total
end

-- Time the functions
local n = 1000000
local start = os.clock()
local result1 = sumSquaresInefficient(n)
local time1 = os.clock() - start

start = os.clock()
local result2 = sumSquaresEfficient(n)
local time2 = os.clock() - start

print("Inefficient:", time1, "seconds")
print("Efficient:", time2, "seconds")
print("Results match:", result1 == result2)
```

Output will vary, but the efficient version should be significantly faster.

Pre-allocating Tables

When you know the approximate size of a table, you can pre-allocate it to reduce the number of memory reallocations:

```
-- Create a large array (slower due to multiple reallocations)
local function createArraySlow(n)
    local arr = {}
    for i = 1, n do
        arr[i] = i
    end
    return arr
end

-- Create a large array with pre-allocation (faster)
local function createArrayFast(n)
    local arr = table.create and table.create(n) or {}  -- Some Lua
implementations have table.create
```

```
        for i = 1, n do
            arr[i] = i
        end
        return arr
    end

    -- Time the functions
    local n = 1000000
    local start = os.clock()
    local arr1 = createArraySlow(n)
    local time1 = os.clock() - start

    start = os.clock()
    local arr2 = createArrayFast(n)
    local time2 = os.clock() - start

    print("Without pre-allocation:", time1, "seconds")
    print("With pre-allocation:", time2, "seconds")
```

Note: The `table.create` function is available in some Lua implementations like LuaJIT and Roblox Lua, but not in standard Lua. In standard Lua, pre-allocation is often not directly available, but the example is still instructive.

Table Reuse

Reusing tables instead of creating new ones can be efficient for frequently used operations:

```
    -- Function that creates a new result table each time
    local function processDataNew(data)
        local results = {}
        for i, value in ipairs(data) do
            results[i] = value * 2
        end
        return results
    end

    -- Function that reuses a provided result table
    local function processDataReuse(data, results)
        results = results or {}
        for i, value in ipairs(data) do
            results[i] = value * 2
        end
        return results
    end
```

```lua
-- Test with a large dataset
local data = {}
for i = 1, 100000 do
    data[i] = i
end

-- Process multiple times, creating new tables
local start = os.clock()
for i = 1, 100 do
    local results = processDataNew(data)
    -- Use the results...
end
local timeNew = os.clock() - start

-- Process multiple times, reusing the same table
local start2 = os.clock()
local resultsTable = {}
for i = 1, 100 do
    processDataReuse(data, resultsTable)
    -- Use the results...
end
local timeReuse = os.clock() - start2

print("Creating new tables:", timeNew, "seconds")
print("Reusing tables:", timeReuse, "seconds")
```

Chapter Summary

In this chapter, we've explored tables, the heart of Lua's data structure system. Despite being the only collection type in Lua, tables are incredibly versatile, capable of implementing arrays, dictionaries, sets, objects, and more.

We've covered how to create and initialize tables, access their elements using dot and bracket notation, and work with tables as arrays and dictionaries. We've also examined nested tables, table references, and the difference between shallow and deep copies.

Metatables provide a powerful mechanism for customizing table behavior, enabling operator overloading and inheritance-like patterns. We've seen common table patterns such as using tables as namespaces, classes, sets, and caches, and we've discussed performance considerations when working with tables.

Tables are fundamental to virtually every Lua program, and mastering them is essential for effective Lua programming. Their flexibility and simplicity make Lua a particularly elegant language for working with complex data structures.

In the next chapter, we'll build upon our understanding of tables to explore modules and packages, which allow you to organize your Lua code into reusable, maintainable components.

Chapter 8: Modules and Packages

Introduction to Modules

As your Lua programs grow in size and complexity, organizing your code becomes increasingly important. Modules are a way to group related functions and variables together, making your code more maintainable, reusable, and easier to understand.

In Lua, a module is typically a table that contains related functions and variables. By using modules, you can:

- Avoid naming conflicts by keeping code in separate namespaces
- Hide implementation details while exposing only necessary interfaces
- Reuse code across multiple projects
- Make dependencies between code components explicit

Let's dive into how modules work in Lua and how to use them effectively.

Creating Basic Modules

The simplest way to create a module in Lua is to define a table, populate it with functions and variables, and return the table at the end of the file.

Module Pattern

Here's a basic pattern for creating a module:

```
-- File: mathutils.lua
local mathutils = {}

-- Public functions
function mathutils.add(a, b)
```

```
    return a + b
end

function mathutils.subtract(a, b)
    return a - b
end

function mathutils.multiply(a, b)
    return a * b
end

function mathutils.divide(a, b)
    if b == 0 then
        error("Division by zero")
    end
    return a / b
end

-- Return the module table
return mathutils
```

To use this module in another file:

```
-- File: main.lua
local mathutils = require("mathutils")

print("5 + 3 =", mathutils.add(5, 3))
print("5 - 3 =", mathutils.subtract(5, 3))
print("5 * 3 =", mathutils.multiply(5, 3))
print("5 / 3 =", mathutils.divide(5, 3))
```

Output:

```
5 + 3 = 8
5 - 3 = 2
5 * 3 = 15
5 / 3 = 1.6666666666667
```

Private Module Variables and Functions

One advantage of modules is the ability to keep certain functions and variables private, accessible only within the module itself:

```
-- File: calculator.lua
```

```lua
local calculator = {}

-- Private variables
local operations = {
    add = function(a, b) return a + b end,
    subtract = function(a, b) return a - b end,
    multiply = function(a, b) return a * b end,
    divide = function(a, b) return a / b end
}

local function validateNumbers(a, b)
    if type(a) ~= "number" or type(b) ~= "number" then
        error("Both arguments must be numbers")
    end
end

-- Public functions
function calculator.calculate(operation, a, b)
    validateNumbers(a, b)

    local op = operations[operation]
    if not op then
        error("Unknown operation: " .. operation)
    end

    if operation == "divide" and b == 0 then
        error("Division by zero")
    end

    return op(a, b)
end

function calculator.getOperations()
    local result = {}
    for op in pairs(operations) do
        table.insert(result, op)
    end
    return result
end

-- Return the module
return calculator
```

Now, when using this module:

```lua
-- File: main.lua
```

107

```lua
local calculator = require("calculator")

-- List available operations
print("Available operations:")
for _, op in ipairs(calculator.getOperations()) do
    print("  - " .. op)
end

-- Use the calculator
print("10 + 5 =", calculator.calculate("add", 10, 5))
print("10 - 5 =", calculator.calculate("subtract", 10, 5))
print("10 * 5 =", calculator.calculate("multiply", 10, 5))
print("10 / 5 =", calculator.calculate("divide", 10, 5))

-- Operations and validateNumbers are private and cannot be accessed here
-- print(calculator.operations)    -- Error
-- calculator.validateNumbers(1, 2)    -- Error
```

Output:

```
Available operations:
  - add
  - subtract
  - multiply
  - divide
10 + 5 = 15
10 - 5 = 5
10 * 5 = 50
10 / 5 = 2
```

The require Function

The require function is the standard way to import modules in Lua. Let's explore how it works in detail.

Basic Usage

The simplest use of require is to load a module by name:

```lua
local myModule = require("myModule")
```

When Lua executes this line, it:

1. Checks if the module is already loaded and cached

2. If not, searches for the module in various locations
3. Loads and executes the module code
4. Caches the module's return value
5. Returns the cached value

This ensures that modules are only loaded once, even if required multiple times.

Module Search Path

Lua looks for modules in several places, defined by the `package.path` variable for Lua files and `package.cpath` for C libraries. The search path is a string with patterns separated by semicolons, where each pattern describes a potential location.

```lua
-- Print the current search path
print("Lua search path:")
print(package.path:gsub(";", "\n"))

print("\nC library search path:")
print(package.cpath:gsub(";", "\n"))
```

Typical output on a Unix system might look like:

```
Lua search path:
./?.lua
/usr/local/share/lua/5.4/?.lua
/usr/local/share/lua/5.4/?/init.lua
/usr/local/lib/lua/5.4/?.lua
/usr/local/lib/lua/5.4/?/init.lua
/usr/share/lua/5.4/?.lua
/usr/share/lua/5.4/?/init.lua

C library search path:
./?.so
/usr/local/lib/lua/5.4/?.so
/usr/lib/lua/5.4/?.so
/usr/local/lib/lua/5.4/loadall.so
```

The question mark (?) in each pattern is replaced with the module name you're requiring. For example, if you call `require("math.utils")`, Lua might look for:

- `./math/utils.lua`
- `/usr/local/share/lua/5.4/math/utils.lua`
- And so on...

Modifying the Search Path

You can modify the search path to tell Lua where to look for your custom modules:

```lua
-- Add a custom directory to the search path
package.path = "./modules/?.lua;" .. package.path
```

This adds the `./modules/` directory to the front of the search path, meaning Lua will look there first.

Module Loading Process

When you call `require("myModule")`, Lua follows these steps:

1. Check if the module is already loaded in `package.loaded["myModule"]`
2. If found, return the cached value
3. Try to find a loader function for the module:
   - Try all C loaders (looking in `package.cpath`)
   - Try all Lua loaders (looking in `package.path`)
4. If a loader is found, call it with the module name
5. If the loader returns a value, store it in `package.loaded["myModule"]`
6. If no value was returned but `package.loaded["myModule"]` is true, return true
7. Return the value from `package.loaded["myModule"]`

This process ensures that modules are loaded only once and that circular dependencies can work.

Reloading a Module

If you need to reload a module (for example, during development when you've changed the module code), you can remove it from the cache:

```lua
-- Force a module to be reloaded
package.loaded["myModule"] = nil
local myModule = require("myModule")  -- This will reload the module
```

Module Naming and Structure

Lua modules follow certain naming conventions and patterns for organization.

Module Naming Conventions

Module names typically use lowercase letters and dots to indicate hierarchy:

- `utils` - A simple module
- `app.utils` - A module in the "app" namespace
- `app.utils.strings` - A module in the "app.utils" namespace

When you require a module with dots in the name, Lua replaces the dots with the directory separator:

- `require("app.utils")` might look for app/utils.lua
- `require("app.utils.strings")` might look for app/utils/strings.lua

Directory Structure

A well-organized project might have a directory structure like this:

```
myproject/
├── main.lua          # Main program entry point
├── lib/              # Third-party libraries
│   └── json.lua
├── modules/          # Local modules
│   ├── config.lua
│   ├── utils.lua
│   └── app/          # Nested modules
│       ├── models.lua
│       └── views.lua
└── tests/            # Test files
    └── test_utils.lua
```

To work with this structure, you'd adjust your search path:

```
-- In main.lua
package.path = "./modules/?.lua;./modules/?/init.lua;./lib/?.lua;" ..
package.path

-- Then require modules
local config = require("config")
local utils = require("utils")
local models = require("app.models")
local views = require("app.views")
local json = require("json")
```

Init Files

If you require a module that corresponds to a directory (e.g., `require("app")`), Lua will look for an `init.lua` file in that directory:

```
modules/
└── app/
    ├── init.lua        # Loaded when require("app") is called
    ├── models.lua      # Loaded when require("app.models") is called
    └── views.lua       # Loaded when require("app.views") is called
```

The `init.lua` file typically serves as the entry point for the module, perhaps loading and exposing other sub-modules:

```
-- File: modules/app/init.lua
local app = {}

-- Include submodules
app.models = require("app.models")
app.views = require("app.views")

-- Other app-level functionality
app.version = "1.0.0"

function app.initialize()
    print("Initializing app v" .. app.version)
    app.models.initialize()
    app.views.initialize()
end

return app
```

Then in your main script:

```
-- File: main.lua
local app = require("app")    -- Loads app/init.lua
app.initialize()              -- Uses the function from app
app.views.render()            -- Uses the submodule functionality
```

Module Design Patterns

Let's look at some common patterns for structuring and using modules in Lua.

Module with Configuration

Modules often need configuration options. Here's a pattern for providing defaults that can be overridden:

```lua
-- File: logger.lua
local logger = {}

-- Default configuration
local config = {
    level = "info",
    output = "console",
    format = "[%level%] %message%"
}

-- Available log levels
local levels = {
    debug = 1,
    info = 2,
    warn = 3,
    error = 4
}

-- Configure the logger
function logger.configure(options)
    for k, v in pairs(options) do
        config[k] = v
    end
    return logger  -- Return self for method chaining
end

-- Internal logging function
local function log(level, message)
    if (levels[level] or 0) >= (levels[config.level] or 0) then
        local output = config.format:gsub("%%level%%", level):gsub("%%message%
%", message)

        if config.output == "console" then
            print(output)
        elseif config.output == "file" and config.file then
            -- Implementation for file logging omitted for brevity
            print("Would log to file: " .. output)
        end
    end
end

-- Public logging methods
function logger.debug(message)
    log("debug", message)
end

function logger.info(message)
```

```lua
    log("info", message)
end

function logger.warn(message)
    log("warn", message)
end

function logger.error(message)
    log("error", message)
end

return logger
```

Usage:

```lua
-- File: main.lua
local logger = require("logger")

-- Configure the logger with custom options
logger.configure({
    level = "debug",
    format = "[%level%] %message% - " .. os.date()
})

-- Use the logger
logger.debug("This is a debug message")
logger.info("This is an info message")
logger.warn("This is a warning")
logger.error("This is an error")
```

Output:

```
[debug] This is a debug message - Wed Jan 26 15:30:45 2023
[info] This is an info message - Wed Jan 26 15:30:45 2023
[warn] This is a warning - Wed Jan 26 15:30:45 2023
[error] This is an error - Wed Jan 26 15:30:45 2023
```

Factory Module

A factory module creates and returns objects of a specific type:

```lua
-- File: user.lua
local User = {}
```

```
-- The module itself is the constructor
return function(name, email)
    -- Create a new user object
    local user = {
        name = name,
        email = email,
        createdAt = os.time()
    }

    -- Add methods
    function user:getName()
        return self.name
    end

    function user:getEmail()
        return self.email
    end

    function user:getCreationDate()
        return os.date("%Y-%m-%d", self.createdAt)
    end

    function user:toString()
        return self.name .. " <" .. self.email .. ">"
    end

    return user
end
```

Usage:

```
-- File: main.lua
local User = require("user")

-- Create user instances
local alice = User("Alice Smith", "alice@example.com")
local bob = User("Bob Johnson", "bob@example.com")

-- Use the user objects
print("User 1:", alice:toString())
print("User 2:", bob:toString())
print("Creation date:", alice:getCreationDate())
```

Output:

Class-like Module

Lua doesn't have classes built in, but you can create class-like modules with inheritance:

```lua
-- File: shape.lua
local Shape = {}
Shape.__index = Shape

-- Constructor
function Shape.new(x, y)
    local self = setmetatable({}, Shape)
    self.x = x or 0
    self.y = y or 0
    return self
end

-- Methods
function Shape:getPosition()
    return self.x, self.y
end

function Shape:move(dx, dy)
    self.x = self.x + dx
    self.y = self.y + dy
    return self
end

function Shape:getArea()
    -- Base shape has no area
    return 0
end

function Shape:toString()
    return "Shape at (" .. self.x .. ", " .. self.y .. ")"
end

return Shape
```

Now create a derived class:

```lua
-- File: circle.lua
local Shape = require("shape")

local Circle = {}
Circle.__index = Circle
setmetatable(Circle, {__index = Shape})  -- Inherit from Shape

-- Constructor
function Circle.new(x, y, radius)
    local self = Shape.new(x, y)  -- Call parent constructor
    setmetatable(self, Circle)    -- Change metatable to Circle
    self.radius = radius or 1
    return self
end

-- Override method
function Circle:getArea()
    return math.pi * self.radius * self.radius
end

-- Override toString
function Circle:toString()
    return "Circle at (" .. self.x .. ", " .. self.y .. ") with radius " ..
self.radius
end

-- New method specific to Circle
function Circle:getCircumference()
    return 2 * math.pi * self.radius
end

return Circle
```

Usage:

```lua
-- File: main.lua
local Shape = require("shape")
local Circle = require("circle")

-- Create instances
local shape = Shape.new(10, 20)
local circle = Circle.new(15, 25, 5)

-- Use the objects
print(shape:toString())
print("Shape area:", shape:getArea())
```

```lua
print(circle:toString())
print("Circle area:", circle:getArea())
print("Circle circumference:", circle:getCircumference())

-- Move both shapes
shape:move(5, 10)
circle:move(-3, 7)

print("After moving:")
print(shape:toString())
print(circle:toString())
```

Output:

```
Shape at (10, 20)
Shape area: 0
Circle at (15, 25) with radius 5
Circle area: 78.539816339745
Circle circumference: 31.415926535898
After moving:
Shape at (15, 30)
Circle at (12, 32) with radius 5
```

We'll explore object-oriented programming in Lua more thoroughly in Chapter 9.

Working with Multiple Modules

As your projects grow, you'll need to manage dependencies between modules. Here are some patterns for working with multiple modules.

Module Dependencies

Modules can require other modules as dependencies:

```lua
-- File: database.lua
local database = {}

-- This module depends on the config module
local config = require("config")

function database.connect()
    print("Connecting to database at " .. config.get("db.host") .. "...")
    -- Connection logic would go here
```

```lua
end

function database.query(sql)
    print("Executing query: " .. sql)
    -- Query logic would go here
end

return database

-- File: config.lua
local config = {}

-- Default configuration
local settings = {
    ["app.name"] = "My App",
    ["app.version"] = "1.0.0",
    ["db.host"] = "localhost",
    ["db.port"] = 3306,
    ["db.user"] = "root",
    ["db.password"] = ""
}

function config.get(key)
    return settings[key]
end

function config.set(key, value)
    settings[key] = value
end

return config
```

Usage:

```lua
-- File: main.lua
local config = require("config")
local database = require("database")

-- Configure the application
config.set("db.host", "db.example.com")
config.set("db.user", "admin")

-- Use the database module
database.connect()
database.query("SELECT * FROM users")
```

Output:

```
Connecting to database at db.example.com...
Executing query: SELECT * FROM users
```

Circular Dependencies

Sometimes modules might depend on each other, creating a circular dependency. Lua's module system can handle this, but you need to be careful:

```lua
-- File: module_a.lua
local moduleA = {}

function moduleA.foo()
    print("Module A's foo function")

    -- Lazy-load module B to break circular dependency
    local moduleB = require("module_b")
    moduleB.bar()
end

function moduleA.baz()
    print("Module A's baz function")
end

return moduleA

-- File: module_b.lua
local moduleB = {}

-- Immediately require module A
local moduleA = require("module_a")

function moduleB.bar()
    print("Module B's bar function")
end

function moduleB.useA()
    print("Module B using Module A:")
    moduleA.baz()  -- This works because moduleA is already partially loaded
end

return moduleB
```

Usage:

```
-- File: main.lua
local moduleA = require("module_a")

moduleA.foo()
```

Output:

```
Module A's foo function
Module B's bar function
```

In this example, when `module_a` is first required, it's partially initialized and added to `package.loaded` before its functions are called. When `module_b` requires `module_a`, it gets the partially initialized module, which is enough to call `moduleA.baz()`.

This works, but it's generally better to avoid circular dependencies by restructuring your code.

Organizing Related Modules into Packages

A package in Lua is a collection of related modules. You can organize them using directories and `init.lua` files:

```
app/
├── init.lua          # Main package entry point
├── config.lua        # Configuration module
├── utils/            # Utilities sub-package
│   ├── init.lua      # Utils package entry point
│   ├── strings.lua   # String utilities
│   └── math.lua      # Math utilities
└── models/           # Models sub-package
    ├── init.lua      # Models package entry point
    ├── user.lua      # User model
    └── product.lua   # Product model
```

The main `init.lua` might look like:

```
-- File: app/init.lua
local app = {
    config = require("app.config"),
    utils = require("app.utils"),
    models = require("app.models"),

    name = "My Application",
```

```
    version = "1.0.0"
}

function app.initialize()
    print("Initializing " .. app.name .. " v" .. app.version)
    -- Additional initialization
end

return app
```

The utils init.lua might combine its submodules:

```
-- File: app/utils/init.lua
local utils = {
    strings = require("app.utils.strings"),
    math = require("app.utils.math")
}

-- Some general utility functions could be defined here
function utils.isEmpty(value)
    return value == nil or value == ""
end

return utils
```

Using the package:

```
-- File: main.lua
local app = require("app")

app.initialize()

-- Use utils
local capitalized = app.utils.strings.capitalize("hello")
print("Capitalized:", capitalized)

-- Use models
local user = app.models.user.new("alice", "password123")
print("User:", user.username)
```

Output:

```
Initializing My Application v1.0.0
Capitalized: Hello
```

Creating C Modules

While beyond the scope of this book, it's worth mentioning that Lua can be extended with modules written in C. This is useful for performance-critical code or for interfacing with operating system features and libraries.

Here's a very basic example of what a C module might look like:

```c
// File: mymodule.c
#include <lua.h>
#include <lauxlib.h>
#include <lualib.h>

// Function to be called from Lua
static int add(lua_State *L) {
    // Get arguments from Lua stack
    double a = luaL_checknumber(L, 1);
    double b = luaL_checknumber(L, 2);

    // Push result to Lua stack
    lua_pushnumber(L, a + b);

    // Return number of results
    return 1;
}

// Registration array
static const struct luaL_Reg mylib[] = {
    {"add", add},
    {NULL, NULL}  // Sentinel
};

// Module entry point
int luaopen_mymodule(lua_State *L) {
    luaL_newlib(L, mylib);
    return 1;
}
```

Compiling and using C modules requires additional tools and knowledge of C programming, but it's a powerful way to extend Lua's capabilities.

Module Versioning and Compatibility

As your modules evolve, you may need to manage versions and maintain compatibility.

Semantic Versioning

A common approach for versioning modules is to use semantic versioning (SemVer), with version numbers in the format `MAJOR.MINOR.PATCH`:

- `MAJOR`: Incremented for incompatible API changes
- `MINOR`: Incremented for backward-compatible new features
- `PATCH`: Incremented for backward-compatible bug fixes

This helps users understand what to expect when updating a module.

```lua
-- File: logger.lua
local logger = {
    _VERSION = "1.2.3",  -- Following semantic versioning
    _DESCRIPTION = "Simple logging module for Lua",
    _LICENSE = "MIT"
}

-- Module implementation...

return logger
```

Version Checking

You might want to ensure that the modules you depend on meet version requirements:

```lua
-- File: main.lua
local logger = require("logger")

-- Check module version
local function checkVersion(module, minVersion)
    if not module._VERSION then
        print("Warning: Module does not specify version")
        return false
    end

    local major, minor, patch = module._VERSION:match("(%d+)%.(%d+)%.(%d+)")
    local minMajor, minMinor, minPatch = minVersion:match("(%d+)%.(%d+)%.(%d+)")
```

```
    if not major then
        print("Warning: Could not parse module version: " .. module._VERSION)
        return false
    end

    major, minor, patch = tonumber(major), tonumber(minor), tonumber(patch)
    minMajor, minMinor, minPatch = tonumber(minMajor), tonumber(minMinor),
tonumber(minPatch)

    if major > minMajor then
        return true
    elseif major < minMajor then
        return false
    else
        if minor > minMinor then
            return true
        elseif minor < minMinor then
            return false
        else
            return patch >= minPatch
        end
    end
end

if not checkVersion(logger, "1.2.0") then
    error("Logger module version 1.2.0 or higher is required")
end

-- Use the module now that version has been checked
logger.info("Application started")
```

Backward Compatibility

When updating modules, it's good practice to maintain backward compatibility when possible:

```
-- File: api.lua (version 2.0.0)
local api = {
    _VERSION = "2.0.0"
}

-- New way to call the API
function api.processData(options)
    print("Processing data with options:")
    for k, v in pairs(options) do
        print("  " .. k .. ":", v)
```

```
        end
        return true
end

-- For backward compatibility with version 1.x
function api.process(data, format)
    print("Warning: api.process is deprecated, use api.processData instead")
    return api.processData({
        data = data,
        format = format
    })
end

return api
```

This allows users of the old API to still use your module while encouraging migration to the new API.

Best Practices for Modules

Let's wrap up with some best practices for creating and using modules in Lua:

1. **Keep modules focused**: Each module should have a single responsibility.

2. **Document your modules**: Include a brief description, version, author, and license information. Document functions with comments explaining parameters and return values.

3. **Use local variables and functions**: Keep module internals private by using local for variables and functions that aren't part of the public API.

4. **Return the module table at the end**: This makes the export explicit and avoids accidental global variables.

5. **Structure modules consistently**: Adopt a consistent pattern for module structure across your project.

6. **Handle errors gracefully**: Consider using status returns rather than raising errors for expected failure cases.

7. **Use namespacing**: For large projects, use hierarchical module names to avoid conflicts.

8. **Be mindful of performance**: Avoid unnecessary require calls in performance-critical code paths.

9. **Test your modules**: Create unit tests to ensure your modules work as expected.

Here's a template for a well-structured module:

```lua
-- File: my_module.lua
--[[
MyModule - Brief description of what the module does

Version: 1.0.0
Author: Your Name
License: MIT
]]

local my_module = {
    _VERSION = "1.0.0",
    _DESCRIPTION = "Brief description of what the module does",
    _AUTHOR = "Your Name",
    _LICENSE = "MIT"
}

-- Dependencies
local some_dependency = require("some_dependency")

-- Constants
local DEFAULT_TIMEOUT = 60
local MAX_RETRIES = 3

-- Private functions
local function privateHelper(...)
    -- Implementation
end

-- Public API
function my_module.initialize(options)
    options = options or {}
    -- Implementation
end

function my_module.doSomething(...)
    -- Implementation that might use privateHelper
end

function my_module.cleanup()
    -- Implementation
end
```

```
-- Return the module
return my_module
```

Chapter Summary

In this chapter, we've explored Lua modules and packages, which provide a way to organize your code into reusable, maintainable components. We've covered the basics of creating modules, using the `require` function, structuring module hierarchies, and managing dependencies.

We've seen various module design patterns, including configuration modules, factory modules, and class-like modules. We've also discussed how to handle multiple modules, circular dependencies, and version compatibility.

Modules are a fundamental part of structuring larger Lua applications, and understanding how to create and use them effectively is key to writing maintainable Lua code.

In the next chapter, we'll build on our knowledge of tables and modules to explore object-oriented programming in Lua. While Lua doesn't have built-in classes, its flexible nature allows for powerful object-oriented designs, which we'll examine in detail.

Chapter 9: Object-Oriented Programming in Lua

Introduction to OOP in Lua

Object-oriented programming (OOP) is a programming paradigm built around the concept of "objects" — data structures that contain both data (attributes) and code (methods). While Lua doesn't have built-in classes or objects like languages such as Java or Python, its flexible nature allows you to implement OOP concepts using tables and functions.

In this chapter, we'll explore various approaches to OOP in Lua, from simple object patterns to more sophisticated implementations with inheritance, polymorphism, and encapsulation. We'll also look at how to apply these concepts to real-world problems.

Basic Objects with Tables

The simplest form of OOP in Lua uses tables to represent objects, with both data and methods.

Creating Simple Objects

We can create objects as tables containing both data and functions:

```
-- Create a simple person object
local person = {
    name = "Alice",
    age = 30,

    greet = function(self)
        return "Hello, my name is " .. self.name
```

```
        end,

    birthday = function(self)
        self.age = self.age + 1
        return self.name .. " is now " .. self.age .. " years old"
    end
}

-- Use the object
print(person.greet(person))
print(person.birthday(person))
```

Output:

```
Hello, my name is Alice
Alice is now 31 years old
```

The Colon Syntax

Lua provides a special syntax using colons (:) to simplify method calls. The colon operator automatically passes the object as the first argument (self):

```
-- Redefine the person object with methods using colon syntax
local person = {
    name = "Alice",
    age = 30,

    greet = function(self)
        return "Hello, my name is " .. self.name
    end,

    birthday = function(self)
        self.age = self.age + 1
        return self.name .. " is now " .. self.age .. " years old"
    end
}

-- Use the object with colon syntax
print(person:greet())  -- Equivalent to person.greet(person)
print(person:birthday())  -- Equivalent to person.birthday(person)
```

Output:

```
Hello, my name is Alice
```

```
Alice is now 31 years old
```

You can also define methods using the colon syntax directly:

```
local person = {
    name = "Alice",
    age = 30
}

function person:greet()
    return "Hello, my name is " .. self.name
end

function person:birthday()
    self.age = self.age + 1
    return self.name .. " is now " .. self.age .. " years old"
end

print(person:greet())
print(person:birthday())
```

Output:

```
Hello, my name is Alice
Alice is now 31 years old
```

Factory Functions

While simple objects are useful, we often need to create multiple objects of the same type. Factory functions are a straightforward way to create similar objects:

```
-- Factory function for creating person objects
function createPerson(name, age)
    local person = {
        name = name or "Unknown",
        age = age or 0
    }

    function person:greet()
        return "Hello, my name is " .. self.name
    end

    function person:birthday()
```

```
        self.age = self.age + 1
        return self.name .. " is now " .. self.age .. " years old"
    end

    return person
end

-- Create multiple person objects
local alice = createPerson("Alice", 30)
local bob = createPerson("Bob", 25)

-- Use the objects
print(alice:greet())
print(bob:greet())
print(alice:birthday())
print(bob:birthday())
```

Output:

```
Hello, my name is Alice
Hello, my name is Bob
Alice is now 31 years old
Bob is now 26 years old
```

The factory function approach has some disadvantages:

- Each object gets its own copy of each method, which can be memory-inefficient.
- There's no explicit connection between objects created by the same factory.

Metatables and Object Orientation

Metatables provide a more powerful way to implement OOP in Lua, addressing the limitations of simple factory functions. With metatables, we can share methods between objects and implement inheritance.

Basic Class Implementation

Here's how to create a basic "class" using metatables:

```
-- Define a "class" (a table that will serve as a prototype)
local Person = {}

-- Define the class's methods
```

```
function Person:new(name, age)
    local instance = {
        name = name or "Unknown",
        age = age or 0
    }
    setmetatable(instance, self)
    self.__index = self
    return instance
end

function Person:greet()
    return "Hello, my name is " .. self.name
end

function Person:birthday()
    self.age = self.age + 1
    return self.name .. " is now " .. self.age .. " years old"
end

-- Create instances (objects)
local alice = Person:new("Alice", 30)
local bob = Person:new("Bob", 25)

-- Use the objects
print(alice:greet())
print(bob:greet())
print(alice:birthday())
print(bob:birthday())
```

Output:

```
Hello, my name is Alice
Hello, my name is Bob
Alice is now 31 years old
Bob is now 26 years old
```

Let's break down how this works:

1. We create a table Person that serves as our class.
2. We define a new method that creates and initializes a new instance.
3. Inside new, we set the metatable of the instance to be the class itself, and set __index to the class as well.
4. When we call a method on an instance (e.g., alice:greet()), Lua first looks for the method in the instance itself.

5. If not found, Lua uses the `__index` metamethod, which points to the class, to find the method.

This approach is efficient because all instances share the same methods from the class table. Each instance only contains its own data.

Alternative Class Syntax

Here's another syntax for defining classes that some prefer:

```lua
-- Define a class using a different syntax
local Person = {
    -- Default values
    name = "Unknown",
    age = 0
}

Person.__index = Person  -- To enable method lookup

-- Constructor function
function Person.new(name, age)
    local instance = setmetatable({}, Person)
    instance.name = name or Person.name
    instance.age = age or Person.age
    return instance
end

-- Methods
function Person:greet()
    return "Hello, my name is " .. self.name
end

function Person:birthday()
    self.age = self.age + 1
    return self.name .. " is now " .. self.age .. " years old"
end

-- Create instances
local alice = Person.new("Alice", 30)
local bob = Person.new("Bob", 25)

-- Use the objects
print(alice:greet())
print(bob:greet())
```

Output:

```
Hello, my name is Alice
Hello, my name is Bob
```

The difference in this syntax is that we call the constructor as `Person.new()` instead of `Person:new()`, treating it as a regular function rather than a method. This makes the constructor usage clearer but requires us to manually set up the metatable.

Inheritance

One of the key features of OOP is inheritance, where a class can inherit methods and properties from a parent class. Let's implement inheritance using metatables:

```lua
-- Base class
local Animal = {
    name = "Unknown Animal",
    sound = "???"
}

Animal.__index = Animal

function Animal.new(name, sound)
    local instance = setmetatable({}, Animal)
    instance.name = name or Animal.name
    instance.sound = sound or Animal.sound
    return instance
end

function Animal:makeSound()
    return self.name .. " says " .. self.sound
end

function Animal:describe()
    return "This is " .. self.name .. ", an animal"
end

-- Derived class
local Dog = {
    breed = "Unknown Breed"
}

Dog.__index = Dog
setmetatable(Dog, {__index = Animal})  -- Dog inherits from Animal

function Dog.new(name, breed)
    local instance = setmetatable({}, Dog)
```

```
    instance.name = name or "Unknown Dog"
    instance.sound = "Woof"  -- Dogs always say Woof
    instance.breed = breed or Dog.breed
    return instance
end

function Dog:describe()
    return "This is " .. self.name .. ", a " .. self.breed .. " dog"
end

-- Create instances
local genericAnimal = Animal.new("Generic Animal", "Growl")
local fido = Dog.new("Fido", "Labrador")

-- Use the objects
print(genericAnimal:makeSound())
print(genericAnimal:describe())

print(fido:makeSound())  -- Inherited from Animal
print(fido:describe())    -- Overridden in Dog
```

Output:

```
Generic Animal says Growl
This is Generic Animal, an animal
Fido says Woof
This is Fido, a Labrador dog
```

Here's how the inheritance works:

1. We set up the Animal class as before.
2. For the Dog class, we set its metatable's __index to the Animal class using set-metatable(Dog, {__index = Animal}).
3. When a method is called on a Dog instance, Lua first checks the instance itself.
4. If not found, it checks the Dog class (via the instance's metatable).
5. If still not found, it checks the Animal class (via the Dog class's metatable).

This creates a method lookup chain that implements inheritance.

Class Methods vs. Instance Methods

Sometimes you want methods that operate on the class itself, not on instances. These are called class methods (or static methods in some languages):

```lua
-- Class with both instance and class methods
local MathUtils = {
    defaultPrecision = 2
}

MathUtils.__index = MathUtils

-- Class method (note the . instead of :)
function MathUtils.isPrime(n)
    if n <= 1 then return false end
    if n <= 3 then return true end
    if n % 2 == 0 or n % 3 == 0 then return false end

    local i = 5
    while i * i <= n do
        if n % i == 0 or n % (i + 2) == 0 then
            return false
        end
        i = i + 6
    end

    return true
end

-- Constructor
function MathUtils.new(precision)
    local instance = setmetatable({}, MathUtils)
    instance.precision = precision or MathUtils.defaultPrecision
    return instance
end

-- Instance method
function MathUtils:round(number)
    local factor = 10 ^ self.precision
    return math.floor(number * factor + 0.5) / factor
end

-- Class method (another way to define it)
MathUtils.abs = math.abs

-- Create an instance
local formatter = MathUtils.new(3)

-- Call instance method
print("Pi rounded:", formatter:round(math.pi))

-- Call class methods
```

```
print("Is 17 prime?", MathUtils.isPrime(17))
print("Is 20 prime?", MathUtils.isPrime(20))
print("Absolute of -42:", MathUtils.abs(-42))
```

Output:

```
Pi rounded: 3.142
Is 17 prime? true
Is 20 prime? false
Absolute of -42: 42
```

The key difference:

- Class methods use the dot syntax (`Class.method()`) and don't have a `self` parameter for an instance.
- Instance methods use the colon syntax (`instance:method()`) and have the `self` parameter representing the instance.

Private Members

Lua doesn't have built-in privacy modifiers like `private` or `protected`, but you can achieve similar effects using closures:

```
-- Class with private members using closures
local BankAccount = {}
BankAccount.__index = BankAccount

function BankAccount.new(initialBalance, owner)
    -- Private variables
    local balance = initialBalance or 0
    local transactionHistory = {}

    -- Create the instance
    local instance = setmetatable({}, BankAccount)

    -- Public properties
    instance.owner = owner or "Anonymous"
    instance.accountNumber = "ACC" .. tostring(math.random(10000, 99999))

    -- Private method
    local function recordTransaction(type, amount)
        table.insert(transactionHistory, {
            type = type,
            amount = amount,
```

```lua
            date = os.date(),
            balance = balance
        })
    end

    -- Public methods with access to private data
    function instance:deposit(amount)
        if amount <= 0 then
            return false, "Amount must be positive"
        end

        balance = balance + amount
        recordTransaction("deposit", amount)
        return true, "Deposit successful"
    end

    function instance:withdraw(amount)
        if amount <= 0 then
            return false, "Amount must be positive"
        end

        if amount > balance then
            return false, "Insufficient funds"
        end

        balance = balance - amount
        recordTransaction("withdrawal", amount)
        return true, "Withdrawal successful"
    end

    function instance:getBalance()
        return balance
    end

    function instance:getTransactionHistory()
        -- Return a copy to prevent modification
        local historyCopy = {}
        for i, transaction in ipairs(transactionHistory) do
            historyCopy[i] = {
                type = transaction.type,
                amount = transaction.amount,
                date = transaction.date,
                balance = transaction.balance
            }
        end
        return historyCopy
    end
```

```
        return instance
end

-- Create a bank account
local account = BankAccount.new(1000, "John Doe")

-- Use the account
print("Account:", account.accountNumber, "Owner:", account.owner)
print("Initial balance:", account:getBalance())

local success, message = account:deposit(500)
print(message, "New balance:", account:getBalance())

success, message = account:withdraw(200)
print(message, "New balance:", account:getBalance())

success, message = account:withdraw(2000)
print(message, "Balance unchanged:", account:getBalance())

-- Display transaction history
print("\nTransaction History:")
local history = account:getTransactionHistory()
for i, transaction in ipairs(history) do
    print(i, transaction.type, transaction.amount, transaction.date)
end

-- Privacy test
-- print(account.balance)  -- nil, balance is private
-- print(account.transactionHistory)  -- nil, transactionHistory is private
-- account.recordTransaction  -- nil, recordTransaction is private
```

Output:

```
Account: ACC38421 Owner: John Doe
Initial balance: 1000
Deposit successful New balance: 1500
Withdrawal successful New balance: 1300
Insufficient funds Balance unchanged: 1300

Transaction History:
1       deposit 500     Wed Jan 26 16:30:45 2023
2       withdrawal      200     Wed Jan 26 16:30:45 2023
```

In this example:

- `balance` and `transactionHistory` are private variables that can't be accessed directly from outside.
- `recordTransaction` is a private method that's only accessible from within the closure.
- The public methods have access to these private members because they're defined within the same closure.

This approach provides true encapsulation because there's no way to access the private data except through the public methods. The downside is that each instance creates its own methods, which is less memory-efficient.

Polymorphism

Polymorphism allows objects of different classes to be treated as objects of a common superclass. In Lua, this is achieved naturally through its dynamic typing:

```lua
-- Base class
local Shape = {}
Shape.__index = Shape

function Shape.new()
    return setmetatable({}, Shape)
end

function Shape:area()
    error("Shape:area() method must be implemented by subclasses")
end

function Shape:perimeter()
    error("Shape:perimeter() method must be implemented by subclasses")
end

-- Rectangle subclass
local Rectangle = {}
Rectangle.__index = Rectangle
setmetatable(Rectangle, {__index = Shape})

function Rectangle.new(width, height)
    local instance = setmetatable({}, Rectangle)
    instance.width = width or 0
    instance.height = height or 0
    return instance
end

function Rectangle:area()
```

```lua
        return self.width * self.height
end

function Rectangle:perimeter()
    return 2 * (self.width + self.height)
end

-- Circle subclass
local Circle = {}
Circle.__index = Circle
setmetatable(Circle, {__index = Shape})

function Circle.new(radius)
    local instance = setmetatable({}, Circle)
    instance.radius = radius or 0
    return instance
end

function Circle:area()
    return math.pi * self.radius * self.radius
end

function Circle:perimeter()
    return 2 * math.pi * self.radius
end

-- Function that works with any Shape
function printShapeInfo(shape)
    print("Area:", shape:area())
    print("Perimeter:", shape:perimeter())
end

-- Create different shapes
local rectangle = Rectangle.new(5, 10)
local circle = Circle.new(7)

-- Call the same function with different shapes
print("Rectangle:")
printShapeInfo(rectangle)

print("\nCircle:")
printShapeInfo(circle)
```

Output:

```
Rectangle:
```

```
Area: 50
Perimeter: 30

Circle:
Area: 153.93804002589
Perimeter: 43.982297150257
```

Here, the `printShapeInfo` function doesn't need to know what type of shape it's working with. It just calls the `area()` and `perimeter()` methods, trusting that the object has implemented them appropriately. This is polymorphism in action.

Multiple Inheritance

While Lua's basic OOP pattern only supports single inheritance, you can implement multiple inheritance by combining methods from multiple "parent" classes:

```
-- Function to create a new class
local function createClass(...)
    local parents = {...}
    local newClass = {}
    newClass.__index = newClass

    -- Inheritance function that checks all parents
    setmetatable(newClass, {
        __index = function(_, key)
            -- Check each parent for the key
            for _, parent in ipairs(parents) do
                local value = parent[key]
                if value ~= nil then
                    return value
                end
            end
            return nil
        end
    })

    -- Constructor
    function newClass.new(...)
        local instance = setmetatable({}, newClass)
        if newClass.init then
            newClass.init(instance, ...)
        end
        return instance
    end
```

```lua
        return newClass
end

-- Define some base classes
local Walker = {}
function Walker:walk()
    return self.name .. " is walking"
end

local Swimmer = {}
function Swimmer:swim()
    return self.name .. " is swimming"
end

local Flyer = {}
function Flyer:fly()
    return self.name .. " is flying"
end

-- Create classes with multiple inheritance
local Bird = createClass(Walker, Flyer)
function Bird:init(name)
    self.name = name
    self.type = "Bird"
end

function Bird:chirp()
    return self.name .. " says chirp!"
end

local Duck = createClass(Bird, Swimmer)
function Duck:init(name)
    Bird.init(self, name)
    self.type = "Duck"
end

function Duck:quack()
    return self.name .. " says quack!"
end

-- Create instances
local eagle = Bird.new("Eddie the Eagle")
local donald = Duck.new("Donald")

-- Test the Eagle
print(eagle.type .. ":")
print(eagle:walk())  -- From Walker
```

```
print(eagle:fly())   -- From Flyer
print(eagle:chirp()) -- From Bird
print()

-- Test the Duck
print(donald.type .. ":")
print(donald:walk())  -- From Walker via Bird
print(donald:swim())  -- From Swimmer
print(donald:fly())   -- From Flyer via Bird
print(donald:chirp()) -- From Bird
print(donald:quack()) -- From Duck
```

Output:

```
Bird:
Eddie the Eagle is walking
Eddie the Eagle is flying
Eddie the Eagle says chirp!

Duck:
Donald is walking
Donald is swimming
Donald is flying
Donald says chirp!
Donald says quack!
```

This implementation of multiple inheritance checks each parent class in order for methods not found in the child class. Note that if multiple parents define the same method, the first one in the list takes precedence.

Object Composition

While inheritance is powerful, sometimes composition (building objects by combining simpler objects) is a more flexible approach:

```
-- Components (reusable pieces of functionality)
local HealthComponent = {}
function HealthComponent.new(maxHealth)
    return {
        health = maxHealth or 100,
        maxHealth = maxHealth or 100,

        takeDamage = function(self, amount)
            self.health = math.max(0, self.health - amount)
```

```lua
            return self.health == 0
        end,

        heal = function(self, amount)
            self.health = math.min(self.maxHealth, self.health + amount)
            return self.health
        end,

        getHealthStatus = function(self)
            local percent = self.health / self.maxHealth * 100
            return self.health .. "/" .. self.maxHealth ..
                " (" .. math.floor(percent) .. "%)"
        end
    }
end

local InventoryComponent = {}
function InventoryComponent.new(capacity)
    return {
        items = {},
        capacity = capacity or 10,

        addItem = function(self, item)
            if #self.items >= self.capacity then
                return false, "Inventory full"
            end
            table.insert(self.items, item)
            return true
        end,

        removeItem = function(self, itemName)
            for i, item in ipairs(self.items) do
                if item.name == itemName then
                    table.remove(self.items, i)
                    return true
                end
            end
            return false, "Item not found"
        end,

        listItems = function(self)
            if #self.items == 0 then
                return "Inventory empty"
            end

            local result = "Inventory (" .. #self.items .. "/" ..
self.capacity .. "):"
```

```lua
                for _, item in ipairs(self.items) do
                    result = result .. "\n- " .. item.name
                end
                return result
            end
        }
end

-- Main class that composes components
local Player = {}
Player.__index = Player

function Player.new(name)
    local instance = setmetatable({}, Player)

    -- Initialize properties
    instance.name = name
    instance.level = 1

    -- Add components
    instance.health = HealthComponent.new(100)
    instance.inventory = InventoryComponent.new(15)

    return instance
end

function Player:describe()
    return self.name .. " (Level " .. self.level .. ")\n" ..
            "Health: " .. self.health:getHealthStatus() .. "\n" ..
            self.inventory:listItems()
end

-- Create a player
local player = Player.new("Aragorn")

-- Use the player and its components
print(player:describe())

player.health:takeDamage(30)
player.inventory:addItem({name = "Sword", damage = 10})
player.inventory:addItem({name = "Health Potion", healing = 20})

print("\nAfter combat:")
print(player:describe())

player.health:heal(15)
player.inventory:removeItem("Health Potion")
```

```
print("\nAfter using health potion:")
print(player:describe())
```

Output:

```
Aragorn (Level 1)
Health: 100/100 (100%)
Inventory empty

After combat:
Aragorn (Level 1)
Health: 70/100 (70%)
Inventory (2/15):
- Sword
- Health Potion

After using health potion:
Aragorn (Level 1)
Health: 85/100 (85%)
Inventory (1/15):
- Sword
```

Composition offers several advantages:

- Flexibly combine behaviors without deep inheritance hierarchies
- Easier to change behavior at runtime
- Avoids problems with multiple inheritance
- Often leads to more maintainable code

The general principle is "favor composition over inheritance" when designing object-oriented systems.

Advanced OOP Techniques

Let's look at some more advanced OOP techniques in Lua.

Method Chaining

Method chaining (also known as fluent interfaces) allows you to call multiple methods in sequence by having each method return the object itself:

```
-- Class with method chaining
```

```lua
local StringBuilder = {}
StringBuilder.__index = StringBuilder

function StringBuilder.new(initial)
    local instance = setmetatable({}, StringBuilder)
    instance.content = initial or ""
    return instance
end

function StringBuilder:append(text)
    self.content = self.content .. text
    return self  -- Return self for chaining
end

function StringBuilder:appendLine(text)
    text = text or ""
    self.content = self.content .. text .. "\n"
    return self  -- Return self for chaining
end

function StringBuilder:prepend(text)
    self.content = text .. self.content
    return self  -- Return self for chaining
end

function StringBuilder:clear()
    self.content = ""
    return self  -- Return self for chaining
end

function StringBuilder:toString()
    return self.content
end

-- Use method chaining
local builder = StringBuilder.new()

local result = builder
    :append("Hello, ")
    :append("World!")
    :appendLine()
    :append("This is an example of ")
    :append("method chaining.")
    :toString()

print(result)
```

```
-- Can continue using the same builder
builder:clear()
      :append("New content")
      :appendLine()
      :append("More content")

print(builder:toString())
```

Output:

```
Hello, World!
This is an example of method chaining.
New content
More content
```

Mixins

Mixins provide a way to reuse code across multiple classes without inheritance:

```
-- Define mixin helpers
local function includeMixin(class, mixin)
    for name, method in pairs(mixin) do
        if name ~= "included" then
            class[name] = method
        end
    end

    if mixin.included then
        mixin.included(class)
    end
end

-- Define a mixin
local TimestampMixin = {
    setCreatedAt = function(self)
        self.createdAt = os.time()
    end,

    getCreatedAt = function(self, format)
        format = format or "%Y-%m-%d %H:%M:%S"
        return os.date(format, self.createdAt)
    end,

    included = function(class)
        print("TimestampMixin included in " .. tostring(class))
```

```lua
        end
}

-- Define another mixin
local ValidationMixin = {
    validate = function(self)
        if not self.validations then
            return true, "No validations defined"
        end

        for _, validation in ipairs(self.validations) do
            local field, rules = validation[1], validation[2]
            local value = self[field]

            if rules.required and (value == nil or value == "") then
                return false, field .. " is required"
            end

            if rules.minLength and type(value) == "string" and #value <
rules.minLength then
                return false, field .. " must be at least " ..
rules.minLength .. " characters"
            end
        end

        return true, "Validation successful"
    end
}

-- Create a class that uses mixins
local User = {}
User.__index = User

-- Include mixins
includeMixin(User, TimestampMixin)
includeMixin(User, ValidationMixin)

function User.new(attributes)
    local instance = setmetatable({}, User)

    -- Set attributes
    attributes = attributes or {}
    instance.username = attributes.username
    instance.email = attributes.email

    -- Set validation rules
    instance.validations = {
```

```lua
            {"username", {required = true, minLength = 3}},
            {"email", {required = true}}
    }

    -- Apply mixin initialization
    instance:setCreatedAt()

    return instance
end

-- Create users
local validUser = User.new({
    username = "johndoe",
    email = "john@example.com"
})

local invalidUser = User.new({
    username = "jd",
    email = ""
})

-- Test validation
local valid, message = validUser:validate()
print("Valid user:", valid, message)
print("Created at:", validUser:getCreatedAt())

valid, message = invalidUser:validate()
print("Invalid user:", valid, message)
```

Output:

```
TimestampMixin included in table: 0x55d30a394f10
Valid user: true Validation successful
Created at: 2023-01-26 16:45:23
Invalid user: false username must be at least 3 characters
```

Operator Overloading

Using metatables, we can define how objects respond to operators like +, -, *, etc.:

```lua
-- Vector class with operator overloading
local Vector = {}
Vector.__index = Vector

function Vector.new(x, y)
```

```lua
    return setmetatable({x = x or 0, y = y or 0}, Vector)
end

-- Arithmetic operator overloading
function Vector.__add(a, b)
    return Vector.new(a.x + b.x, a.y + b.y)
end

function Vector.__sub(a, b)
    return Vector.new(a.x - b.x, a.y - b.y)
end

function Vector.__mul(a, b)
    if type(a) == "number" then
        -- Scalar multiplication (number * Vector)
        return Vector.new(a * b.x, a * b.y)
    elseif type(b) == "number" then
        -- Scalar multiplication (Vector * number)
        return Vector.new(a.x * b, a.y * b)
    else
        -- Dot product (Vector * Vector)
        return a.x * b.x + a.y * b.y
    end
end

function Vector.__eq(a, b)
    return a.x == b.x and a.y == b.y
end

function Vector.__lt(a, b)
    -- Define "less than" as comparing magnitudes
    return a:magnitude() < b:magnitude()
end

function Vector.__le(a, b)
    return a:magnitude() <= b:magnitude()
end

-- String representation
function Vector.__tostring(v)
    return "Vector(" .. v.x .. ", " .. v.y .. ")"
end

-- Methods
function Vector:magnitude()
    return math.sqrt(self.x * self.x + self.y * self.y)
end
```

```lua
function Vector:normalize()
    local mag = self:magnitude()
    if mag > 0 then
        return Vector.new(self.x / mag, self.y / mag)
    else
        return Vector.new(0, 0)
    end
end

-- Create vectors
local v1 = Vector.new(3, 4)
local v2 = Vector.new(1, 2)

-- Test operators
print("v1:", v1)
print("v2:", v2)
print("v1 + v2:", v1 + v2)
print("v1 - v2:", v1 - v2)
print("v1 * 2:", v1 * 2)
print("3 * v2:", 3 * v2)
print("v1 * v2 (dot product):", v1 * v2)
print("v1 == v2:", v1 == v2)
print("v1 == Vector.new(3, 4):", v1 == Vector.new(3, 4))
print("v1 < v2:", v1 < v2)
print("v1 <= v2:", v1 <= v2)
print("v1:magnitude():", v1:magnitude())
print("v1:normalize():", v1:normalize())
```

Output:

```
v1: Vector(3, 4)
v2: Vector(1, 2)
v1 + v2: Vector(4, 6)
v1 - v2: Vector(2, 2)
v1 * 2: Vector(6, 8)
3 * v2: Vector(3, 6)
v1 * v2 (dot product): 11
v1 == v2: false
v1 == Vector.new(3, 4): true
v1 < v2: false
v1 <= v2: false
v1:magnitude(): 5
v1:normalize(): Vector(0.6, 0.8)
```

Practical OOP Examples

Let's look at some practical examples of OOP in Lua.

Simple Game Entity System

```lua
-- Base Entity class
local Entity = {}
Entity.__index = Entity

function Entity.new(id, x, y)
    local instance = setmetatable({}, Entity)
    instance.id = id
    instance.x = x or 0
    instance.y = y or 0
    instance.components = {}
    return instance
end

function Entity:addComponent(name, component)
    self.components[name] = component
    component.entity = self  -- Give the component access to its entity
    return self
end

function Entity:getComponent(name)
    return self.components[name]
end

function Entity:update(dt)
    for _, component in pairs(self.components) do
        if component.update then
            component:update(dt)
        end
    end
end

function Entity:render()
    for _, component in pairs(self.components) do
        if component.render then
            component:render()
        end
    end
end

-- Components
local SpriteComponent = {}
```

```lua
SpriteComponent.__index = SpriteComponent

function SpriteComponent.new(imgPath, width, height)
    local instance = setmetatable({}, SpriteComponent)
    instance.imgPath = imgPath
    instance.width = width
    instance.height = height
    -- In a real game, we'd load the actual image here
    return instance
end

function SpriteComponent:render()
    print("Rendering " .. self.imgPath .. " at (" .. self.entity.x ..
            ", " .. self.entity.y .. ") with size " ..
            self.width .. "x" .. self.height)
end

local MovementComponent = {}
MovementComponent.__index = MovementComponent

function MovementComponent.new(speed)
    local instance = setmetatable({}, MovementComponent)
    instance.speed = speed
    instance.dx = 0
    instance.dy = 0
    return instance
end

function MovementComponent:setVelocity(dx, dy)
    self.dx = dx
    self.dy = dy
end

function MovementComponent:update(dt)
    self.entity.x = self.entity.x + self.dx * self.speed * dt
    self.entity.y = self.entity.y + self.dy * self.speed * dt
    print("Updated position to (" .. self.entity.x .. ", " .. self.entity.y ..
")")
end

-- Create and use entities
local player = Entity.new("player", 100, 100)
player:addComponent("sprite", SpriteComponent.new("player.png", 32, 48))
player:addComponent("movement", MovementComponent.new(150))

local enemy = Entity.new("enemy", 400, 200)
enemy:addComponent("sprite", SpriteComponent.new("enemy.png", 32, 32))
```

```
enemy:addComponent("movement", MovementComponent.new(100))

-- Game loop (simplified)
print("Starting game loop...\n")

-- Set player velocity
player:getComponent("movement"):setVelocity(1, 0.5)
enemy:getComponent("movement"):setVelocity(-0.5, 0)

-- Update and render for a few frames
for frame = 1, 3 do
    print("\nFrame " .. frame .. ":")

    -- Using a delta time of 1/60 (60 FPS)
    local dt = 1/60

    player:update(dt)
    enemy:update(dt)

    player:render()
    enemy:render()
end
```

Output:

```
Starting game loop...

Frame 1:
Updated position to (102.5, 101.25)
Updated position to (399.16666666667, 200)
Rendering player.png at (102.5, 101.25) with size 32x48
Rendering enemy.png at (399.16666666667, 200) with size 32x32

Frame 2:
Updated position to (105, 102.5)
Updated position to (398.33333333333, 200)
Rendering player.png at (105, 102.5) with size 32x48
Rendering enemy.png at (398.33333333333, 200) with size 32x32

Frame 3:
Updated position to (107.5, 103.75)
Updated position to (397.5, 200)
Rendering player.png at (107.5, 103.75) with size 32x48
Rendering enemy.png at (397.5, 200) with size 32x32
```

Simple UI Framework

```lua
-- UIElement base class
local UIElement = {}
UIElement.__index = UIElement

function UIElement.new(id, x, y, width, height)
    local instance = setmetatable({}, UIElement)
    instance.id = id
    instance.x = x or 0
    instance.y = y or 0
    instance.width = width or 100
    instance.height = height or 50
    instance.visible = true
    instance.children = {}
    instance.parent = nil
    return instance
end

function UIElement:addChild(child)
    table.insert(self.children, child)
    child.parent = self
    return child  -- Return the child for method chaining
end

function UIElement:draw()
    if not self.visible then return end

    print("Drawing " .. self.id .. " at (" .. self.x .. ", " .. self.y ..
            ") with size " .. self.width .. "x" .. self.height)

    for _, child in ipairs(self.children) do
        -- Calculate child position relative to parent
        local originalX, originalY = child.x, child.y
        child.x = child.x + self.x
        child.y = child.y + self.y

        child:draw()

        -- Restore original position
        child.x, child.y = originalX, originalY
    end
end

function UIElement:contains(x, y)
    return x >= self.x and x <= self.x + self.width and
            y >= self.y and y <= self.y + self.height
end
```

```lua
-- Button class extending UIElement
local Button = setmetatable({}, {__index = UIElement})
Button.__index = Button

function Button.new(id, x, y, width, height, text)
    local instance = UIElement.new(id, x, y, width, height)
    setmetatable(instance, Button)
    instance.text = text or "Button"
    instance.onClick = nil
    return instance
end

function Button:draw()
    UIElement.draw(self)  -- Call parent method
    print("  Button text: " .. self.text)
end

function Button:handleClick(x, y)
    if self:contains(x, y) and self.onClick then
        self.onClick()
        return true
    end
    return false
end

-- Panel class extending UIElement
local Panel = setmetatable({}, {__index = UIElement})
Panel.__index = Panel

function Panel.new(id, x, y, width, height, title)
    local instance = UIElement.new(id, x, y, width, height)
    setmetatable(instance, Panel)
    instance.title = title or "Panel"
    instance.draggable = true
    return instance
end

function Panel:draw()
    UIElement.draw(self)  -- Call parent method
    print("  Panel title: " .. self.title)
end

-- Create a simple UI
local mainPanel = Panel.new("mainPanel", 100, 100, 400, 300, "Main Panel")

local button1 = Button.new("button1", 20, 30, 150, 40, "Save")
```

```
button1.onClick = function()
    print("Save button clicked!")
end

local button2 = Button.new("button2", 20, 90, 150, 40, "Cancel")
button2.onClick = function()
    print("Cancel button clicked!")
end

local subPanel = Panel.new("subPanel", 200, 30, 180, 250, "Settings")
local button3 = Button.new("button3", 15, 40, 150, 40, "Apply")
subPanel:addChild(button3)

mainPanel:addChild(button1)
mainPanel:addChild(button2)
mainPanel:addChild(subPanel)

-- Draw the UI
print("Drawing UI Hierarchy:")
mainPanel:draw()

-- Simulate clicks
print("\nSimulating clicks:")
local function simulateClick(x, y)
    print("Click at (" .. x .. ", " .. y .. ")")

    -- Check if button1 was clicked
    local absoluteX1 = button1.x + mainPanel.x
    local absoluteY1 = button1.y + mainPanel.y
    if button1:contains(x - mainPanel.x, y - mainPanel.y) then
        button1.onClick()
    end

    -- Check if button3 inside subPanel was clicked
    local absoluteX3 = button3.x + subPanel.x + mainPanel.x
    local absoluteY3 = button3.y + subPanel.y + mainPanel.y
    if button3:contains(x - subPanel.x - mainPanel.x, y - subPanel.y -
mainPanel.y) then
        button3.onClick = function() print("Apply button clicked!") end
        button3.onClick()
    end
end

simulateClick(170, 140)  -- Should hit button1
simulateClick(330, 180)  -- Should hit button3
```

Output:

```
Drawing UI Hierarchy:
Drawing mainPanel at (100, 100) with size 400x300
  Panel title: Main Panel
Drawing button1 at (120, 130) with size 150x40
  Button text: Save
Drawing button2 at (120, 190) with size 150x40
  Button text: Cancel
Drawing subPanel at (300, 130) with size 180x250
  Panel title: Settings
Drawing button3 at (315, 170) with size 150x40
  Button text: Apply

Simulating clicks:
Click at (170, 140)
Save button clicked!
Click at (330, 180)
Apply button clicked!
```

Best Practices for OOP in Lua

To wrap up, here are some best practices for object-oriented programming in Lua:

1. **Choose the right approach for your needs:**

   - Simple objects are fine for small scripts
   - Factory functions work well for medium-sized projects
   - Full class-based OOP with metatables is better for larger applications

2. **Be consistent with syntax:**

   - Choose one way to create objects/classes and stick with it
   - Standardize how methods are defined and called

3. **Document your class structure:**

   - Comment the purpose of each class, its properties, and methods
   - Specify the expected types for constructor parameters

4. **Use meaningful names:**

   - Class names should be singular nouns (e.g., Person, not People)
   - Method names should typically be verbs or verb phrases

5. **Keep classes focused:**

   - Each class should have a single responsibility
   - If a class is doing too much, split it into multiple classes

6. **Favor composition over inheritance:**

- Complex hierarchies can become difficult to maintain
- Composition is often more flexible and easier to reason about

7. **Be careful with shared state**:

- Avoid putting mutable state in class tables (vs. instance tables)
- Clearly document when state is shared between instances

8. **Don't expose implementation details**:

- Use closure-based private members for truly encapsulated data
- Prefix "private" methods with underscore as a convention

9. **Validate inputs in constructors**:

- Check that parameters are of the expected types
- Provide sensible defaults for optional parameters

10. **Consider performance implications**:

- Method lookup through metatables has some overhead
- For performance-critical code, you might need to optimize

Chapter Summary

In this chapter, we've explored object-oriented programming in Lua. Though Lua doesn't have built-in classes, it provides flexible mechanisms through tables, functions, and metatables to implement OOP concepts.

We've covered basic objects, factory functions, metatables, inheritance, polymorphism, and composition. We've also explored advanced techniques like method chaining, mixins, and operator overloading. Through practical examples, we've seen how these concepts can be applied to real-world problems.

Lua's approach to OOP is both simple and powerful. It doesn't force a specific paradigm but gives you the tools to implement the style that best fits your needs. This flexibility is one of Lua's strengths, allowing you to use as much or as little OOP as your project requires.

In the next chapter, we'll explore file I/O operations in Lua, which will allow your programs to read from and write to files on disk. This is essential for many applications, from configuration and data storage to log files and document processing.

Chapter 10: File I/O Operations

Introduction to File I/O

File input/output (I/O) operations allow your programs to interact with files on disk. This capability is essential for many applications, such as reading configuration files, saving user data, processing log files, or generating reports.

Lua provides a comprehensive set of functions for file operations through its `io` library. In this chapter, we'll explore how to read from and write to files, handle different file formats, and implement common file manipulation patterns.

Basic File Operations

Let's start with the fundamental file operations: opening, reading, writing, and closing files.

Opening and Closing Files

Before you can read from or write to a file, you need to open it. The `io.open` function is used for this purpose:

```
-- Open a file for reading
local file = io.open("example.txt", "r")
if file then
    print("File opened successfully")
    file:close()  -- Always close files when done
else
    print("Failed to open file")
end
```

The `io.open` function takes two parameters:

1. The filename or path
2. The mode, which specifies how the file should be opened

Here are the common file modes:

Mode	Description
"r"	Read mode (default)
"w"	Write mode (creates a new file or truncates an existing one)
"a"	Append mode (opens for writing, but doesn't truncate; positions at EOF)
"r+"	Update mode (for both reading and writing)
"w+"	Update mode (creates a new file or truncates an existing one)
"a+"	Append update mode (opens or creates for reading and appending)
"rb", "wb", etc.	Binary modes (important on Windows)

If the file cannot be opened (e.g., it doesn't exist for reading, or you don't have permission), `io.open` returns `nil` plus an error message.

Always close files when you're done with them using the `close` method:

```
file:close()
```

Closing files releases system resources and ensures that all data is properly written to disk.

Reading from Files

Lua provides several methods for reading from files:

```lua
-- Open a file for reading
local file = io.open("sample.txt", "r")
if not file then
    print("Failed to open file")
    return
end

-- Read the entire file at once
local contents = file:read("*all")
print("File contents:\n" .. contents)

-- Close and reopen to start from the beginning
```

```
file:close()
file = io.open("sample.txt", "r")

-- Read one line at a time
print("\nReading line by line:")
local line = file:read("*line")
while line do
    print(line)
    line = file:read("*line")
end

-- Close and reopen
file:close()
file = io.open("sample.txt", "r")

-- Read a specific number of characters
print("\nReading 5 characters:")
local chars = file:read(5)
print(chars)

-- Read the next line
print("\nReading next line:")
local nextLine = file:read("*line")
print(nextLine)

-- Close the file
file:close()
```

The read method accepts different arguments that determine what is read:

Argument	Description
"*all" or "a"	Reads the entire file
"*line" or "l"	Reads the next line (without the newline character)
"*number" or "n"	Reads a number
n (a number)	Reads up to n characters

When reading line by line, the read method returns nil when it reaches the end of the file, which makes it convenient to use in a while loop.

Writing to Files

To write to a file, open it in write or append mode, then use the write method:

```
-- Open a file for writing
```

```lua
local file = io.open("output.txt", "w")
if not file then
    print("Failed to open file for writing")
    return
end

-- Write strings to the file
file:write("Hello, world!\n")
file:write("This is a test file.\n")
file:write("Created on ", os.date(), "\n")

-- Close the file
file:close()
print("File written successfully")

-- Append to the file
file = io.open("output.txt", "a")
if not file then
    print("Failed to open file for appending")
    return
end

-- Append more text
file:write("This line was appended.\n")
file:write("The file now has more content.\n")

-- Close the file
file:close()
print("Content appended successfully")

-- Read and display the final result
file = io.open("output.txt", "r")
if file then
    print("\nFinal file contents:")
    print(file:read("*all"))
    file:close()
end
```

Output (the date will vary):

```
File written successfully
Content appended successfully

Final file contents:
Hello, world!
This is a test file.
```

```
Created on Wed Jan 26 17:30:45 2023
This line was appended.
The file now has more content.
```

The `write` method accepts multiple arguments and writes them in sequence. Note that unlike `print`, it doesn't automatically add spaces between arguments or a newline at the end.

File Positions and Seeking

Lua allows you to control the current position within a file using the `seek` method:

```
-- Open a file
local file = io.open("positions.txt", "w+")  -- Open for reading and writing
if not file then
    print("Failed to open file")
    return
end

-- Write some content
file:write("Line 1: This is the first line.\n")
file:write("Line 2: This is the second line.\n")
file:write("Line 3: This is the third line.\n")

-- Get the current position
local position = file:seek()  -- Current position (end of file)
print("Current position:", position)

-- Seek to the beginning of the file
file:seek("set", 0)
print("After seeking to start, position:", file:seek())

-- Read the first line
local line1 = file:read("*line")
print("First line:", line1)
print("After reading first line, position:", file:seek())

-- Seek relative to current position (skip ahead 10 bytes)
file:seek("cur", 10)
print("After seeking ahead 10 bytes, position:", file:seek())

-- Read from current position
local partial = file:read("*line")
print("Partial line:", partial)
```

```
-- Seek to end minus 20 bytes
file:seek("end", -20)
print("After seeking to end-20, position:", file:seek())

-- Read the last part
local lastPart = file:read("*all")
print("Last part:", lastPart)

-- Close the file
file:close()
```

Output (positions may vary slightly):

```
Current position: 87
After seeking to start, position: 0
First line: Line 1: This is the first line.
After reading first line, position: 30
After seeking ahead 10 bytes, position: 40
Partial line: is the second line.
After seeking to end-20, position: 67
Last part: he third line.
```

The seek method takes two optional arguments:

1. whence: The reference point ("set" for beginning, "cur" for current position, "end" for end of file)
2. offset: The number of bytes to move (positive or negative)

If called without arguments, seek returns the current position.

Standard Input, Output, and Error

Lua provides three standard file handles:

- io.stdin: The standard input (keyboard)
- io.stdout: The standard output (console)
- io.stderr: The standard error output (console)

These can be used like any other file handle:

```
-- Write to standard output
io.stdout:write("Enter your name: ")

-- Read from standard input
```

```lua
local name = io.stdin:read("*line")

-- Write to standard output again
io.stdout:write("Hello, " .. name .. "!\n")

-- Write an error message to standard error
io.stderr:write("This is an error message.\n")
```

Output (after the user types "John"):

```
Enter your name: John
Hello, John!
This is an error message.
```

Simplified I/O Functions

Lua provides some simplified I/O functions for common operations:

```lua
-- Set the default input file
local file = io.open("input.txt", "w")
file:write("Line 1\nLine 2\nLine 3\n")
file:close()

file = io.open("input.txt", "r")
io.input(file)  -- Sets this as the default input file

-- Read from the default input file
local line1 = io.read("*line")
local line2 = io.read("*line")
print("First line:", line1)
print("Second line:", line2)

-- Close the default input file
io.input():close()

-- Set the default output file
local outFile = io.open("simple_output.txt", "w")
io.output(outFile)  -- Sets this as the default output file

-- Write to the default output file
io.write("This text goes to the file.\n")
io.write("More text for the file.\n")

-- Close the default output file
```

```lua
io.output():close()

-- Read and display the output file
file = io.open("simple_output.txt", "r")
print("\nOutput file contents:")
print(file:read("*all"))
file:close()
```

Output:

```
First line: Line 1
Second line: Line 2

Output file contents:
This text goes to the file.
More text for the file.
```

The simplified functions include:

- `io.input([file])`: Gets or sets the default input file
- `io.output([file])`: Gets or sets the default output file
- `io.read(...)`: Reads from the default input file
- `io.write(...)`: Writes to the default output file
- `io.lines([filename])`: Iterates through the lines of a file

Reading Files Line by Line

A common task is reading a file line by line, and Lua provides several ways to do this:

```lua
-- Create a sample file
local file = io.open("lines.txt", "w")
file:write("Line 1: First line of the file\n")
file:write("Line 2: Second line of the file\n")
file:write("Line 3: Third line of the file\n")
file:write("Line 4: Fourth line of the file\n")
file:write("Line 5: Fifth line of the file\n")
file:close()

-- Method 1: Using a while loop with read
print("Method 1: while loop with read")
file = io.open("lines.txt", "r")
if file then
    local line = file:read("*line")
    local lineNum = 1
```

```lua
    while line do
        print(lineNum .. ": " .. line)
        line = file:read("*line")
        lineNum = lineNum + 1
    end
    file:close()
end

-- Method 2: Using io.lines() iterator
print("\nMethod 2: io.lines() iterator")
lineNum = 1
for line in io.lines("lines.txt") do
    print(lineNum .. ": " .. line)
    lineNum = lineNum + 1
end

-- Method 3: Using file:lines() iterator
print("\nMethod 3: file:lines() iterator")
file = io.open("lines.txt", "r")
if file then
    lineNum = 1
    for line in file:lines() do
        print(lineNum .. ": " .. line)
        lineNum = lineNum + 1
    end
    file:close()
end
```

Output:

```
Method 1: while loop with read
1: Line 1: First line of the file
2: Line 2: Second line of the file
3: Line 3: Third line of the file
4: Line 4: Fourth line of the file
5: Line 5: Fifth line of the file

Method 2: io.lines() iterator
1: Line 1: First line of the file
2: Line 2: Second line of the file
3: Line 3: Third line of the file
4: Line 4: Fourth line of the file
5: Line 5: Fifth line of the file

Method 3: file:lines() iterator
1: Line 1: First line of the file
```

```
2: Line 2: Second line of the file
3: Line 3: Third line of the file
4: Line 4: Fourth line of the file
5: Line 5: Fifth line of the file
```

The `io.lines` and `file:lines` iterators are convenient because they automatically handle opening and closing the file (in the case of `io.lines`) and reading each line.

Working with Binary Files

Lua can also work with binary files, which is useful for reading and writing non-text data like images or custom data formats:

```lua
-- Create a binary file with some sample data
local file = io.open("binary.dat", "wb")  -- Open in binary write mode
if not file then
    print("Failed to open binary file for writing")
    return
end

-- Write some binary data
file:write(string.char(0x48, 0x65, 0x6C, 0x6C, 0x6F))  -- "Hello" in ASCII
file:write(string.char(0, 1, 2, 3, 4))                 -- Some binary values
file:close()

-- Read the binary file
file = io.open("binary.dat", "rb")  -- Open in binary read mode
if not file then
    print("Failed to open binary file for reading")
    return
end

-- Read all bytes
local data = file:read("*all")
file:close()

-- Display the data in hexadecimal
print("Binary file length: " .. #data .. " bytes")
print("Hex dump:")
for i = 1, #data do
    local byte = string.byte(data, i)
    io.write(string.format("%02X ", byte))
    if i % 8 == 0 then io.write("\n") end
end
io.write("\n")
```

```
-- Convert ASCII part back to a string
local text = string.sub(data, 1, 5)
print("ASCII text: " .. text)
```

Output:

```
Binary file length: 10 bytes
Hex dump:
48 65 6C 6C 6F 00 01 02
03 04
ASCII text: Hello
```

When working with binary files, it's important to:

1. Use "rb", "wb", etc. modes to ensure binary treatment (especially on Windows)
2. Use `string.char` and `string.byte` to convert between binary data and Lua values
3. Be careful with encoding issues when working with text in binary files

File Existence and Properties

Lua doesn't provide built-in functions to check if a file exists or get its properties, but we can implement these ourselves:

```
-- Function to check if a file exists
function fileExists(path)
    local file = io.open(path, "r")
    if file then
        file:close()
        return true
    end
    return false
end

-- Function to get file size
function getFileSize(path)
    local file = io.open(path, "r")
    if not file then return nil end

    local size = file:seek("end")
    file:close()
```

```lua
        return size
end

-- Function to get last modified time (using os.execute and returning output)
function getFileModTime(path)
    if not fileExists(path) then return nil end

    local result
    if package.config:sub(1,1) == '/' then
        -- Unix-like system
        local handle = io.popen('stat -c %Y "'..path..'"')
        result = handle:read("*a")
        handle:close()
    else
        -- Windows
        local handle = io.popen('dir "'..path..'" /TC')
        local output = handle:read("*a")
        handle:close()
        -- Extract date from the output (simplified)
        result = output
    end

    return result
end

-- Create a test file
local file = io.open("testfile.txt", "w")
file:write("This is a test file.\n")
file:write("It has multiple lines.\n")
file:close()

-- Test the functions
print("File exists:", fileExists("testfile.txt"))
print("File exists:", fileExists("nonexistent.txt"))
print("File size:", getFileSize("testfile.txt") .. " bytes")

-- The modified time function may not work on all systems
local modTime = getFileModTime("testfile.txt")
if modTime then
    print("Modified time:", modTime)
end
```

Output (may vary):

```
File exists: true
File exists: false
```

```
File size: 40 bytes
Modified time: 1643215845
```

These functions provide basic file information. Note that the modified time function uses io.popen, which isn't available in all Lua implementations and may have security implications.

Error Handling in File I/O

When working with files, errors can occur for various reasons (file not found, permission denied, disk full, etc.). It's important to handle these errors gracefully:

```lua
-- Basic error handling: check the return value
local file, errorMsg = io.open("nonexistent.txt", "r")
if not file then
    print("Error opening file: " .. errorMsg)
else
    -- Process the file...
    file:close()
end

-- Using pcall for more comprehensive error handling
local function processFile(filename)
    local file, errorMsg = io.open(filename, "r")
    if not file then
        error("Unable to open file: " .. errorMsg)
    end

    local contents = file:read("*all")
    file:close()

    -- Process the contents...
    return #contents  -- Return the size
end

-- Use pcall to catch errors
local success, result = pcall(processFile, "example.txt")
if success then
    print("File processed successfully. Size: " .. result .. " bytes")
else
    print("An error occurred: " .. result)
end

-- More comprehensive error handling
local function safelyProcessFile(filename)
```

```lua
    -- Open the file
    local file, openError = io.open(filename, "r")
    if not file then
        return false, "Open error: " .. openError
    end

    -- Read the file (using pcall to catch potential errors)
    local success, content = pcall(function() return file:read("*all") end)

    -- Always close the file, even if an error occurred
    file:close()

    -- Check for read errors
    if not success then
        return false, "Read error: " .. content
    end

    -- Process the content (another potential source of errors)
    local success, result = pcall(function()
        -- Some processing that might error
        if #content == 0 then
            error("File is empty")
        end
        return #content  -- Return the size
    end)

    if not success then
        return false, "Processing error: " .. result
    end

    return true, result
end

-- Test the safer function
local success, result = safelyProcessFile("nonexistent.txt")
if success then
    print("File processed successfully. Size: " .. result .. " bytes")
else
    print(result)
end
```

Output:

```
Error opening file: no such file or directory
An error occurred: Unable to open file: no such file or directory
Open error: no such file or directory
```

The key principles for error handling in file I/O are:

1. Always check the return values from file operations
2. Use `pcall` for more complex error handling
3. Ensure files are closed even when errors occur
4. Provide meaningful error messages

Working with File Paths

When working with files, you often need to manipulate file paths. Lua doesn't provide a standard library for this, but we can implement some useful functions:

```lua
-- Function to get the directory part of a path
function getDirectory(path)
    local dirPattern = "(.*[\\/])[^\\/]*$"
    return string.match(path, dirPattern) or ""
end

-- Function to get the filename part of a path
function getFilename(path)
    local filenamePattern = ".*[\\/]([^\\/]*)$"
    return string.match(path, filenamePattern) or path
end

-- Function to get the file extension
function getExtension(path)
    local extensionPattern = ".*%.([^%.]*)$"
    return string.match(path, extensionPattern) or ""
end

-- Function to get the filename without extension
function getBasename(path)
    local basename = getFilename(path)
    local extPattern = "(.*)%.([^%.]*)$"
    local name = string.match(basename, extPattern)
    return name or basename
end

-- Function to join path components
function joinPaths(...)
    local separator = package.config:sub(1,1)  -- Get system separator (/ or \)
    local parts = {...}

    -- Remove trailing separators from all but the last part
    for i = 1, #parts - 1 do
        parts[i] = parts[i]:gsub("[\\/]*$", "") .. separator
```

```
        end

        -- Remove leading separators from all but the first part
        for i = 2, #parts do
            parts[i] = parts[i]:gsub("^[\\/]*", "")
        end

        return table.concat(parts)
end

-- Test the functions
local paths = {
    "/home/user/documents/file.txt",
    "C:\\Windows\\System32\\drivers\\etc\\hosts",
    "document.pdf",
    ".hidden",
    "/var/log/"
}

for _, path in ipairs(paths) do
    print("Path: " .. path)
    print("  Directory: " .. getDirectory(path))
    print("  Filename: " .. getFilename(path))
    print("  Extension: " .. getExtension(path))
    print("  Basename: " .. getBasename(path))
    print()
end

-- Test path joining
print("Joined path: " .. joinPaths("/home/user", "documents",
"project/file.txt"))
print("Joined path: " .. joinPaths("C:\\", "Program Files", "Application"))
```

Output:

```
Path: /home/user/documents/file.txt
  Directory: /home/user/documents/
  Filename: file.txt
  Extension: txt
  Basename: file

Path: C:\Windows\System32\drivers\etc\hosts
  Directory: C:\Windows\System32\drivers\etc\
  Filename: hosts
  Extension:
  Basename: hosts
```

```
Path: document.pdf
  Directory:
  Filename: document.pdf
  Extension: pdf
  Basename: document

Path: .hidden
  Directory:
  Filename: .hidden
  Extension: hidden
  Basename:

Path: /var/log/
  Directory: /var/log/
  Filename:
  Extension:
  Basename:

Joined path: /home/user/documents/project/file.txt
Joined path: C:/Program Files/Application
```

These functions provide basic path manipulation capabilities, but be aware that they may not handle all edge cases, especially with unusual path formats.

Working with Temporary Files

Sometimes you need to create temporary files for intermediate processing:

```lua
-- Function to create a temporary file
function createTempFile(prefix)
    prefix = prefix or "lua_temp"
    local tempDir

    -- Get system temp directory
    if package.config:sub(1,1) == '/' then
        -- Unix-like system
        tempDir = os.getenv("TMPDIR") or "/tmp"
    else
        -- Windows
        tempDir = os.getenv("TEMP") or os.getenv("TMP") or "."
    end

    local filename = joinPaths(tempDir, prefix .. "_" .. os.time() .. "_" ..
math.random(1000, 9999))
```

```lua
    local file, err = io.open(filename, "w")
    if not file then
        return nil, "Failed to create temporary file: " .. err
    end

    return file, filename
end

-- Function to safely perform operations with a temporary file
function withTempFile(func, prefix)
    local file, filename = createTempFile(prefix)
    if not file then
        return nil, filename  -- Error message
    end

    local success, result = pcall(function()
        return func(file, filename)
    end)

    -- Close and remove the temporary file
    file:close()
    os.remove(filename)

    if not success then
        return nil, result  -- Error message
    end

    return result
end

-- Test the temporary file functions
-- Initialize random seed
math.randomseed(os.time())

-- Example usage: Count lines in a file using a temporary file
local function countLines(inputFilename)
    return withTempFile(function(tempFile, tempFilename)
        -- Create a test input file
        local inputFile = io.open(inputFilename, "w")
        inputFile:write("Line 1\nLine 2\nLine 3\nLine 4\nLine 5\n")
        inputFile:close()

        -- Process input file and write to temp file
        local input = io.open(inputFilename, "r")
        local lineCount = 0
```

```
        for line in input:lines() do
            lineCount = lineCount + 1
            tempFile:write(lineCount .. ": " .. line .. "\n")
        end

        input:close()
        tempFile:flush()  -- Ensure all data is written

        -- Return the result
        return lineCount
    end, "linecount")
end

local lines, err = countLines("input_for_temp.txt")
if lines then
    print("The file has " .. lines .. " lines")
else
    print("Error: " .. err)
end

-- Clean up the test file
os.remove("input_for_temp.txt")
```

Output:

```
The file has 5 lines
```

Working with temporary files is useful for scenarios where:

1. You need to process a large amount of data that doesn't fit in memory
2. You need to pass data between different parts of your application
3. You need to create intermediate results before producing a final output

File Locking and Concurrent Access

When multiple processes might access the same file, you need to ensure data integrity through file locking. Lua doesn't provide this functionality directly, but there are options:

```
-- Simple file locking using lock files
function acquireLock(lockFilePath, timeout)
    timeout = timeout or 10  -- Default timeout in seconds
    local startTime = os.time()
```

```lua
    -- Try to create the lock file
    while os.time() - startTime < timeout do
        local lockFile, err = io.open(lockFilePath, "r")

        if lockFile then
            -- Lock file exists, check if it's stale
            local content = lockFile:read("*all")
            lockFile:close()

            local lockTime = tonumber(content) or 0
            if os.time() - lockTime > 300 then  -- 5 minutes timeout
                -- Stale lock, break it
                print("Breaking stale lock")
                break
            end

            -- Lock exists and is valid, wait and retry
            print("Lock exists, waiting...")
            os.execute("sleep 1")  -- Wait 1 second (Unix)
        else
            -- No lock file, try to create it
            lockFile, err = io.open(lockFilePath, "w")
            if lockFile then
                lockFile:write(tostring(os.time()))
                lockFile:close()
                return true  -- Successfully acquired lock
            else
                print("Failed to create lock file: " .. err)
                return false
            end
        end
    end

    -- Timeout occurred
    if os.time() - startTime >= timeout then
        print("Timeout waiting for lock")
        return false
    end

    -- Breaking stale lock
    local lockFile, err = io.open(lockFilePath, "w")
    if lockFile then
        lockFile:write(tostring(os.time()))
        lockFile:close()
        return true
    else
        print("Failed to create lock file: " .. err)
```

```lua
            return false
        end
end

function releaseLock(lockFilePath)
    os.remove(lockFilePath)
end

-- Example using the locking mechanism
local function updateSharedFile(filename, newContent)
    local lockFile = filename .. ".lock"

    -- Acquire lock
    print("Attempting to acquire lock...")
    if not acquireLock(lockFile, 5) then
        return false, "Failed to acquire lock"
    end

    print("Lock acquired, updating file...")

    -- Perform file operations
    local success, err = pcall(function()
        -- Open the file for reading
        local file = io.open(filename, "r")
        local content = ""
        if file then
            content = file:read("*all")
            file:close()
        end

        -- Append new content
        content = content .. newContent .. "\n"

        -- Write back to file
        file = io.open(filename, "w")
        file:write(content)
        file:close()
    end)

    -- Release lock
    releaseLock(lockFile)
    print("Lock released")

    if not success then
        return false, "Error updating file: " .. err
    end
```

```lua
        return true
end

-- Test the locking mechanism
local result, err = updateSharedFile("shared_data.txt", "Update at " ..
os.date())
if result then
    print("File updated successfully")

    -- Display the file contents
    local file = io.open("shared_data.txt", "r")
    if file then
        print("\nFile contents:")
        print(file:read("*all"))
        file:close()
    end
else
    print("Failed to update file: " .. err)
end

-- Clean up
os.remove("shared_data.txt")
os.remove("shared_data.txt.lock")
```

Output (may vary):

```
Attempting to acquire lock...
Lock acquired, updating file...
Lock released
File updated successfully

File contents:
Update at Wed Jan 26 17:45:30 2023
```

This example implements a simple file locking mechanism using lock files. In real-world applications, you might want to use:

1. OS-specific locking mechanisms via LuaFileSystem or similar libraries
2. Database locks if you're working with a database
3. More robust distributed locking mechanisms for multi-server applications

File I/O Patterns and Techniques

Let's explore some common patterns and techniques for file I/O.

Safely Writing to Files

When writing important data to files, it's a good practice to write to a temporary file first, then rename it to the final filename:

```lua
-- Function to safely write to a file
function safeWrite(filename, content)
    -- Create a temporary filename
    local tempFilename = filename .. ".tmp"

    -- Write to the temporary file
    local file, err = io.open(tempFilename, "w")
    if not file then
        return false, "Failed to open temporary file: " .. err
    end

    -- Write the content
    local success, writeErr = pcall(function()
        file:write(content)
    end)

    -- Close the file
    file:close()

    if not success then
        os.remove(tempFilename)  -- Clean up the temporary file
        return false, "Failed to write data: " .. writeErr
    end

    -- Rename the temporary file to the final filename
    local renameSuccess, renameErr

    if package.config:sub(1,1) == '/' then
        -- Unix-like system
        renameSuccess = os.rename(tempFilename, filename)
        renameErr = "Failed to rename file"
    else
        -- Windows might not allow renaming if target exists
        os.remove(filename)  -- Remove the existing file if any
        renameSuccess = os.rename(tempFilename, filename)
        renameErr = "Failed to rename file"
    end

    if not renameSuccess then
        os.remove(tempFilename)  -- Clean up the temporary file
        return false, renameErr
    end
```

```
        return true
end

-- Test the safe write function
local content = "This is important data that should be written safely.\n"
            .. "We don't want to lose this information if the program crashes.\
n"
            .. "Using the safe write technique helps prevent data corruption.\n"

local success, err = safeWrite("important_data.txt", content)
if success then
    print("Data written safely")

    -- Verify the file contents
    local file = io.open("important_data.txt", "r")
    if file then
        local readContent = file:read("*all")
        file:close()

        if readContent == content then
            print("File verification successful")
        else
            print("File verification failed: content doesn't match")
        end
    end
else
    print("Failed to write data: " .. err)
end

-- Clean up
os.remove("important_data.txt")
```

Output:

```
Data written safely
File verification successful
```

This pattern ensures that the file is either completely written or not modified at all, avoiding partial writes that could corrupt data.

Buffered Reading for Large Files

When dealing with large files, reading the entire file into memory might not be practical. Instead, you can process the file in chunks:

```lua
-- Function to process a large file in chunks
function processLargeFile(filename, chunkSize, processFunc)
    chunkSize = chunkSize or 4096  -- Default to 4KB chunks

    local file, err = io.open(filename, "r")
    if not file then
        return false, "Failed to open file: " .. err
    end

    local chunk = file:read(chunkSize)
    local totalProcessed = 0

    while chunk do
        local success, result = pcall(function()
            return processFunc(chunk)
        end)

        if not success then
            file:close()
            return false, "Processing error: " .. result
        end

        totalProcessed = totalProcessed + #chunk
        chunk = file:read(chunkSize)
    end

    file:close()
    return true, totalProcessed
end

-- Create a large-ish test file
local function createTestFile(filename, size)
    local file = io.open(filename, "w")
    if not file then return false end

    for i = 1, size do
        file:write("Line " .. i .. ": This is some test data that will be
repeated many times.\n")
    end

    file:close()
    return true
end

-- Create a test file with 10,000 lines
createTestFile("large_test.txt", 10000)
```

```lua
-- Process the file in chunks
local lineCount = 0
local byteCount = 0

local success, totalBytes = processLargeFile("large_test.txt", 1024,
function(chunk)
    -- Count lines in this chunk
    for _ in chunk:gmatch("\n") do
        lineCount = lineCount + 1
    end

    -- Count specific patterns
    local matches = chunk:gsub("test data", "")
    byteCount = byteCount + matches

    return true
end)

if success then
    print("Processed " .. totalBytes .. " bytes")
    print("Found approximately " .. lineCount .. " lines")
    print("Found approximately " .. byteCount .. " occurrences of 'test data'")
else
    print("Failed to process file: " .. totalBytes)
end

-- Clean up
os.remove("large_test.txt")
```

Output (numbers may vary slightly due to chunk boundaries):

```
Processed 610000 bytes
Found approximately 10000 lines
Found approximately 10000 occurrences of 'test data'
```

This approach allows you to process files that are too large to fit in memory, by reading and processing manageable chunks at a time.

Working with CSV Files

CSV (Comma-Separated Values) is a common format for data exchange. Here's a simple CSV parser and writer:

```lua
-- Function to parse CSV data
function parseCSV(data, separator, header)
```

```lua
        separator = separator or ","
        header = header ~= false  -- Default to true

        local lines = {}
        for line in data:gmatch("[^\r\n]+") do
            table.insert(lines, line)
        end

        if #lines == 0 then
            return {}
        end

        local result = {}
        local headers = {}

        -- Parse header line if specified
        if header then
            local headerLine = lines[1]
            local i = 1
            for field in headerLine:gmatch("([^" .. separator .. "]*)(" .. separator
.. "?)") do
                if field ~= "" or i == 1 then
                    headers[i] = field:match("^%s*(.-)%s*$")  -- Trim whitespace
                    i = i + 1
                end
            end
            table.remove(lines, 1)
        end

        -- Parse data lines
        for _, line in ipairs(lines) do
            if line:match("%S") then  -- Skip empty lines
                local record = {}
                local i = 1
                for field in line:gmatch("([^" .. separator .. "]*)(" ..
separator .. "?)") do
                    if field ~= "" or i == 1 then
                        field = field:match("^%s*(.-)%s*$")  -- Trim whitespace

                        if header then
                            record[headers[i] or i] = field
                        else
                            record[i] = field
                        end

                        i = i + 1
                    end
            end
```

```lua
                end
                table.insert(result, record)
            end
        end

    return result, headers
end

-- Function to write a table to CSV
function writeCSV(data, separator, headers)
    separator = separator or ","
    local lines = {}

    -- Write header line if headers are provided
    if headers then
        local headerLine = table.concat(headers, separator)
        table.insert(lines, headerLine)
    end

    -- Write data lines
    for _, record in ipairs(data) do
        local line = {}

        if headers then
            -- Write record as a map using headers
            for _, header in ipairs(headers) do
                table.insert(line, record[header] or "")
            end
        else
            -- Write record as an array
            for i = 1, #record do
                table.insert(line, record[i] or "")
            end
        end

        table.insert(lines, table.concat(line, separator))
    end

    return table.concat(lines, "\n")
end

-- Test with a sample CSV file
local csvData = [[
Name,Age,City,Country
John Doe,30,New York,USA
Jane Smith,25,London,UK
Bob Johnson,45,Paris,France
```

```lua
Alice Brown,35,Tokyo,Japan
]]

-- Parse the CSV data
local records, headers = parseCSV(csvData)
print("Parsed " .. #records .. " records")

-- Display the parsed data
print("\nCSV Data:")
for i, record in ipairs(records) do
    print("Record " .. i .. ":")
    for key, value in pairs(record) do
        print("  " .. key .. ": " .. value)
    end
end

-- Modify some data
records[1].Age = "31"
table.insert(records, {Name = "Carlos Rodriguez", Age = "28", City = "Madrid",
Country = "Spain"})

-- Write back to CSV
local newCSV = writeCSV(records, ",", headers)
print("\nNew CSV Data:")
print(newCSV)

-- Write to a file
local file = io.open("people.csv", "w")
if file then
    file:write(newCSV)
    file:close()
    print("\nCSV written to people.csv")
end

-- Read from the file and parse again
file = io.open("people.csv", "r")
if file then
    local fileContent = file:read("*all")
    file:close()

    local newRecords = parseCSV(fileContent)
    print("\nRead " .. #newRecords .. " records from the file")
end

-- Clean up
os.remove("people.csv")
```

Output:

```
Parsed 4 records

CSV Data:
Record 1:
  Name: John Doe
  Country: USA
  City: New York
  Age: 30
Record 2:
  Name: Jane Smith
  Country: UK
  City: London
  Age: 25
Record 3:
  Name: Bob Johnson
  Country: France
  City: Paris
  Age: 45
Record 4:
  Name: Alice Brown
  Country: Japan
  City: Tokyo
  Age: 35

New CSV Data:
Name,Age,City,Country
John Doe,31,New York,USA
Jane Smith,25,London,UK
Bob Johnson,45,Paris,France
Alice Brown,35,Tokyo,Japan
Carlos Rodriguez,28,Madrid,Spain

CSV written to people.csv

Read 5 records from the file
```

While this CSV parser is simple, it handles basic CSV files. For more complex CSV handling, you might want to use a dedicated library, as CSV can have many edge cases (quoted fields, escaped quotes, multiline fields, etc.).

Configuration Files

Lua files themselves can be used as configuration files, which offers great flexibility:

```lua
-- Example of a Lua configuration file
local configContent = [[
-- My Application Configuration

config = {
    -- General settings
    app = {
        name = "My Application",
        version = "1.0.0",
        debug = true
    },

    -- Database settings
    database = {
        host = "localhost",
        port = 3306,
        user = "admin",
        password = "secret",
        name = "myapp_db"
    },

    -- Server settings
    server = {
        host = "0.0.0.0",
        port = 8080,
        maxConnections = 100,
        timeout = 30
    },

    -- Logging settings
    logging = {
        level = "info",  -- debug, info, warn, error
        file = "/var/log/myapp.log",
        console = true
    }
}

-- Return the configuration
return config
]]

-- Write the configuration to a file
local file = io.open("config.lua", "w")
file:write(configContent)
file:close()

-- Function to load a Lua-based configuration file
```

```lua
function loadConfig(filename)
    local chunk, err = loadfile(filename)
    if not chunk then
        return nil, "Failed to load config file: " .. err
    end

    local success, result = pcall(chunk)
    if not success then
        return nil, "Failed to execute config file: " .. result
    end

    return result
end

-- Load the configuration
local config, err = loadConfig("config.lua")
if not config then
    print("Error loading config: " .. err)
else
    print("Configuration loaded successfully")

    -- Access configuration values
    print("\nApplication name: " .. config.app.name)
    print("Database host: " .. config.database.host)
    print("Server port: " .. config.server.port)
    print("Logging level: " .. config.logging.level)

    -- Modify and save configuration
    config.app.debug = false
    config.server.port = 9000

    -- Write modified config back to file
    local newConfigContent = "return " .. table.tostring(config)

    -- We need a helper function to convert tables to strings
    function table.tostring(tbl, indent)
        indent = indent or 0
        local indentStr = string.rep("    ", indent)
        local result = "{\n"

        for k, v in pairs(tbl) do
            result = result .. indentStr .. "    "

            -- Format key
            if type(k) == "number" then
                result = result .. "[" .. k .. "]"
```

```
            elseif type(k) == "string" and k:match("^[A-Za-z_][A-Za-z0-9_]*$")
then
                result = result .. k
            else
                result = result .. "[\"" .. tostring(k) .. "\"]"
            end

            result = result .. " = "

            -- Format value
            if type(v) == "table" then
                result = result .. table.tostring(v, indent + 1)
            elseif type(v) == "string" then
                result = result .. "\"" .. v .. "\""
            elseif type(v) == "boolean" or type(v) == "number" then
                result = result .. tostring(v)
            else
                result = result .. "\"" .. tostring(v) .. "\""
            end

            result = result .. ",\n"
        end

        result = result .. indentStr .. "}"
        return result
    end

    file = io.open("modified_config.lua", "w")
    file:write(newConfigContent)
    file:close()

    print("\nModified configuration saved to modified_config.lua")
end

-- Clean up
os.remove("config.lua")
os.remove("modified_config.lua")
```

Output:

```
Configuration loaded successfully

Application name: My Application
Database host: localhost
Server port: 8080
Logging level: info
```

```
Modified configuration saved to modified_config.lua
```

Using Lua files as configuration has several advantages:

1. Configuration can include comments and complex data structures
2. Configuration can include logic and calculated values
3. You can validate the configuration as it loads
4. It's a familiar format for Lua developers

Chapter Summary

In this chapter, we've explored Lua's file I/O capabilities in depth. We've covered the basics of opening, reading from, writing to, and closing files, as well as more advanced topics like file positioning, binary files, and error handling.

We've also examined practical patterns and techniques for working with files, including safe writing strategies, processing large files in chunks, and working with common file formats like CSV. Additionally, we've looked at how to use Lua files themselves as flexible configuration files.

File I/O is a fundamental capability for many applications, allowing programs to persist data, communicate with other systems, and process information from various sources. With the techniques covered in this chapter, you should be well-equipped to handle a wide range of file-related tasks in your Lua applications.

In the next chapter, we'll explore error handling and debugging in Lua, which are crucial skills for developing robust and maintainable applications. We'll learn how to anticipate and handle errors gracefully, and how to debug problems when they arise.

Chapter 11: Error Handling and Debugging

Understanding Errors in Lua

Errors are an inevitable part of programming, and handling them gracefully is a crucial skill. In Lua, errors can occur for various reasons: invalid syntax, attempting to use nil values, division by zero, file I/O issues, and many other cases.

When an error occurs during execution, Lua typically stops the program and prints an error message. However, Lua also provides mechanisms to catch and handle errors, allowing your programs to recover from problems rather than simply crashing.

In this chapter, we'll explore how errors work in Lua, how to handle them effectively, and how to debug your programs when errors do occur.

Types of Errors

In Lua, errors generally fall into three categories:

Syntax Errors

Syntax errors occur when the code doesn't conform to Lua's grammar rules. These are detected when Lua tries to parse your code:

```
-- Syntax error: missing the 'then' keyword
if x > 10
    print("x is greater than 10")
end
```

Error message:

```
stdin:2: 'then' expected near 'print'
```

Syntax errors must be fixed before your program can run at all.

Runtime Errors

Runtime errors occur during program execution. Common examples include:

```
-- Attempt to perform arithmetic on a nil value
local x
print(x + 1)
```

Error message:

```
stdin:2: attempt to perform arithmetic on a nil value (local 'x')

-- Attempt to index a non-table value
local str = "hello"
print(str.length)  -- Strings don't have a 'length' field
```

Error message:

```
stdin:2: attempt to index a string value (field 'length')

-- Division by zero
local result = 10 / 0
```

Error message:

```
stdin:1: attempt to divide by zero

-- Attempt to call a non-function value
local notAFunction = 42
notAFunction()
```

Error message:

```
stdin:2: attempt to call a number value
```

User-Defined Errors

You can also generate your own errors using the `error` function:

```lua
function divide(a, b)
    if b == 0 then
        error("Division by zero is not allowed")
    end
    return a / b
end

print(divide(10, 0))
```

Error message:

```
stdin:3: Division by zero is not allowed
stack traceback:
        stdin:3: in function 'divide'
        stdin:7: in main chunk
```

Basic Error Handling

Lua provides the `pcall` (protected call) function to run code in a protected environment, catching any errors that might occur:

```lua
-- Basic error handling with pcall
local success, result = pcall(function()
    return 10 / 0  -- This will cause an error
end)

if success then
    print("The operation succeeded. Result:", result)
else
    print("The operation failed. Error:", result)
end

-- Another example with pcall
success, result = pcall(function()
    return 10 / 2  -- This will succeed
end)

if success then
    print("The operation succeeded. Result:", result)
else
```

```
      print("The operation failed. Error:", result)
end
```

Output:

```
The operation failed. Error: stdin:2: attempt to divide by zero
The operation succeeded. Result: 5
```

The pcall function takes a function as its argument and returns two values:

1. A boolean indicating success (true) or failure (false)
2. Either the function's return value (on success) or the error message (on failure)

Advanced Error Handling with xpcall

For more control over error handling, Lua provides xpcall, which allows you to specify an error handler function:

```
-- Error handler function for xpcall
local function errorHandler(err)
    print("An error occurred: " .. err)
    print("Stack traceback:")
    print(debug.traceback("", 2))  -- Get traceback, skipping this function
    return "Error handled: " .. err
end

-- Using xpcall with an error handler
local success, result = xpcall(function()
    error("Something went wrong!")
end, errorHandler)

print("Success:", success)
print("Result:", result)

-- Another example with a calculation that works
success, result = xpcall(function()
    return 10 * 5
end, errorHandler)

print("Success:", success)
print("Result:", result)
```

Output:

```
An error occurred: Something went wrong!
Stack traceback:
stack traceback:
        stdin:2: in function <stdin:1>
        [C]: in function 'xpcall'
        stdin:7: in main chunk
Success: false
Result: Error handled: Something went wrong!
Success: true
Result: 50
```

The error handler function receives the error message as an argument and can perform additional operations like logging or cleanup before returning a value that becomes the second result of xpcall.

Creating and Raising Errors

You can generate your own errors using the error function:

```
-- Generate an error with a message
function validateAge(age)
    if type(age) ~= "number" then
        error("Age must be a number", 2)  -- The 2 indicates the error position
in the stack
    end

    if age < 0 or age > 150 then
        error("Age must be between 0 and 150", 2)
    end

    return true
end

-- Test the function with pcall
local function testValidation(age)
    local success, result = pcall(function()
        return validateAge(age)
    end)

    if success then
        print("Age " .. age .. " is valid")
    else
        print("Validation failed: " .. result)
    end
end
```

```
testValidation(25)
testValidation("not a number")
testValidation(-5)
testValidation(200)
```

Output:

```
Age 25 is valid
Validation failed: stdin:3: Age must be a number
Validation failed: stdin:7: Age must be between 0 and 150
Validation failed: stdin:7: Age must be between 0 and 150
```

The second argument to error specifies the level at which to report the error. This affects which function is shown as the source of the error in the error message.

Error Handling Patterns

Let's explore some common patterns for error handling in Lua.

Return Values for Error Reporting

A common pattern in Lua libraries is to return nil plus an error message for failures:

```
-- Function that returns nil plus error message on failure
function divide(a, b)
    if type(a) ~= "number" or type(b) ~= "number" then
        return nil, "Both arguments must be numbers"
    end

    if b == 0 then
        return nil, "Division by zero"
    end

    return a / b
end

-- Using the function
local result, err = divide(10, 2)
if result then
    print("Result: " .. result)
else
    print("Error: " .. err)
end
```

```lua
result, err = divide(10, 0)
if result then
    print("Result: " .. result)
else
    print("Error: " .. err)
end

result, err = divide("10", 2)
if result then
    print("Result: " .. result)
else
    print("Error: " .. err)
end
```

Output:

```
Result: 5
Error: Division by zero
Error: Both arguments must be numbers
```

This pattern is used extensively in Lua's built-in libraries, especially for I/O operations.

Error Objects

For more structured error handling, you can create error objects:

```lua
-- Define an error class
local Error = {}
Error.__index = Error

function Error.new(code, message, details)
    local self = setmetatable({}, Error)
    self.code = code
    self.message = message
    self.details = details or {}
    self.timestamp = os.time()
    return self
end

function Error:__tostring()
    return string.format("Error %s: %s", self.code, self.message)
end
```

```lua
-- Function that generates error objects
function getUserData(userId)
    if type(userId) ~= "number" then
        local err = Error.new("INVALID_TYPE", "User ID must be a number", {
            providedType = type(userId),
            paramName = "userId"
        })
        return nil, err
    end

    if userId <= 0 then
        local err = Error.new("INVALID_RANGE", "User ID must be positive", {
            providedValue = userId,
            paramName = "userId"
        })
        return nil, err
    end

    -- Simulate a database lookup
    if userId > 1000 then
        local err = Error.new("NOT_FOUND", "User not found", {
            userId = userId
        })
        return nil, err
    end

    -- Success case
    return {
        id = userId,
        name = "User " .. userId,
        email = "user" .. userId .. "@example.com"
    }
end

-- Test the function
function processUser(userId)
    local user, err = getUserData(userId)
    if not user then
        print("Failed to get user: " .. tostring(err))

        -- Different handling based on error code
        if err.code == "NOT_FOUND" then
            print("User does not exist. Creating a new user...")
        elseif err.code == "INVALID_TYPE" then
            print("Please provide a valid user ID number")
        elseif err.code == "INVALID_RANGE" then
            print("User ID must be greater than 0")
```

```
        end

        return false
    end

    print("Got user data:")
    print("  ID: " .. user.id)
    print("  Name: " .. user.name)
    print("  Email: " .. user.email)
    return true
end

-- Try with different user IDs
print("Test 1:")
processUser(42)

print("\nTest 2:")
processUser("abc")

print("\nTest 3:")
processUser(-5)

print("\nTest 4:")
processUser(9999)
```

Output:

```
Test 1:
Got user data:
  ID: 42
  Name: User 42
  Email: user42@example.com

Test 2:
Failed to get user: Error INVALID_TYPE: User ID must be a number
Please provide a valid user ID number

Test 3:
Failed to get user: Error INVALID_RANGE: User ID must be positive
User ID must be greater than 0

Test 4:
Failed to get user: Error NOT_FOUND: User not found
User does not exist. Creating a new user...
```

This pattern provides richer error information and allows for more sophisticated error handling based on error types.

Assertions

Lua provides the `assert` function, which raises an error if its first argument evaluates to false:

```lua
-- Using assert for parameter validation
function calculateArea(length, width)
    assert(type(length) == "number", "Length must be a number")
    assert(type(width) == "number", "Width must be a number")
    assert(length > 0, "Length must be positive")
    assert(width > 0, "Width must be positive")

    return length * width
end

-- Test with pcall
local function testCalculation(length, width)
    local success, result = pcall(function()
        return calculateArea(length, width)
    end)

    if success then
        print("Area: " .. result)
    else
        print("Calculation failed: " .. result)
    end
end

testCalculation(5, 10)
testCalculation("5", 10)
testCalculation(5, -10)
```

Output:

```
Area: 50
Calculation failed: stdin:2: Length must be a number
Calculation failed: stdin:4: Width must be positive
```

The `assert` function is a convenient way to check conditions and automatically raise an error with a meaningful message when they fail.

Combining pcall with Return Values

You can combine pcall with the return value pattern for more robust error handling:

```lua
-- Function that uses both pcall and return values
function safelyProcessFile(filename)
    -- Check if the file exists
    local exists, err = pcall(function()
        local file = io.open(filename, "r")
        if not file then
            error("File not found")
        end
        file:close()
        return true
    end)

    if not exists then
        return nil, "File access error: " .. err
    end

    -- Process the file
    local success, content = pcall(function()
        local file = io.open(filename, "r")
        local content = file:read("*all")
        file:close()
        return content
    end)

    if not success then
        return nil, "File read error: " .. content
    end

    -- Process the content (could potentially fail)
    local success, result = pcall(function()
        -- Some processing that might throw an error
        if #content == 0 then
            error("File is empty")
        end

        -- Count lines and words
        local lines = 0
        local words = 0

        for _ in content:gmatch("\n") do
            lines = lines + 1
        end

        for _ in content:gmatch("%w+") do
```

```lua
                words = words + 1
            end

            return {
                size = #content,
                lines = lines + 1,   -- +1 because the last line might not end with \
n
                words = words
            }
        end)

        if not success then
            return nil, "Processing error: " .. result
        end

        return result
end

-- Create a test file
local function createTestFile(filename, content)
        local file = io.open(filename, "w")
        if file then
            file:write(content)
            file:close()
            return true
        end
        return false
end

-- Test with different scenarios
local testFile = "test_file.txt"
local testContent = "This is a test file.\nIt has multiple lines.\nWe'll use it
to test our error handling."

-- Create the test file
if createTestFile(testFile, testContent) then
        print("Test file created")

        -- Test with the existing file
        local result, err = safelyProcessFile(testFile)
        if result then
            print("File processed successfully:")
            print("  Size: " .. result.size .. " bytes")
            print("  Lines: " .. result.lines)
            print("  Words: " .. result.words)
        else
            print("Error: " .. err)
```

```
        end

        -- Test with a non-existent file
        result, err = safelyProcessFile("nonexistent.txt")
        if result then
            print("File processed successfully")
        else
            print("Error: " .. err)
        end

        -- Test with an empty file
        createTestFile("empty.txt", "")
        result, err = safelyProcessFile("empty.txt")
        if result then
            print("File processed successfully")
        else
            print("Error: " .. err)
        end

        -- Clean up
        os.remove(testFile)
        os.remove("empty.txt")
else
        print("Failed to create test file")
end
```

Output:

```
Test file created
File processed successfully:
  Size: 90 bytes
  Lines: 3
  Words: 19
Error: File access error: stdin:6: File not found
Error: Processing error: stdin:37: File is empty
```

This pattern combines the safety of pcall with the readability of the return value pattern, making it suitable for complex operations with multiple potential failure points.

Debugging in Lua

Even with good error handling, bugs can still occur. Lua provides several techniques for debugging your code.

Basic Debugging with Print Statements

The simplest debugging technique is to add print statements to your code:

```lua
-- Debugging with print statements
function factorial(n)
    print("factorial called with n =", n)

    if n <= 1 then
        print("base case: returning 1")
        return 1
    else
        print("calculating factorial for n - 1 =", n - 1)
        local subResult = factorial(n - 1)
        print("got subResult =", subResult)

        local result = n * subResult
        print("returning result =", result)
        return result
    end
end

print("Starting factorial calculation")
local result = factorial(5)
print("Final result:", result)
```

Output:

```
Starting factorial calculation
factorial called with n = 5
calculating factorial for n - 1 = 4
factorial called with n = 4
calculating factorial for n - 1 = 3
factorial called with n = 3
calculating factorial for n - 1 = 2
factorial called with n = 2
calculating factorial for n - 1 = 1
factorial called with n = 1
base case: returning 1
got subResult = 1
returning result = 2
got subResult = 2
returning result = 6
got subResult = 6
returning result = 24
got subResult = 24
returning result = 120
```

```
Final result: 120
```

While simple, print statements can be very effective for tracking the flow of your program and the values of variables at different points.

The Debug Library

Lua provides a debug library with more sophisticated debugging tools:

```lua
-- Using the debug library
function exampleFunction(a, b)
    local c = a + b
    local d = a * b

    -- Get information about the current function
    local info = debug.getinfo(1)
    print("Function name:", info.name)
    print("Source:", info.source)
    print("Line:", info.currentline)

    -- Get local variables
    local names = {}
    local values = {}
    for i = 1, math.huge do
        local name, value = debug.getlocal(1, i)
        if not name then break end
        names[i] = name
        values[i] = value
    end

    print("Local variables:")
    for i, name in ipairs(names) do
        print("  " .. name .. " = " .. tostring(values[i]))
    end

    return c + d
end

local result = exampleFunction(5, 10)
print("Result:", result)

-- Get the call stack
print("\nCall stack:")
print(debug.traceback())
```

Output:

```
Function name: exampleFunction
Source: stdin
Line: 8
Local variables:
  a = 5
  b = 10
  c = 15
  d = 50
  info = table: 0x565189292530
  names = table: 0x55518927ab30
  values = table: 0x565189292b10
Result: 65

Call stack:
stack traceback:
        stdin:31: in main chunk
```

The debug library provides functions to inspect call stacks, local variables, function information, and more. It's a powerful tool for debugging complex issues.

Interactive Debugging

For more interactive debugging, you can create a simple REPL (Read-Eval-Print Loop):

```lua
-- Simple interactive debugger
function debug_repl(env)
    env = env or _G  -- Default to the global environment

    local function printTable(t, indent)
        indent = indent or 0
        local indentStr = string.rep("  ", indent)

        for k, v in pairs(t) do
            if type(v) == "table" and indent < 2 then
                print(indentStr .. tostring(k) .. " = {")
                printTable(v, indent + 1)
                print(indentStr .. "}")
            else
                print(indentStr .. tostring(k) .. " = " .. tostring(v))
            end
        end
    end

    print("Entering debug REPL. Type 'exit' to leave.")
```

```lua
    while true do
        io.write("> ")
        local line = io.read()

        if line == "exit" then
            break
        elseif line == "vars" then
            print("Variables in environment:")
            printTable(env)
        else
            local func, err = load("return " .. line, "debug", "t", env)
            if not func then
                func, err = load(line, "debug", "t", env)
            end

            if not func then
                print("Error: " .. err)
            else
                local success, result = pcall(func)
                if success then
                    if result ~= nil then
                        if type(result) == "table" then
                            print("Result table:")
                            printTable(result)
                        else
                            print(result)
                        end
                    end
                else
                    print("Error: " .. result)
                end
            end
        end
    end

    print("Exiting debug REPL.")
end

-- Example usage in a function
function processData(data)
    local result = {}

    for i, value in ipairs(data) do
        if i == 3 then
            print("Breaking at i = 3 for debugging")
            debug_repl({
                i = i,
```

```
                value = value,
                data = data,
                result = result,
                -- Add any other variables you want to expose
                processData = processData
            })
        end

        result[i] = value * 2
    end

    return result
end

-- Test the function
local data = {10, 20, 30, 40, 50}
local processedData = processData(data)
print("Processed data:")
for i, value in ipairs(processedData) do
    print(i, value)
end
```

This simple REPL allows you to inspect variables and execute arbitrary code during program execution. In an interactive session, you could examine variables, call functions, and experiment with code to understand what's happening.

Conditional Breakpoints

You can implement conditional breakpoints by combining debugging with conditional statements:

```
-- Function with a conditional breakpoint
function processItems(items, threshold)
    local results = {}

    for i, item in ipairs(items) do
        local value = item.value

        -- Conditional breakpoint
        if value > threshold and os.getenv("DEBUG") == "1" then
            print("Breakpoint triggered for item " .. i)
            print("Item value " .. value .. " exceeds threshold " .. threshold)

            -- You could call debug_repl() here, or just print debugigng info
            print("Item details:")
            for k, v in pairs(item) do
```

```lua
                print("  " .. k .. ": " .. tostring(v))
            end

            io.write("Press Enter to continue...")
            io.read()
        end

        results[i] = value * 2
    end

    return results
end

-- Test data
local items = {
    {name = "Item 1", value = 10},
    {name = "Item 2", value = 20},
    {name = "Item 3", value = 30},
    {name = "Item 4", value = 40},
    {name = "Item 5", value = 50}
}

-- Process the items with a threshold
local results = processItems(items, 25)
print("Results:", table.concat(results, ", "))
```

In this example, the breakpoint only triggers if the DEBUG environment variable is set to "1". This allows you to leave debugging code in place but only activate it when needed.

Logging

For longer-running applications, logging is often more practical than interactive debugging:

```lua
-- Simple logging system
local Logger = {}

-- Log levels
Logger.LEVELS = {
    DEBUG = 1,
    INFO = 2,
    WARN = 3,
    ERROR = 4,
    FATAL = 5
```

```lua
}

-- Configuration
Logger.config = {
    level = Logger.LEVELS.INFO,  -- Default level
    useFile = false,
    filePath = "app.log",
    showTimestamp = true
}

-- Configure the logger
function Logger.configure(config)
    for key, value in pairs(config) do
        Logger.config[key] = value
    end
end

-- Write a log message
function Logger.log(level, message, ...)
    if level < Logger.config.level then
        return
    end

    -- Get level name
    local levelName
    for name, value in pairs(Logger.LEVELS) do
        if value == level then
            levelName = name
            break
        end
    end

    -- Format message with optional arguments
    if select("#", ...) > 0 then
        message = string.format(message, ...)
    end

    -- Add timestamp if configured
    local timestamp = ""
    if Logger.config.showTimestamp then
        timestamp = os.date("%Y-%m-%d %H:%M:%S") .. " "
    end

    -- Format the full log line
    local logLine = string.format("%s[%s] %s", timestamp, levelName, message)

    -- Write to console
```

```lua
    print(logLine)

    -- Write to file if configured
    if Logger.config.useFile then
        local file = io.open(Logger.config.filePath, "a")
        if file then
            file:write(logLine .. "\n")
            file:close()
        end
    end
end

-- Convenience methods for each log level
function Logger.debug(message, ...)
    Logger.log(Logger.LEVELS.DEBUG, message, ...)
end

function Logger.info(message, ...)
    Logger.log(Logger.LEVELS.INFO, message, ...)
end

function Logger.warn(message, ...)
    Logger.log(Logger.LEVELS.WARN, message, ...)
end

function Logger.error(message, ...)
    Logger.log(Logger.LEVELS.ERROR, message, ...)
end

function Logger.fatal(message, ...)
    Logger.log(Logger.LEVELS.FATAL, message, ...)
end

-- Test the logger
Logger.configure({
    level = Logger.LEVELS.DEBUG,
    useFile = true,
    filePath = "debug.log"
})

Logger.debug("This is a debug message")
Logger.info("Processing item %d: %s", 42, "Example Item")
Logger.warn("Warning: approaching resource limit (%d%%)", 85)
Logger.error("Failed to connect to %s: %s", "database", "connection timeout")
Logger.fatal("Critical error: %s", "out of memory")

-- Clean up
```

```lua
os.remove("debug.log")
```

Output (timestamps will vary):

```
2023-01-26 17:55:30 [DEBUG] This is a debug message
2023-01-26 17:55:30 [INFO] Processing item 42: Example Item
2023-01-26 17:55:30 [WARN] Warning: approaching resource limit (85%)
2023-01-26 17:55:30 [ERROR] Failed to connect to database: connection timeout
2023-01-26 17:55:30 [FATAL] Critical error: out of memory
```

A logging system allows you to:

1. Record events at different severity levels
2. Control which messages are displayed or saved based on configuration
3. Include contextual information like timestamps
4. Save logs to files for later analysis

Performance Profiling

To identify bottlenecks in your code, you can implement simple profiling:

```lua
-- Simple profiling utility
local Profiler = {}

function Profiler.start(name)
    local startTime = os.clock()

    return function()
        local endTime = os.clock()
        local elapsed = endTime - startTime
        print(string.format("Profile '%s': %.6f seconds", name, elapsed))
        return elapsed
    end
end

-- Profile a function
function Profiler.profileFunc(func, name, ...)
    name = name or "function"
    local startTime = os.clock()
    local results = {func(...)}
    local endTime = os.clock()

    print(string.format("Profile '%s': %.6f seconds", name, endTime -
startTime))
```

```lua
        return table.unpack(results)
end

-- Example functions to profile
function fibonacci(n)
    if n <= 1 then
        return n
    else
        return fibonacci(n-1) + fibonacci(n-2)
    end
end

function factorial(n)
    if n <= 1 then
        return 1
    else
        return n * factorial(n-1)
    end
end

-- Profile using stop function
print("Using start/stop:")
local stop = Profiler.start("fibonacci(30)")
fibonacci(30)
stop()

-- Profile using profileFunc
print("\nUsing profileFunc:")
local fibResult = Profiler.profileFunc(fibonacci, "fibonacci(30)", 30)
print("Result:", fibResult)

local factResult = Profiler.profileFunc(factorial, "factorial(20)", 20)
print("Result:", factResult)

-- More complex example: Compare two implementations
function slowSum(n)
    local sum = 0
    for i = 1, n do
        sum = sum + i
    end
    return sum
end

function fastSum(n)
    return n * (n + 1) / 2
end
```

```
print("\nComparing implementations:")
local n = 1000000

local slowResult = Profiler.profileFunc(slowSum, "slowSum(" .. n .. ")", n)
print("Result:", slowResult)

local fastResult = Profiler.profileFunc(fastSum, "fastSum(" .. n .. ")", n)
print("Result:", fastResult)
```

Output (times will vary):

```
Using start/stop:
Profile 'fibonacci(30)': 0.406250 seconds

Using profileFunc:
Profile 'fibonacci(30)': 0.437500 seconds
Result: 832040
Profile 'factorial(20)': 0.000000 seconds
Result: 2432902008176640000

Comparing implementations:
Profile 'slowSum(1000000)': 0.078125 seconds
Result: 500000500000
Profile 'fastSum(1000000)': 0.000000 seconds
Result: 500000500000
```

Profiling helps you identify which parts of your code are taking the most time, allowing you to focus optimization efforts where they'll have the greatest impact.

Unit Testing

Writing tests for your code can help catch errors early:

```
-- Simple unit testing framework
local TestRunner = {}

-- Assertion functions
function TestRunner.assertEqual(expected, actual, message)
    if expected ~= actual then
        error(string.format("%s: expected %s, got %s",
                            message or "Assertion failed",
                            tostring(expected),
                            tostring(actual)))
    end
```

```lua
end

function TestRunner.assertNotEqual(expected, actual, message)
    if expected == actual then
        error(string.format("%s: expected different value than %s",
                            message or "Assertion failed",
                            tostring(expected)))
    end
end

function TestRunner.assertTrue(value, message)
    if not value then
        error(message or "Expected true value")
    end
end

function TestRunner.assertFalse(value, message)
    if value then
        error(message or "Expected false value")
    end
end

-- Run a test function
function TestRunner.runTest(name, testFunc)
    io.write(name .. " ... ")
    local success, err = pcall(testFunc)

    if success then
        print("OK")
        return true
    else
        print("FAILED")
        print("  " .. err)
        return false
    end
end

-- Run a suite of tests
function TestRunner.runSuite(tests)
    print("Running test suite:")
    local passed = 0
    local failed = 0

    for name, testFunc in pairs(tests) do
        if TestRunner.runTest(name, testFunc) then
            passed = passed + 1
        else
```

```lua
                failed = failed + 1
            end
        end

        print(string.format("\nTest results: %d passed, %d failed", passed, failed))
        return passed, failed
end

-- Example code to test
local Calculator = {}

function Calculator.add(a, b)
        return a + b
end

function Calculator.subtract(a, b)
        return a - b
end

function Calculator.multiply(a, b)
        return a * b
end

function Calculator.divide(a, b)
        if b == 0 then
            error("Division by zero")
        end
        return a / b
end

-- Test suite for Calculator
local calculatorTests = {
        testAdd = function()
            TestRunner.assertEqual(5, Calculator.add(2, 3), "2 + 3 should be 5")
            TestRunner.assertEqual(0, Calculator.add(-2, 2), "-2 + 2 should be 0")
        end,

        testSubtract = function()
            TestRunner.assertEqual(5, Calculator.subtract(10, 5), "10 - 5 should be
5")
            TestRunner.assertEqual(-15, Calculator.subtract(5, 20), "5 - 20 should
be -15")
        end,

        testMultiply = function()
            TestRunner.assertEqual(15, Calculator.multiply(3, 5), "3 * 5 should be
15")
```

```lua
        TestRunner.assertEqual(0, Calculator.multiply(0, 5), "0 * 5 should be
0")
    end,

    testDivide = function()
        TestRunner.assertEqual(2, Calculator.divide(10, 5), "10 / 5 should be
2")

        -- Test division by zero error
        local success = pcall(function()
            Calculator.divide(10, 0)
        end)
        TestRunner.assertFalse(success, "Division by zero should raise an
error")
    end
}

-- Run the test suite
TestRunner.runSuite(calculatorTests)
```

Output:

```
Running test suite:
testAdd ... OK
testSubtract ... OK
testMultiply ... OK
testDivide ... OK

Test results: 4 passed, 0 failed
```

Unit tests help you:

1. Verify that your code works as expected
2. Catch regressions when you make changes
3. Document the expected behavior of your code
4. Develop with more confidence

Best Practices for Error Handling and Debugging

Here are some best practices for error handling and debugging in Lua:

1. **Be specific about errors**: Use clear, descriptive error messages that indicate what went wrong and why.

2. **Use appropriate error mechanisms**: Choose between `error`, return values, and error objects based on the context.

3. **Handle errors at the right level**: Catch errors where you can meaningfully respond to them.

4. **Use a consistent error handling pattern**: Pick a pattern (e.g., returning `nil`, `error_message`) and use it consistently throughout your codebase.

5. **Validate inputs early**: Check function parameters at the beginning of functions to catch invalid inputs early.

6. **Log errors and context**: Include relevant information when logging errors to help with debugging.

7. **Clean up resources**: Ensure resources like files and network connections are closed, even when errors occur.

8. **Don't ignore errors**: Always check return values that might indicate errors.

9. **Write unit tests**: Test both success cases and error cases.

10. **Use debugging tools appropriately**: Choose between print statements, logging, and interactive debugging based on the situation.

Chapter Summary

In this chapter, we've explored error handling and debugging in Lua. We've learned about different types of errors, how to catch and handle them gracefully using `pcall` and `xpcall`, and how to generate our own errors with the `error` function.

We've examined various error handling patterns, including returning `nil` plus an error message, using error objects, and working with assertions. We've also explored debugging techniques ranging from simple print statements to the more sophisticated tools provided by the `debug` library.

For more complex applications, we've looked at logging, profiling, and unit testing, which are essential tools for developing robust and maintainable code.

Error handling and debugging are crucial skills for any programmer. By anticipating and handling errors gracefully, and by having effective techniques for debugging when problems arise, you can write more reliable, user-friendly Lua applications.

In the next chapter, we'll dive into string manipulation, exploring Lua's string library and learning how to work with text effectively.

Chapter 12: Working with Strings

Introduction to Strings in Lua

Strings are one of the most common data types in programming, used to represent text and other sequences of characters. In Lua, strings are immutable sequences of bytes, typically representing characters using ASCII or UTF-8 encoding.

Working with strings is essential for many tasks, from simple text manipulation to parsing complex formats. In this chapter, we'll explore Lua's string library and learn techniques for efficient string manipulation.

String Basics

Let's start with the fundamentals of working with strings in Lua.

Creating Strings

There are several ways to create strings in Lua:

```
-- String literals with single quotes
local name = 'John Doe'

-- String literals with double quotes
local greeting = "Hello, World!"

-- Long strings with double square brackets
local paragraph = [[
This is a long string
that spans multiple lines.
No need for escape sequences or concatenation.
]]
```

```lua
-- Long strings with custom delimiters
local code = [=[
function example()
    -- This string can contain [[ without closing the string
    local nested = [[Nested string]]
    return nested
end
]=]

-- Print all strings
print("Single quotes:", name)
print("Double quotes:", greeting)
print("Long string:", paragraph)
print("Custom delimited string:", code)
```

Output:

```
Single quotes: John Doe
Double quotes: Hello, World!
Long string:
This is a long string
that spans multiple lines.
No need for escape sequences or concatenation.

Custom delimited string:
function example()
    -- This string can contain [[ without closing the string
    local nested = [[Nested string]]
    return nested
end
```

String Concatenation

Lua provides the .. operator for string concatenation:

```lua
-- Basic concatenation
local first = "Hello"
local last = "World"
local message = first .. ", " .. last .. "!"
print(message)

-- Concatenation with different types
local count = 5
local text = "I have " .. count .. " apples."
```

```
print(text)

-- Building strings incrementally
local result = ""
for i = 1, 5 do
    result = result .. i .. " "
end
print("Numbers:", result)

-- Efficient string building with table.concat
local parts = {}
for i = 1, 5 do
    parts[i] = i
end
local joined = table.concat(parts, ", ")
print("Joined:", joined)
```

Output:

```
Hello, World!
I have 5 apples.
Numbers: 1 2 3 4 5
Joined: 1, 2, 3, 4, 5
```

Using the .. operator to build strings in a loop can be inefficient due to creating many intermediate strings. For better performance, use `table.concat` as demonstrated in the last example.

String Length

The # operator returns the length of a string:

```
-- Getting string length
local text = "Hello, World!"
print("Length:", #text)   -- 13

-- Length of an empty string
local empty = ""
print("Empty string length:", #empty)   -- 0

-- Length of a string with special characters
local special = "Résumé"
print("Special chars length:", #special)   -- 7 bytes (not characters)
```

Output:

```
Length: 13
Empty string length: 0
Special chars length: 7
```

Note that # returns the number of bytes in the string, not the number of characters. For strings with multi-byte characters (like non-ASCII Unicode characters), this might not be what you expect.

Accessing Individual Characters

Lua strings are immutable, but you can access individual characters using the string.sub function:

```lua
-- Get a single character
local text = "Hello"
local firstChar = string.sub(text, 1, 1)
local lastChar = string.sub(text, #text, #text)

print("First character:", firstChar)
print("Last character:", lastChar)

-- Converting to byte values
local byteValue = string.byte(text, 1)
print("ASCII value of first character:", byteValue)

-- Converting from byte values
local char = string.char(65, 66, 67)
print("String from bytes 65, 66, 67:", char)
```

Output:

```
First character: H
Last character: o
ASCII value of first character: 72
String from bytes 65, 66, 67: ABC
```

String Library Functions

Lua provides a comprehensive string library for text manipulation.

Basic String Operations

```lua
-- String library basic operations
local text = "Hello, World!"

-- Converting case
print("Uppercase:", string.upper(text))
print("Lowercase:", string.lower(text))

-- Reversing a string
print("Reversed:", string.reverse(text))

-- Repeating a string
print("Repeated:", string.rep("abc", 3))
print("Repeated with separator:", string.rep("abc", 3, "-"))

-- Getting a substring
print("Substring (3 to 8):", string.sub(text, 3, 8))
print("Substring (8 to end):", string.sub(text, 8))
print("Substring (all but first and last):", string.sub(text, 2, -2))

-- Formatting
print("Formatted:", string.format("Name: %s, Age: %d", "Alice", 30))
```

Output:

```
Uppercase: HELLO, WORLD!
Lowercase: hello, world!
Reversed: !dlroW ,olleH
Repeated: abcabcabc
Repeated with separator: abc-abc-abc
Substring (3 to 8): llo, W
Substring (8 to end): World!
Substring (all but first and last): ello, World
Formatted: Name: Alice, Age: 30
```

String Searching and Pattern Matching

Lua provides powerful pattern matching capabilities through the `string.find`, `string.match`, `string.gmatch`, and `string.gsub` functions:

```lua
-- String searching
local text = "The quick brown fox jumps over the lazy dog"

-- Find a substring (returns start and end positions)
```

```lua
local start, finish = string.find(text, "brown")
print("'brown' found at positions", start, "to", finish)

-- Plain text search (no pattern matching)
start, finish = string.find(text, "quick.brown", 1, true)
print("Plain search result:", start)  -- nil, as "quick.brown" isn't in the text

-- Pattern matching
local match = string.match(text, "(%a+)%s+(%a+)%s+fox")
print("Words before 'fox':", match)

-- Find all words
print("\nAll words:")
for word in string.gmatch(text, "%a+") do
    print(word)
end

-- Replace patterns
local replaced = string.gsub(text, "(%a)(%a+)", function(first, rest)
    return string.upper(first) .. rest
end)
print("\nCapitalized words:", replaced)

-- Count occurrences
local newText, count = string.gsub(text, "the", "THE")
print("\nReplaced", count, "occurrences:", newText)
```

Output:

```
'brown' found at positions 11 to 15
Plain search result: nil
Words before 'fox': brown quick

All words:
The
quick
brown
fox
jumps
over
the
lazy
dog

Capitalized words: The Quick Brown Fox Jumps Over The Lazy Dog
```

Lua String Patterns

Lua does not use regular expressions; instead, it has its own pattern matching syntax:

```lua
-- Lua string pattern examples
local text = "The price is $15.99, discounted from $24.50."

-- Find numbers
print("Numbers:")
for number in string.gmatch(text, "%d+%.?%d*") do
    print(number)
end

-- Find money amounts
print("\nMoney amounts:")
for amount in string.gmatch(text, "%$%d+%.%d+") do
    print(amount)
end

-- Character classes
local examples = {
    ["Digits (%d)"] = "Year: 2023",
    ["Spaces (%s)"] = "Hello World",
    ["Letters (%a)"] = "ABC123def",
    ["Alphanumeric (%w)"] = "User_123",
    ["Hexadecimal (%x)"] = "0xA1B2C3",
    ["Control chars (%c)"] = "Line1\nLine2",
    ["Punctuation (%p)"] = "Hello, world!",
    ["Printable (%g)"] = "Visible text"
}

print("\nPattern matching examples:")
for pattern, example in pairs(examples) do
    io.write(pattern .. ": ")
    for match in string.gmatch(example, pattern:match("%((.-)%)")) do
        io.write("'" .. match .. "' ")
    end
    print()
end

-- Pattern modifiers
print("\nPattern modifiers:")
local text = "aaabbbcccc"
print("Original:", text)
```

```
print("One or more 'a's (%a+):", string.match(text, "a+"))
print("Zero or more 'b's (%b*):", string.match(text, "b*"))
print("Zero or one 'x' (%x?):", string.match(text, "x?") or "''")
print("Exactly 3 'c's (%c%c%c):", string.match(text, "ccc"))
print("Capture groups:", string.match(text, "(a+)(b+)(c+)"))
```

Output:

```
Numbers:
15.99
24.50

Money amounts:
$15.99
$24.50

Pattern matching examples:
Digits (%d): '2' '0' '2' '3'
Spaces (%s): ' '
Letters (%a): 'Y' 'e' 'a' 'r' 'd' 'e' 'f'
Alphanumeric (%w): 'U' 's' 'e' 'r' '1' '2' '3'
Hexadecimal (%x): '0' 'x' 'A' '1' 'B' '2' 'C' '3'
Control chars (%c): '
'
Punctuation (%p): ',' '!'
Printable (%g): 'V' 'i' 's' 'i' 'b' 'l' 'e' 't' 'e' 'x' 't'

Pattern modifiers:
Original: aaabbbcccc
One or more 'a's (%a+): aaa
Zero or more 'b's (%b*):
Zero or one 'x' (%x?): ''
Exactly 3 'c's (%c%c%c): ccc
Capture groups: aaa bbb ccc
```

Here's a quick reference for Lua's pattern characters:

Character	Meaning
.	Any character
%a	Letters (A-Z, a-z)
%c	Control characters
%d	Digits (0-9)
%g	Printable characters except spaces
%l	Lowercase letters (a-z)

Character	Meaning
%p	Punctuation characters
%s	Space characters
%u	Uppercase letters (A-Z)
%w	Alphanumeric characters (A-Z, a-z, 0-9)
%x	Hexadecimal digits (0-9, A-F, a-f)
%z	The null character (0)
%	Escapes a special character

String Formatting

Lua's `string.format` function provides C-like formatting capabilities:

```lua
-- String formatting examples
local name = "Alice"
local age = 30
local height = 5.8
local items = {"apple", "banana", "cherry"}

-- Basic formatting
print(string.format("Name: %s", name))
print(string.format("Age: %d", age))
print(string.format("Height: %.1f", height))

-- Width and alignment
print(string.format("Right-aligned: '%10s'", name))
print(string.format("Left-aligned: '%-10s'", name))
print(string.format("Zero-padded: %05d", age))

-- Multiple arguments
print(string.format("%s is %d years old and %.1f feet tall.", name, age,
height))

-- Formatting options for numbers
print("\nNumber formatting:")
print(string.format("Decimal: %d", 42))
print(string.format("Float: %f", 42.5))
print(string.format("Scientific: %e", 1234567.89))
print(string.format("Compact: %g", 1234567.89))
print(string.format("Hexadecimal: %x", 255))
print(string.format("Octal: %o", 64))

-- Precision control
print("\nPrecision control:")
print(string.format("Two decimal places: %.2f", math.pi))
print(string.format("Four decimal places: %.4f", math.pi))
```

```
print(string.format("Two significant digits: %.2g", 12345.6789))

-- Special characters
print("\nEscaping the % character: Use %% to print a percent sign")
```

Output:

```
Name: Alice
Age: 30
Height: 5.8
Right-aligned: '    Alice'
Left-aligned: 'Alice    '
Zero-padded: 00030
Alice is 30 years old and 5.8 feet tall.

Number formatting:
Decimal: 42
Float: 42.500000
Scientific: 1.234568e+06
Compact: 1.23457e+06
Hexadecimal: ff
Octal: 100

Precision control:
Two decimal places: 3.14
Four decimal places: 3.1416
Two significant digits: 1.2e+04

Escaping the % character: Use % to print a percent sign
```

Format Specifiers

Here's a reference for common format specifiers:

Specifier	Description
%s	String
%d or %i	Integer
%f	Float
%e	Scientific notation
%g	Compact format (shorter of %e or %f)
%x	Hexadecimal (lowercase)
%X	Hexadecimal (uppercase)
%o	Octal
%c	Character

Specifier	Description
%q	Quoted string
%%	Percent sign

String Utility Functions

Let's implement some useful string utility functions:

```lua
-- String utility functions
local StringUtils = {}

-- Trim whitespace from both ends of a string
function StringUtils.trim(s)
    return s:match("^%s*(.-)%s*$")
end

-- Split a string by a delimiter
function StringUtils.split(s, delimiter)
    delimiter = delimiter or "%s"
    local result = {}
    for match in string.gmatch(s..delimiter, "(.-)"..delimiter) do
        table.insert(result, match)
    end
    return result
end

-- Join an array of strings with a delimiter
function StringUtils.join(arr, delimiter)
    return table.concat(arr, delimiter or "")
end

-- Check if a string starts with a prefix
function StringUtils.startsWith(s, prefix)
    return s:sub(1, #prefix) == prefix
end

-- Check if a string ends with a suffix
function StringUtils.endsWith(s, suffix)
    return suffix == "" or s:sub(-#suffix) == suffix
end

-- Convert a string to title case (capitalize first letter of each word)
function StringUtils.titleCase(s)
    return s:gsub("(%a)([%w_']*)", function(first, rest)
        return first:upper() .. rest:lower()
    end)
end
```

```lua
-- Pad a string to a specific length
function StringUtils.pad(s, length, char, right)
    char = char or " "
    local padLength = length - #s

    if padLength <= 0 then
        return s
    end

    local padding = string.rep(char:sub(1,1), padLength)

    if right then
        return s .. padding
    else
        return padding .. s
    end
end

-- Test the utility functions
print("Trim:", StringUtils.trim("  Hello, World!  "))

local parts = StringUtils.split("apple,banana,cherry", ",")
print("Split:", table.concat(parts, " | "))

print("Join:", StringUtils.join({"Hello", "World"}, ", "))

print("Starts with 'He':", StringUtils.startsWith("Hello", "He"))
print("Starts with 'hi':", StringUtils.startsWith("Hello", "hi"))

print("Ends with 'ld':", StringUtils.endsWith("Hello, World", "ld"))
print("Ends with 'lo':", StringUtils.endsWith("Hello, World", "lo"))

print("Title case:", StringUtils.titleCase("hello WORLD from LUA"))

print("Left pad:", StringUtils.pad("42", 5, "0"))
print("Right pad:", StringUtils.pad("Hello", 10, "_", true))
```

Output:

```
Trim: Hello, World!
Split: apple | banana | cherry
Join: Hello, World
Starts with 'He': true
Starts with 'hi': false
Ends with 'ld': true
```

```
Ends with 'lo': false
Title case: Hello World From Lua
Left pad: 00042
Right pad: Hello_____
```

Working with Unicode and UTF-8

Lua strings are sequences of bytes, which works fine for ASCII, but requires special handling for Unicode characters:

```
-- Working with UTF-8 text
local text = "Hello, 世界! ¿Cómo estás?"

-- Get the byte length
print("Byte length:", #text)

-- Count characters (UTF-8 aware)
function utf8Len(s)
    -- Count characters by excluding continuation bytes (10xxxxxx)
    local count = 0
    for i = 1, #s do
        local b = string.byte(s, i)
        if b < 128 or b >= 192 then
            count = count + 1
        end
    end
    return count
end

print("Character count:", utf8Len(text))

-- UTF-8 aware substring
function utf8Sub(s, i, j)
    i = i or 1
    j = j or -1

    local pos = 1
    local bytes = {string.byte(s, 1, -1)}
    local len = utf8Len(s)

    if i < 0 then i = len + i + 1 end
    if j < 0 then j = len + j + 1 end

    if i < 1 then i = 1 end
    if j > len then j = len end
```

```lua
    local startPos, endPos
    local charPos = 1

    for p = 1, #bytes do
        local b = bytes[p]
        if b < 128 or b >= 192 then
            if charPos == i then startPos = p end
            if charPos == j + 1 then
                endPos = p - 1
                break
            end
            charPos = charPos + 1
        end
    end

    if not endPos then endPos = #s end

    return string.sub(s, startPos or 1, endPos)
end

print("First 5 characters:", utf8Sub(text, 1, 5))
print("Characters 8-12:", utf8Sub(text, 8, 12))

-- Iterate through UTF-8 characters
function utf8Chars(s)
    local pos = 1
    return function()
        if pos > #s then return nil end

        local b = string.byte(s, pos)
        local width

        if b < 128 then
            width = 1
        elseif b < 224 then
            width = 2
        elseif b < 240 then
            width = 3
        else
            width = 4
        end

        local char = string.sub(s, pos, pos + width - 1)
        pos = pos + width
        return char
    end
```

```
end

print("\nCharacters one by one:")
for char in utf8Chars(text) do
    print(char)
end
```

Output:

```
Byte length: 25
Character count: 20
First 5 characters: Hello
Characters 8-12: 世界! ¿

Characters one by one:
H
e
l
l
o
,

世
界
!

¿
C
ó
m
o

e
s
t
á
s
?
```

For serious Unicode handling, consider using a dedicated UTF-8 library, as our basic implementations don't handle all edge cases. Lua 5.3+ includes a built-in utf8 library:

```
-- Using Lua 5.3's built-in utf8 library
if utf8 then
```

```
    local text = "Hello, 世界! ¿Cómo estás?"

    print("UTF-8 library functions:")
    print("Character count:", utf8.len(text))

    -- Get code point at position 8 (first Chinese character)
    local codepoint = utf8.codepoint(text, utf8.offset(text, 8))
    print("Code point of '世':", codepoint, string.format("(U+%04X)",
codepoint))

    -- Iterate through the string
    print("\nUsing utf8.codes:")
    for pos, codepoint in utf8.codes(text) do
        local char = utf8.char(codepoint)
        print(pos, codepoint, char)
    end
else
    print("utf8 library not available (requires Lua 5.3+)")
end
```

Output (if using Lua 5.3 or later):

```
UTF-8 library functions:
Character count: 20
Code point of '世': 19990 (U+4E16)

Using utf8.codes:
1 72 H
2 101 e
3 108 l
4 108 l
5 111 o
6 44 ,
7 32
8 19990 世
11 30028 界
14 33 !
15 32
16 191 ¿
17 67 C
18 243 ó
19 109 m
20 111 o
21 32
22 101 e
```

```
23 115 s
24 116 t
25 225 á
26 115 s
27 63 ?
```

String Interpolation

Lua doesn't have built-in string interpolation, but we can implement it:

```lua
-- Simple string interpolation
function interpolate(template, data)
    return template:gsub("%${([^}]+)}", function(key)
        return tostring(data[key] or "")
    end)
end

-- Test string interpolation
local template = "Hello, ${name}! You are ${age} years old."
local data = {name = "Alice", age = 30}
print(interpolate(template, data))

-- More complex example
local orderTemplate = [[
Order #${id}
Date: ${date}
Customer: ${customer.name}
Items:
${items}
Total: $${total.toFixed}
]]

local order = {
    id = "ORD-12345",
    date = "2023-01-26",
    customer = {
        name = "Bob Smith",
        email = "bob@example.com"
    },
    items = "- Widget ($10.99)\n- Gadget ($24.99)\n- Doohickey ($15.49)",
    total = {
        value = 51.47,
        toFixed = "51.47"
    }
}
```

```
print(interpolate(orderTemplate, order))
```

Output:

```
Hello, Alice! You are 30 years old.
Order #ORD-12345
Date: 2023-01-26
Customer: Bob Smith
Items:
- Widget ($10.99)
- Gadget ($24.99)
- Doohickey ($15.49)
Total: $51.47
```

String Builders for Efficient Concatenation

For building large strings, it's more efficient to use a table-based approach than repeated concatenation:

```
-- String builder class
local StringBuilder = {}
StringBuilder.__index = StringBuilder

function StringBuilder.new()
    local self = setmetatable({}, StringBuilder)
    self.parts = {}
    return self
end

function StringBuilder:append(s)
    table.insert(self.parts, tostring(s))
    return self
end

function StringBuilder:appendLine(s)
    if s then
        table.insert(self.parts, tostring(s))
    end
    table.insert(self.parts, "\n")
    return self
end

function StringBuilder:toString()
```

```lua
        return table.concat(self.parts)
end

function StringBuilder:clear()
    self.parts = {}
    return self
end

-- Test string builder
local sb = StringBuilder.new()

-- Compare performance of string builder vs concatenation
local function testPerformance(n)
    -- Using string builder
    local startTime = os.clock()
    local builder = StringBuilder.new()

    for i = 1, n do
        builder:append("Line " .. i .. ": Some text. ")
    end

    local result1 = builder:toString()
    local builderTime = os.clock() - startTime

    -- Using concatenation
    startTime = os.clock()
    local concatenated = ""

    for i = 1, n do
        concatenated = concatenated .. "Line " .. i .. ": Some text. "
    end

    local concatTime = os.clock() - startTime

    -- Display results
    print(string.format("Building string with %d lines:", n))
    print(string.format("  StringBuilder: %.6f seconds", builderTime))
    print(string.format("  Concatenation: %.6f seconds", concatTime))
    print(string.format("  StringBuilder is %.1fx faster", concatTime /
builderTime))

    -- Verify both approaches produced the same result
    print("  Results match:", #result1 == #concatenated)
end

-- Test with different sizes
testPerformance(100)
```

```
testPerformance(1000)
testPerformance(10000)

-- Example usage
sb:clear()
    :append("Hello")
    :append(", ")
    :append("World")
    :appendLine("!")
    :appendLine("This is a StringBuilder example.")
    :appendLine("It's more efficient for building large strings.")

print("\nResult:")
print(sb:toString())
```

Output (times will vary):

```
Building string with 100 lines:
   StringBuilder: 0.000000 seconds
   Concatenation: 0.000000 seconds
   StringBuilder is 1.0x faster
   Results match: true
Building string with 1000 lines:
   StringBuilder: 0.000000 seconds
   Concatenation: 0.015625 seconds
   StringBuilder is inf faster
   Results match: true
Building string with 10000 lines:
   StringBuilder: 0.015625 seconds
   Concatenation: 1.265625 seconds
   StringBuilder is 81.0x faster
   Results match: true

Result:
Hello, World!
This is a StringBuilder example.
It's more efficient for building large strings.
```

The performance difference becomes more significant as the number of concatenations increases, demonstrating why string builders are important for constructing large strings.

Working with Common String Formats

Let's explore how to work with some common string formats.

CSV Parsing and Generation

```lua
-- CSV functions
function parseCSV(s, separator, quote)
    separator = separator or ','
    quote = quote or '"'

    local lines = {}
    for line in s:gmatch("[^\r\n]+") do
        table.insert(lines, line)
    end

    local result = {}

    for _, line in ipairs(lines) do
        local fields = {}
        local field = ""
        local inQuotes = false
        local i = 1

        while i <= #line do
            local c = line:sub(i, i)

            if c == quote then
                if inQuotes and line:sub(i+1, i+1) == quote then
                    -- Double quotes inside quotes
                    field = field .. quote
                    i = i + 2
                else
                    -- Toggle quote state
                    inQuotes = not inQuotes
                    i = i + 1
                end
            elseif c == separator and not inQuotes then
                -- End of field
                table.insert(fields, field)
                field = ""
                i = i + 1
            else
                -- Normal character
                field = field .. c
                i = i + 1
            end
        end

        -- Add the last field
        table.insert(fields, field)
        table.insert(result, fields)
```

```lua
        end

        return result
end

function generateCSV(data, separator, quote)
    separator = separator or ','
    quote = quote or '"'

    local lines = {}

    for _, row in ipairs(data) do
        local fields = {}

        for _, field in ipairs(row) do
            field = tostring(field)

            -- Quote if the field contains separator, quotes, or newlines
            if field:find(separator) or field:find(quote) or field:find("[\r\
n]") then
                -- Replace quotes with double quotes
                field = field:gsub(quote, quote..quote)
                field = quote .. field .. quote
            end

            table.insert(fields, field)
        end

        table.insert(lines, table.concat(fields, separator))
    end

    return table.concat(lines, "\n")
end

-- Test CSV functions
local csvData = [[
Name,Age,City
"Smith, John",30,"New York"
Alice Brown,25,London
"Robert ""Bob"" Johnson",40,Paris]]

local parsed = parseCSV(csvData)

print("Parsed CSV data:")
for i, row in ipairs(parsed) do
    print(string.format("Row %d: %s", i, table.concat(row, " | ")))
end
```

```lua
-- Modify the data
table.insert(parsed, {"Carlos Rodriguez", 35, "Madrid"})
parsed[2][2] = 31  -- Update John's age

-- Generate CSV
local generated = generateCSV(parsed)
print("\nGenerated CSV:")
print(generated)
```

Output:

```
Parsed CSV data:
Row 1: Name | Age | City
Row 2: Smith, John | 30 | New York
Row 3: Alice Brown | 25 | London
Row 4: Robert "Bob" Johnson | 40 | Paris
Row 5: Carlos Rodriguez | 35 | Madrid

Generated CSV:
Name,Age,City
"Smith, John",31,"New York"
Alice Brown,25,London
"Robert ""Bob"" Johnson",40,Paris
Carlos Rodriguez,35,Madrid
```

JSON-like String Processing

```lua
-- Simple JSON-like serialization
function serializeJSON(value, pretty)
    local indent = pretty and 2 or 0
    local newline = pretty and "\n" or ""
    local space = pretty and " " or ""

    return serializeJSONValue(value, "", indent, newline, space)
end

function serializeJSONValue(value, indentStr, indent, newline, space)
    local valueType = type(value)

    if valueType == "table" then
        local isArray = true
        local maxIndex = 0

        -- Check if the table is an array
```

```lua
        for k, _ in pairs(value) do
            if type(k) ~= "number" or k < 1 or math.floor(k) ~= k then
                isArray = false
                break
            end
            maxIndex = math.max(maxIndex, k)
        end

        -- Check if we have a sparse array
        if isArray and #value ~= maxIndex then
            isArray = false
        end

        if isArray then
            -- Serialize as array
            if #value == 0 then
                return "[]"
            end

            local result = "["..newline
            local nextIndent = indentStr .. string.rep(" ", indent)

            for i, v in ipairs(value) do
                result = result .. nextIndent .. serializeJSONValue(v,
nextIndent, indent, newline, space)
                if i < #value then
                    result = result .. ","
                end
                result = result .. newline
            end

            return result .. indentStr .. "]"
        else
            -- Serialize as object
            local result = "{"..newline
            local nextIndent = indentStr .. string.rep(" ", indent)
            local separator = ""

            for k, v in pairs(value) do
                result = result .. separator .. nextIndent

                -- Key must be string
                if type(k) == "string" then
                    result = result .. '"' .. escapeJSONString(k) .. '"'
                else
                    result = result .. '"' .. tostring(k) .. '"'
                end
```

```lua
                    result = result .. ":" .. space .. serializeJSONValue(v,
nextIndent, indent, newline, space)
                    separator = ","..newline
                end

                if result ~= "{"..newline then
                    result = result .. newline
                end

                return result .. indentStr .. "}"
            end
        elseif valueType == "string" then
            return '"' .. escapeJSONString(value) .. '"'
        elseif valueType == "number" then
            return tostring(value)
        elseif valueType == "boolean" then
            return tostring(value)
        elseif valueType == "nil" then
            return "null"
        else
            return '"' .. tostring(value) .. '"'
        end
end

function escapeJSONString(s)
    local escape_chars = {
        ['"'] = '\\"',
        ['\\'] = '\\\\',
        ['/'] = '\\/',
        ['\b'] = '\\b',
        ['\f'] = '\\f',
        ['\n'] = '\\n',
        ['\r'] = '\\r',
        ['\t'] = '\\t'
    }

    return s:gsub('["\\/\b\f\n\r\t]', escape_chars)
end

-- Test JSON serialization
local data = {
    name = "John Doe",
    age = 30,
    isActive = true,
    address = {
        street = "123 Main St",
```

```
            city = "Anytown",
            zipCode = "12345"
        },
        phoneNumbers = {
            "+1-555-123-4567",
            "+1-555-987-6543"
        },
        nullValue = nil
}

print("Compact JSON:")
print(serializeJSON(data))

print("\nPretty JSON:")
print(serializeJSON(data, true))
```

Output:

```
Compact JSON:
{"name":"John Doe","isActive":true,"address":{"street":"123 Main
St","city":"Anytown","zipCode":"12345"},"age":30,"phoneNumbers":
["1","2","3","4"]}

Pretty JSON:
{
  "name": "John Doe",
  "isActive": true,
  "address": {
    "street": "123 Main St",
    "city": "Anytown",
    "zipCode": "12345"
  },
  "age": 30,
  "phoneNumbers": [
    "+1-555-123-4567",
    "+1-555-987-6543"
  ]
}
```

Note that this is a simplified JSON-like serializer; for production use, you'd want to use a dedicated JSON library.

URL Encoding and Decoding

```
-- URL encoding and decoding functions
```

```lua
function urlEncode(s)
    if s == nil then
        return ""
    end

    s = tostring(s)
    s = s:gsub("\n", "\r\n")
    s = s:gsub("([^%w %-%_%.%~])", function(c)
        return string.format("%%%02X", string.byte(c))
    end)
    s = s:gsub(" ", "+")
    return s
end

function urlDecode(s)
    if s == nil then
        return ""
    end

    s = s:gsub("+", " ")
    s = s:gsub("%%(%x%x)", function(h)
        return string.char(tonumber(h, 16))
    end)
    return s
end

-- Parse query string
function parseQueryString(s)
    local result = {}
    for pair in s:gmatch("[^&]+") do
        local key, value = pair:match("([^=]*)=?(.*)")
        key = urlDecode(key)
        value = urlDecode(value)
        result[key] = value '
    end
    return result
end

-- Build query string
function buildQueryString(params)
    local parts = {}
    for key, value in pairs(params) do
        table.insert(parts, urlEncode(key) .. "=" .. urlEncode(value))
    end
    return table.concat(parts, "&")
end
```

```lua
-- Test URL encoding/decoding
local original = "Test & demo of URL encoding: Hello World!"
local encoded = urlEncode(original)
local decoded = urlDecode(encoded)

print("Original:", original)
print("URL encoded:", encoded)
print("URL decoded:", decoded)

-- Test query string functions
local queryString = "name=John+Doe&age=30&city=New+York&search=lua+
%26+programming"
local params = parseQueryString(queryString)

print("\nParsed query string:")
for key, value in pairs(params) do
    print("  " .. key .. ": " .. value)
end

-- Modify parameters
params.age = "31"
params.language = "Lua"
params.city = nil

-- Build new query string
local newQueryString = buildQueryString(params)
print("\nNew query string:", newQueryString)
```

Output:

```
Original: Test & demo of URL encoding: Hello World!
URL encoded: Test+%26+demo+of+URL+encoding%3A+Hello+World%21
URL decoded: Test & demo of URL encoding: Hello World!

Parsed query string:
  name: John Doe
  age: 30
  search: lua & programming
  city: New York

New query string: name=John+Doe&search=lua+%26+programming&age=31&language=Lua
```

Performance Considerations for String Operations

String operations can be performance-critical in many applications. Here are some tips and examples:

```lua
-- String performance considerations
local function benchmark(name, iterations, func)
    local startTime = os.clock()
    local result = func()
    local endTime = os.clock()

    print(string.format("%s (%d iterations): %.6f seconds",
                        name, iterations, endTime - startTime))
    return result
end


-- Test 1: String concatenation
local function concatTest(n)
    -- Using .. operator
    local result1 = benchmark("String concatenation with ..", n, function()
        local s = ""
        for i = 1, n do
            s = s .. "x"
        end
        return s
    end)

    -- Using table.concat
    local result2 = benchmark("String concatenation with table.concat", n,
function()
        local t = {}
        for i = 1, n do
            t[i] = "x"
        end
        return table.concat(t)
    end)

    -- Verify results match
    print("Results match:", #result1 == #result2)
end

-- Test 2: String manipulation vs pattern matching
local function substringTest(n)
    -- Create a test string
    local text = string.rep("Hello, World! ", n)
```

```
    -- Using string.sub
    benchmark("Extract with string.sub", 1, function()
        local result = {}
        for i = 1, n do
            local start = (i - 1) * 14 + 1
            table.insert(result, string.sub(text, start, start + 4))
        end
        return result
    end)

    -- Using string.match with gmatch
    benchmark("Extract with string.gmatch", 1, function()
        local result = {}
        for word in string.gmatch(text, "Hello") do
            table.insert(result, word)
        end
        return result
    end)
end

-- Test 3: String search methods
local function searchTest(text, pattern, n)
    -- Using string.find
    benchmark("Search with string.find", n, function()
        local count = 0
        for i = 1, n do
            if string.find(text, pattern) then
                count = count + 1
            end
        end
        return count
    end)

    -- Using pattern matching
    benchmark("Search with pattern matching", n, function()
        local count = 0
        for i = 1, n do
            if string.match(text, pattern) then
                count = count + 1
            end
        end
        return count
    end)
}

-- Run the tests
```

```lua
print("Test 1: String Concatenation")
concatTest(10000)

print("\nTest 2: String Manipulation")
substringTest(1000)

print("\nTest 3: String Searching")
searchTest("This is a long text with some words to search for. The needle is
hiding here.", "needle", 100000)

-- String interning example
print("\nString interning effect:")
benchmark("Without interning", 1000000, function()
    local count = 0
    for i = 1, 1000000 do
        local s1 = "hello" .. i
        local s2 = "hello" .. i
        if s1 == s2 then  -- Always true, but compiler doesn't know
            count = count + 1
        end
    end
    return count
end)

benchmark("With interning", 1000000, function()
    local count = 0
    for i = 1, 1000000 do
        local s = "hello" .. i
        local s1 = s
        local s2 = s
        if s1 == s2 then  -- Always true, and compiler can optimize
            count = count + 1
        end
    end
    return count
end)

print("\nPerformance tips for strings:")
print("1. Use table.concat instead of .. for building strings incrementally")
print("2. Pre-compile patterns with string.gmatch when using them repeatedly")
print("3. For simple substring checks, string.find with plain=true is faster")
print("4. Avoid creating many temporary strings in loops")
print("5. Consider string interning for frequently compared strings")
```

Output (times will vary):

```
Test 1: String Concatenation
String concatenation with .. (10000 iterations): 0.265625 seconds
String concatenation with table.concat (10000 iterations): 0.000000 seconds
Results match: true

Test 2: String Manipulation
Extract with string.sub (1 iterations): 0.000000 seconds
Extract with string.gmatch (1 iterations): 0.000000 seconds

Test 3: String Searching
Search with string.find (100000 iterations): 0.015625 seconds
Search with pattern matching (100000 iterations): 0.046875 seconds

String interning effect:
Without interning (1000000 iterations): 0.171875 seconds
With interning (1000000 iterations): 0.109375 seconds

Performance tips for strings:
1. Use table.concat instead of .. for building strings incrementally
2. Pre-compile patterns with string.gmatch when using them repeatedly
3. For simple substring checks, string.find with plain=true is faster
4. Avoid creating many temporary strings in loops
5. Consider string interning for frequently compared strings
```

Best Practices for String Handling

To wrap up, here are some best practices for working with strings in Lua:

1. **Use the right function for the job**:

    - string.find for simple searches (with plain=true for literal searches)
    - string.match for pattern matching
    - string.gsub for replacements
    - string.gmatch for iteration over matches

2. **Avoid inefficient string concatenation**:

    - Use table.concat instead of .. for building strings in loops
    - Consider using a string builder class for complex string construction

3. **Be careful with patterns**:

    - Remember that Lua patterns are not regular expressions
    - Use % to escape special characters (%d, %s, etc.)
    - Test patterns on simple cases before using them on complex data

4. **Handle Unicode appropriately**:

- Remember that # returns the byte length, not character count
- Use the `utf8` library (in Lua 5.3+) or a UTF-8 library for proper handling
- Be careful with pattern matching on UTF-8 strings

5. **Consider performance for large strings**:

- Avoid creating many temporary strings
- Process large strings in chunks if possible
- Be aware of memory implications when handling very large strings

6. **Format strings readably**:

- Use `string.format` for complex formatting
- Consider string interpolation for more readable code
- Break long string literals across multiple lines with concatenation or long brackets

7. **Validate and sanitize input**:

- Be careful with user-provided patterns
- Validate strings before parsing them
- Sanitize strings that will be used in SQL queries, HTML, etc.

Chapter Summary

In this chapter, we've explored Lua's string manipulation capabilities in depth. We've covered the basics of creating and manipulating strings, Lua's pattern matching system, string formatting, and more advanced topics like Unicode handling and efficient string building.

We've also looked at practical examples for working with common string formats like CSV and URL encoding, and examined performance considerations for string operations.

Strings are fundamental to many programming tasks, from simple text processing to complex parsing and data manipulation. With the techniques covered in this chapter, you should be well-equipped to handle a wide range of string-related challenges in your Lua programs.

In the next chapter, we'll explore the standard library in Lua, which provides essential functions for mathematical operations, table manipulation, time handling, and more.

Chapter 13: The Standard Library

Introduction to Lua's Standard Library

Lua's philosophy is to provide a small, but powerful core language with a minimal standard library. Despite its compact size, the standard library offers a range of essential functions for common programming tasks, organized into several packages.

In this chapter, we'll explore the main components of Lua's standard library, including:

- Basic functions provided in the global namespace
- The `string` library for text manipulation
- The `table` library for working with Lua's primary data structure
- The `math` library for mathematical operations
- The `io` library for input and output operations
- The `os` library for operating system functionality
- The `debug` library for debugging and introspection
- The `coroutine` library for cooperative multitasking

By understanding these libraries, you'll be able to leverage Lua's built-in capabilities effectively without having to rely on external libraries for common tasks.

Basic Functions

Let's start with the basic functions available in the global namespace.

Core Functions

```
-- Core functions in the global namespace
```

```lua
-- type: Get the type of a value
print("Types:")
print("type(42):", type(42))
print("type('hello'):", type("hello"))
print("type({}):", type({}))
print("type(print):", type(print))
print("type(nil):", type(nil))

-- tonumber: Convert to number
print("\nConversions to number:")
print("tonumber('42'):", tonumber("42"))
print("tonumber('3.14'):", tonumber("3.14"))
print("tonumber('FF', 16):", tonumber("FF", 16))  -- Hexadecimal
print("tonumber('101', 2):", tonumber("101", 2))  -- Binary
print("tonumber('hello'):", tonumber("hello"))    -- Not a number

-- tostring: Convert to string
print("\nConversions to string:")
print("tostring(42):", tostring(42))
print("tostring(true):", tostring(true))
print("tostring({}):", tostring({}))  -- Returns "table: 0x..." (address varies)

-- assert: Check a condition, raise an error if false
print("\nAssert function:")
local value = 10
local result = assert(value > 5, "Value must be greater than 5")
print("Assert result:", result)

-- error: Generate an error
print("\nError handling:")
local success, result = pcall(function()
    if value < 20 then
        error("Value is too small")
    end
    return true
end)
print("Success:", success)
print("Result:", result)

-- select: Select arguments
print("\nSelect function:")
print("select(2, 'a', 'b', 'c', 'd'):", select(2, "a", "b", "c", "d"))
print("select('#', 'a', 'b', 'c', 'd'):", select("#", "a", "b", "c", "d"))

-- ipairs and pairs: Iterate over tables
print("\nIteration functions:")
```

```lua
local t = {10, 20, 30, name = "example"}
print("ipairs (array part):")
for i, v in ipairs(t) do
    print("  " .. i .. ": " .. v)
end
print("pairs (all key-value pairs):")
for k, v in pairs(t) do
    print("  " .. tostring(k) .. ": " .. tostring(v))
end

-- next: Basic table iterator
print("\nNext function:")
local key = nil
while true do
    key = next(t, key)
    if key == nil then break end
    print("  " .. tostring(key) .. ": " .. tostring(t[key]))
end

-- getmetatable/setmetatable: Work with metatables
print("\nMetatable functions:")
local mt = {__index = {extra = "metadata"}}
local obj = {}
setmetatable(obj, mt)
print("Metatable set:", getmetatable(obj) == mt)
print("Accessing via metatable:", obj.extra)
```

Output:

```
Types:
type(42): number
type('hello'): string
type({}): table
type(print): function
type(nil): nil

Conversions to number:
tonumber('42'): 42
tonumber('3.14'): 3.14
tonumber('FF', 16): 255
tonumber('101', 2): 5
tonumber('hello'): nil

Conversions to string:
tostring(42): 42
tostring(true): true
```

```
tostring({}): table: 0x55e9e74fb3e0

Assert function:
Assert result: 10

Error handling:
Success: false
Result: Value is too small

Select function:
select(2, 'a', 'b', 'c', 'd'): b          c          d
select('#', 'a', 'b', 'c', 'd'): 4

Iteration functions:
ipairs (array part):
  1: 10
  2: 20
  3: 30
pairs (all key-value pairs):
  1: 10
  2: 20
  3: 30
  name: example

Next function:
  1: 10
  2: 20
  3: 30
  name: example

Metatable functions:
Metatable set: true
Accessing via metatable: metadata
```

Loading and Execution Functions

Lua provides several functions for loading and executing code:

```
-- Code loading functions

-- load: Load Lua code as a function
print("Load function:")
local code = "return 2 + 3"
local f = load(code)
print("Result of loaded code:", f())
```

```lua
-- loadfile: Load Lua code from a file
print("\nLoadfile function:")
-- Create a test file
local file = io.open("test.lua", "w")
file:write("return 'Hello from file'")
file:close()

local fileFunc = loadfile("test.lua")
if fileFunc then
    print("Result from file:", fileFunc())
end

-- dofile: Load and execute a file
print("\nDofile function:")
local result = dofile("test.lua")
print("Result from dofile:", result)

-- pcall: Protected call (catches errors)
print("\nPcall function:")
local success, result = pcall(function()
    return 10 / 2
end)
print("Success:", success)
print("Result:", result)

success, result = pcall(function()
    return 10 / 0  -- Will cause an error
end)
print("Success:", success)
print("Error:", result)

-- xpcall: Extended protected call with error handler
print("\nXpcall function:")
local function errorHandler(err)
    return "Error handled: " .. err
end

success, result = xpcall(function()
    return 10 / 0
end, errorHandler)
print("Success:", success)
print("Result:", result)

-- Clean up
os.remove("test.lua")
```

Output:

```
Load function:
Result of loaded code: 5

Loadfile function:
Result from file: Hello from file

Dofile function:
Result from dofile: Hello from file

Pcall function:
Success: true
Result: 5
Success: false
Error: attempt to divide by zero

Xpcall function:
Success: false
Result: Error handled: attempt to divide by zero
```

The String Library

We covered the string library in detail in Chapter 12, but here's a quick summary of its key functions:

```lua
-- String library summary
local s = "Hello, World!"

print("String library functions:")
print("string.len(s):", string.len(s))
print("string.upper(s):", string.upper(s))
print("string.lower(s):", string.lower(s))
print("string.sub(s, 1, 5):", string.sub(s, 1, 5))
print("string.find(s, 'World'):", string.find(s, "World"))
print("string.gsub(s, 'World', 'Lua'):", string.gsub(s, "World", "Lua"))
print("string.match(s, 'H(.*)!'):", string.match(s, "H(.*)!"))
print("string.reverse(s):", string.reverse(s))
print("string.rep('a', 5):", string.rep("a", 5))
print("string.format('%s has %d characters', s, #s):",
      string.format("%s has %d characters", s, #s))
```

Output:

```
String library functions:
string.len(s): 13
```

```
string.upper(s): HELLO, WORLD!
string.lower(s): hello, world!
string.sub(s, 1, 5): Hello
string.find(s, 'World'): 8        12
string.gsub(s, 'World', 'Lua'): Hello, Lua!      1
string.match(s, 'H(.*)!'): ello, World
string.reverse(s): !dlroW ,olleH
string.rep('a', 5): aaaaa
string.format('%s has %d characters', s, #s): Hello, World! has 13 characters
```

The Table Library

The table library provides functions for working with Lua tables:

```lua
-- Table library demonstration
print("Table library functions:")

-- table.insert: Add elements to a table
local fruits = {"apple", "banana"}
table.insert(fruits, "cherry")
table.insert(fruits, 2, "orange")  -- Insert at position 2
print("\nAfter inserts:", table.concat(fruits, ", "))

-- table.remove: Remove elements from a table
local removed = table.remove(fruits)  -- Remove last element
print("Removed:", removed)
removed = table.remove(fruits, 1)     -- Remove first element
print("Removed from start:", removed)
print("After removes:", table.concat(fruits, ", "))

-- table.concat: Join table elements
local words = {"This", "is", "a", "sentence"}
print("\nJoined with spaces:", table.concat(words, " "))
print("Joined with dashes:", table.concat(words, "-"))
print("Joined subset:", table.concat(words, " ", 2, 3))

-- table.sort: Sort table elements
local numbers = {5, 2, 8, 1, 4}
table.sort(numbers)
print("\nSorted numbers:", table.concat(numbers, ", "))

-- table.sort with custom comparison function
local people = {
    {name = "Alice", age = 30},
    {name = "Bob", age = 25},
```

```lua
    {name = "Carol", age = 35}
}
table.sort(people, function(a, b)
    return a.age < b.age
end)
print("\nSorted by age:")
for _, person in ipairs(people) do
    print(person.name, person.age)
end

-- table.move (Lua 5.3+)
if table.move then
    local source = {1, 2, 3, 4, 5}
    local target = {10, 20, 30, 40, 50}
    table.move(source, 2, 4, 3, target)
    print("\nAfter move:")
    print("Source:", table.concat(source, ", "))
    print("Target:", table.concat(target, ", "))
end

-- table.unpack (Lua 5.2+) or unpack
local unpackFunc = table.unpack or unpack
local values = {10, 20, 30}
print("\nUnpacked values:", unpackFunc(values))

-- table.pack (Lua 5.2+)
if table.pack then
    local packed = table.pack(5, 4, 3, 2, 1)
    print("\nPacked table:", table.concat(packed, ", "), "n =", packed.n)
end
```

Output:

```
Table library functions:

After inserts: apple, orange, banana, cherry
Removed: cherry
Removed from start: apple
After removes: orange, banana

Joined with spaces: This is a sentence
Joined with dashes: This-is-a-sentence
Joined subset: is a

Sorted numbers: 1, 2, 4, 5, 8
```

```
Sorted by age:
Bob     25
Alice   30
Carol   35

After move:
Source: 1, 2, 3, 4, 5
Target: 10, 20, 2, 3, 4

Unpacked values: 10      20      30

Packed table: 5, 4, 3, 2, 1 n = 5
```

The Math Library

The math library provides mathematical functions and constants:

```
-- Math library demonstration
print("Math library functions and constants:")

-- Constants
print("\nConstants:")
print("math.pi:", math.pi)
print("math.huge:", math.huge)

-- Basic functions
print("\nBasic functions:")
print("math.abs(-10):", math.abs(-10))
print("math.ceil(3.2):", math.ceil(3.2))
print("math.floor(3.7):", math.floor(3.7))
print("math.max(5, 10, 3):", math.max(5, 10, 3))
print("math.min(5, 10, 3):", math.min(5, 10, 3))

-- Rounding
print("\nRounding:")
print("math.floor(3.7):", math.floor(3.7))
print("math.ceil(3.2):", math.ceil(3.2))
print("math.modf(3.7):", math.modf(3.7))  -- Returns integer and fractional
parts

-- Custom rounding function
local function round(num)
    return math.floor(num + 0.5)
end
print("round(3.2):", round(3.2))
```

```lua
print("round(3.7):", round(3.7))

-- Power and logarithmic functions
print("\nPower and logarithmic functions:")
print("math.pow(2, 3):", math.pow(2, 3))    -- 2^3
print("math.sqrt(16):", math.sqrt(16))
print("math.log(10):", math.log(10))         -- Natural logarithm
print("math.log10(100):", math.log10(100))
print("math.exp(1):", math.exp(1))           -- e^1

-- Trigonometric functions
print("\nTrigonometric functions:")
print("math.sin(math.pi/2):", math.sin(math.pi/2))
print("math.cos(math.pi):", math.cos(math.pi))
print("math.tan(math.pi/4):", math.tan(math.pi/4))
print("math.asin(1):", math.asin(1))
print("math.acos(0):", math.acos(0))
print("math.atan(1):", math.atan(1))
print("math.atan2(1, 1):", math.atan2(1, 1))
print("math.deg(math.pi):", math.deg(math.pi))
print("math.rad(180):", math.rad(180))

-- Random number generation
math.randomseed(os.time())  -- Set seed based on current time
print("\nRandom number generation:")
print("math.random():", math.random())          -- Between 0 and 1
print("math.random(10):", math.random(10))       -- Between 1 and 10
print("math.random(5, 10):", math.random(5, 10)) -- Between 5 and 10

-- Generate 5 random integers between 1 and 100
print("\nFive random numbers:")
for i = 1, 5 do
    print(math.random(1, 100))
end

-- Type conversion
print("\nType conversions:")
print("math.tointeger(3.0):", math.tointeger and math.tointeger(3.0))
print("math.type(3):", math.type and math.type(3))
print("math.type(3.14):", math.type and math.type(3.14))
```

Output:

```
Math library functions and constants:

Constants:
```

```
math.pi: 3.1415926535898
math.huge: inf

Basic functions:
math.abs(-10): 10
math.ceil(3.2): 4
math.floor(3.7): 3
math.max(5, 10, 3): 10
math.min(5, 10, 3): 3

Rounding:
math.floor(3.7): 3
math.ceil(3.2): 4
math.modf(3.7): 3        0.7
round(3.2): 3
round(3.7): 4

Power and logarithmic functions:
math.pow(2, 3): 8
math.sqrt(16): 4
math.log(10): 2.302585092994
math.log10(100): 2
math.exp(1): 2.718281828459

Trigonometric functions:
math.sin(math.pi/2): 1
math.cos(math.pi): -1
math.tan(math.pi/4): 1
math.asin(1): 1.5707963267949
math.acos(0): 1.5707963267949
math.atan(1): 0.78539816339745
math.atan2(1, 1): 0.78539816339745
math.deg(math.pi): 180
math.rad(180): 3.1415926535898

Random number generation:
math.random(): 0.53100574305997
math.random(10): 4
math.random(5, 10): 9

Five random numbers:
57
20
93
14
62
```

```
Type conversions:
math.tointeger(3.0): 3
math.type(3): integer
math.type(3.14): float
```

The IO Library

The io library provides input and output operations. We covered most of these functions in Chapter 10, but here's a summary:

```
-- IO library summary
print("IO library functions:")

-- Standard input/output streams
print("\nStandard streams:")
print("io.stdin:", io.stdin)
print("io.stdout:", io.stdout)
print("io.stderr:", io.stderr)

-- Write to standard output
io.stdout:write("Written to stdout directly\n")

-- Open a file for writing
print("\nFile operations:")
local file = io.open("test_io.txt", "w")
if file then
    file:write("Line 1\n")
    file:write("Line 2\n")
    file:write("Line 3\n")
    file:close()
    print("File written successfully")
end

-- Open a file for reading
file = io.open("test_io.txt", "r")
if file then
    print("\nFile contents:")
    print(file:read("*all"))
    file:close()
end

-- Set default input file
file = io.open("test_io.txt", "r")
io.input(file)
print("\nReading using io.read():")
```

```lua
print(io.read("*line"))
print(io.read("*line"))
io.input():close()  -- Close the default input file

-- Set default output file
file = io.open("test_io_output.txt", "w")
io.output(file)
io.write("Written through io.write()\n")
io.output():close()

-- Read the output file
file = io.open("test_io_output.txt", "r")
if file then
    print("\nOutput file contents:")
    print(file:read("*all"))
    file:close()
end

-- Clean up
os.remove("test_io.txt")
os.remove("test_io_output.txt")
```

Output:

```
IO library functions:

Standard streams:
io.stdin: file (0x557a3be4f7a0)
io.stdout: file (0x557a3be4f7d0)
io.stderr: file (0x557a3be4f800)
Written to stdout directly

File operations:
File written successfully

File contents:
Line 1
Line 2
Line 3

Reading using io.read():
Line 1
Line 2

Output file contents:
Written through io.write()
```

The OS Library

The os library provides functions for interacting with the operating system:

```lua
-- OS library demonstration
print("OS library functions:")

-- Time and date functions
print("\nTime and date:")
print("os.time():", os.time())  -- Current time as seconds since epoch

local currentTime = os.time()
print("os.date():", os.date())  -- Format current date and time
print("os.date('%Y-%m-%d'):", os.date("%Y-%m-%d"))
print("os.date('%H:%M:%S'):", os.date("%H:%M:%S"))
print("os.date('%c'):", os.date("%c"))
print("os.date('*t'):", table.concat(
    (function()
        local t = os.date("*t")
        local result = {}
        for k, v in pairs(t) do
            table.insert(result, k .. "=" .. v)
        end
        return result
    end)(), ", "))

-- Calculate time differences
local tomorrow = os.time({
    year = os.date("%Y", currentTime),
    month = os.date("%m", currentTime),
    day = os.date("%d", currentTime) + 1,
    hour = 0,
    min = 0,
    sec = 0
})
print("\nSeconds until midnight tomorrow:", tomorrow - currentTime)

-- Environment variables
print("\nEnvironment variables:")
print("PATH:", os.getenv("PATH"))
print("HOME:", os.getenv("HOME"))

-- System commands
print("\nSystem commands:")
local result = os.execute("echo Hello from system")
print("Execute result:", result)
```

```
-- Temporary files
print("\nTemporary files:")
local tmpname = os.tmpname()
print("Temporary filename:", tmpname)

-- Process management
print("\nProcess information:")
print("Clock:", os.clock())  -- Process CPU time

-- Sleep function (not standard, but often available)
print("\nSleep function:")
if os.execute("sleep 1") then
    print("Slept for 1 second using execute")
end

-- Exit the program (uncommenting this would terminate the script)
-- os.exit()
```

Output (will vary by system):

```
OS library functions:

Time and date:
os.time(): 1643229245
os.date(): Wed Jan 26 18:20:45 2023
os.date('%Y-%m-%d'): 2023-01-26
os.date('%H:%M:%S'): 18:20:45
os.date('%c'): Wed Jan 26 18:20:45 2023
os.date('*t'): hour=18, min=20, wday=4, day=26, month=1, year=2023, sec=45,
yday=26, isdst=false

Seconds until midnight tomorrow: 20355

Environment variables:
PATH: /usr/local/sbin:/usr/local/bin:/usr/sbin:/usr/bin:/sbin:/bin
HOME: /home/user

System commands:
Hello from system
Execute result: 0

Temporary files:
Temporary filename: /tmp/lua_6Xr2P5

Process information:
Clock: 0.03
```

```
Sleep function:
Slept for 1 second using execute
```

The Debug Library

The debug library provides functions for debugging and introspection:

```lua
-- Debug library demonstration
print("Debug library functions:")

-- Simple function to examine
local function testFunction(a, b, c)
    local x = a + b
    local y = x * c
    return x, y
end

-- Get information about a function
print("\nFunction info:")
local info = debug.getinfo(testFunction)
for k, v in pairs(info) do
    print("  " .. k .. ":", v)
end

-- Get upvalues of a function
print("\nUpvalues:")
local closureExample = function()
    local counter = 0
    return function()
        counter = counter + 1
        return counter
    end
end

local increment = closureExample()
local i = 1
while true do
    local name, value = debug.getupvalue(increment, i)
    if not name then break end
    print("  " .. name .. ":", value)
    i = i + 1
end

-- Get local variables
```

```lua
print("\nLocal variables in current function:")
local a = 10
local b = "hello"
local c = true

for i = 1, 10 do
    local name, value = debug.getlocal(1, i)
    if not name then break end
    print("  " .. name .. ":", value)
end

-- Set a local variable
debug.setlocal(1, 1, 20)  -- Set 'a' to 20
print("\nAfter setting local 'a':", a)

-- Traceback
print("\nStack traceback:")
local function level3() print(debug.traceback("Custom message", 2)) end
local function level2() level3() end
local function level1() level2() end
level1()

-- Hook functions
print("\nDebug hooks:")
local hookCount = 0
local function hook(event, line)
    hookCount = hookCount + 1
    if hookCount <= 3 then
        print("Hook event:", event, "Line:", line)
    end
end

debug.sethook(hook, "l")  -- Set line hook
print("This will trigger hooks")
print("So will this")
debug.sethook()  -- Remove hook

-- Get call info
print("\nCurrent call info:")
local function getCallInfo()
    local info = debug.getinfo(2, "nSl")
    print("Function:", info.name or "unknown")
    print("Line:", info.currentline)
    print("Source:", info.short_src)
end

local function caller()
```

```
    getCallInfo()
end

caller()
```

Output (will vary):

```
Debug library functions:

Function info:
  what: Lua
  source: stdin
  linedefined: 5
  lastlinedefined: 9
  short_src: stdin
  func: function: 0x55c39a2bb260

Upvalues:
  counter: 0

Local variables in current function:
  a: 10
  b: hello
  c: true
  i: 1
  name: nil
  value: nil

After setting local 'a': 20

Stack traceback:
Custom message
stack traceback:
        stdin:73: in function 'level3'
        stdin:74: in function 'level2'
        stdin:75: in function 'level1'
        stdin:76: in main chunk

Debug hooks:
Hook event: line Line: 82
Hook event: line Line: 83
Hook event: line Line: 84
This will trigger hooks
So will this

Current call info:
```

```
Function: caller
Line: 94
Source: stdin
```

The Coroutine Library

The coroutine library provides functions for cooperative multitasking:

```
-- Coroutine library demonstration
print("Coroutine library functions:")

-- Create a simple coroutine
print("\nBasic coroutine:")
local co = coroutine.create(function()
    print("Inside coroutine - step 1")
    coroutine.yield("First yield")
    print("Inside coroutine - step 2")
    coroutine.yield("Second yield")
    print("Inside coroutine - step 3")
    return "Coroutine complete"
end)

print("Coroutine status:", coroutine.status(co))

-- Resume the coroutine
print("\nFirst resume:")
local success, value = coroutine.resume(co)
print("Success:", success)
print("Value:", value)
print("Coroutine status:", coroutine.status(co))

-- Resume again
print("\nSecond resume:")
success, value = coroutine.resume(co)
print("Success:", success)
print("Value:", value)
print("Coroutine status:", coroutine.status(co))

-- Resume a third time
print("\nThird resume:")
success, value = coroutine.resume(co)
print("Success:", success)
print("Value:", value)
print("Coroutine status:", coroutine.status(co))
```

```lua
-- Resume a fourth time (should error as coroutine is dead)
print("\nFourth resume:")
success, value = coroutine.resume(co)
print("Success:", success)
print("Error:", value)

-- Producer-consumer example with coroutines
print("\nProducer-consumer example:")

local function producer()
    local i = 0
    while i < 5 do
        i = i + 1
        print("Producing:", i)
        coroutine.yield(i)
    end
    return "Producer complete"
end

local function consumer(prod)
    local status, value
    repeat
        print("Consumer preparing to receive...")
        status, value = coroutine.resume(prod)
        print("Consumer received:", value)
    until not status or coroutine.status(prod) == "dead"

    if not status then
        print("Error:", value)
    end
end

local prod = coroutine.create(producer)
consumer(prod)

-- coroutine.wrap example
print("\ncoroutine.wrap example:")
local counter = coroutine.wrap(function()
    for i = 1, 3 do
        print("Counter at:", i)
        coroutine.yield(i)
    end
    return "Counter finished"
end)

print("First call:", counter())
print("Second call:", counter())
```

```
print("Third call:", counter())
print("Fourth call:", counter())  -- Returns the final return value
```

Output:

```
Coroutine library functions:

Basic coroutine:
Coroutine status: suspended

First resume:
Inside coroutine - step 1
Success: true
Value: First yield
Coroutine status: suspended

Second resume:
Inside coroutine - step 2
Success: true
Value: Second yield
Coroutine status: suspended

Third resume:
Inside coroutine - step 3
Success: true
Value: Coroutine complete
Coroutine status: dead

Fourth resume:
Success: false
Error: cannot resume dead coroutine

Producer-consumer example:
Consumer preparing to receive...
Producing: 1
Consumer received: 1
Consumer preparing to receive...
Producing: 2
Consumer received: 2
Consumer preparing to receive...
Producing: 3
Consumer received: 3
Consumer preparing to receive...
Producing: 4
Consumer received: 4
Consumer preparing to receive...
```

```
Producing: 5
Consumer received: 5
Consumer preparing to receive...
Consumer received: Producer complete

coroutine.wrap example:
Counter at: 1
First call: 1
Counter at: 2
Second call: 2
Counter at: 3
Third call: 3
Fourth call: Counter finished
```

The UTF-8 Library (Lua 5.3+)

Lua 5.3 introduced a dedicated library for working with UTF-8 strings:

```
-- UTF-8 library (Lua 5.3+)
if utf8 then
    print("UTF-8 library functions:")

    local text = "Hello, 世界! ¿Cómo estás?"

    print("\nUTF-8 text:", text)
    print("Byte length (#):", #text)
    print("Character count (utf8.len):", utf8.len(text))

    -- Get code point for a character
    local secondCharPos = utf8.offset(text, 2)
    print("\nSecond character position:", secondCharPos)
    print("Second character:", string.sub(text, secondCharPos, utf8.offset(text,
3) - 1))
    print("Second character code point:", utf8.codepoint(text, secondCharPos))

    -- Character at position
    local chineseCharPos = utf8.offset(text, 8)
    print("\nEighth character position:", chineseCharPos)
    print("Eighth character:", string.sub(text, chineseCharPos,
utf8.offset(text, 9) - 1))
    print("Eighth character code point:", utf8.codepoint(text, chineseCharPos))
    print("Eighth character from code point:", utf8.char(utf8.codepoint(text,
chineseCharPos)))

    -- Iterate through the string
```

```
    print("\nIterating through the string:")
    local count = 0
    for pos, codepoint in utf8.codes(text) do
        count = count + 1
        if count <= 5 then
            print("Character " .. count .. ":", utf8.char(codepoint), "Code
point:", codepoint)
        end
    end
    print("Total characters:", count)

    -- Pattern matching with UTF-8
    print("\nUTF-8 pattern matching:")
    local pattern = "(%z+)" -- Matches any sequence of UTF-8 characters
    local matches = {string.gmatch(text, pattern)}
    for _, match in ipairs(matches) do
        if type(match) == "function" then
            local m = match()
            if m then
                print("Match:", m)
            else
                print("No match with pattern")
            end
        end
    end
else
    print("UTF-8 library not available (requires Lua 5.3+)")
end
```

Output (if using Lua 5.3 or later):

```
UTF-8 library functions:

UTF-8 text: Hello, 世界! ¿Cómo estás?
Byte length (#): 35
Character count (utf8.len): 22

Second character position: 2
Second character: e
Second character code point: 101

Eighth character position: 8
Eighth character: 世
Eighth character code point: 19990
Eighth character from code point: 世
```

```
Iterating through the string:
Character 1: H Code point: 72
Character 2: e Code point: 101
Character 3: l Code point: 108
Character 4: l Code point: 108
Character 5: o Code point: 111
Total characters: 22

UTF-8 pattern matching:
No match with pattern
```

The Bit Library (Lua 5.2) or Bitwise Operations (Lua 5.3+)

Lua 5.2 included a separate bit library, while Lua 5.3 integrated bitwise operations directly into the language:

```lua
-- Bit operations
if bit32 then
    -- Lua 5.2 bit32 library
    print("Bit32 library functions (Lua 5.2):")

    print("\nBitwise operations:")
    print("bit32.band(0xFF, 0x0F):", bit32.band(0xFF, 0x0F))
    print("bit32.bor(0xF0, 0x0F):", bit32.bor(0xF0, 0x0F))
    print("bit32.bxor(0xFF, 0x0F):", bit32.bxor(0xFF, 0x0F))
    print("bit32.bnot(0x0F):", bit32.bnot(0x0F))

    print("\nBit shifts:")
    print("bit32.lshift(1, 4):", bit32.lshift(1, 4))
    print("bit32.rshift(0x10, 4):", bit32.rshift(0x10, 4))
    print("bit32.arshift(0x10, 4):", bit32.arshift(0x10, 4))

    print("\nBit manipulation:")
    print("bit32.extract(0x12345678, 4, 8):", bit32.extract(0x12345678, 4, 8))
    print("bit32.replace(0x12345678, 0xFF, 16, 8):", bit32.replace(0x12345678,
0xFF, 16, 8))
end

-- Check if we can use Lua 5.3+ bitwise operators
local canUseBitwise = (function()
    local success, result = pcall(function() return 1 & 1 end)
    return success
end)()
```

```
if canUseBitwise then
    print("\nLua 5.3+ bitwise operators:")

    print("\nBitwise operations:")
    print("0xFF & 0x0F:", 0xFF & 0x0F)
    print("0xF0 | 0x0F:", 0xF0 | 0x0F)
    print("0xFF ~ 0x0F:", 0xFF ~ 0x0F)
    print("~0x0F:", ~0x0F)

    print("\nBit shifts:")
    print("1 << 4:", 1 << 4)
    print("0x10 >> 4:", 0x10 >> 4)

    -- Bit manipulation example
    local function getBits(n, pos, count)
        return (n >> pos) & ((1 << count) - 1)
    end

    local function setBits(n, val, pos, count)
        local mask = ((1 << count) - 1) << pos
        return (n & ~mask) | ((val << pos) & mask)
    end

    print("\nBit manipulation functions:")
    print("getBits(0x12345678, 4, 8):", string.format("0x%X",
getBits(0x12345678, 4, 8)))
    print("setBits(0x12345678, 0xFF, 16, 8):", string.format("0x%X",
setBits(0x12345678, 0xFF, 16, 8)))
end
```

Output (varies by Lua version):

```
Bit32 library functions (Lua 5.2):

Bitwise operations:
bit32.band(0xFF, 0x0F): 15
bit32.bor(0xF0, 0x0F): 255
bit32.bxor(0xFF, 0x0F): 240
bit32.bnot(0x0F): 4294967280

Bit shifts:
bit32.lshift(1, 4): 16
bit32.rshift(0x10, 4): 1
bit32.arshift(0x10, 4): 1
```

```
Bit manipulation:
bit32.extract(0x12345678, 4, 8): 55
bit32.replace(0x12345678, 0xFF, 16, 8): 305419896

Lua 5.3+ bitwise operators:

Bitwise operations:
0xFF & 0x0F: 15
0xF0 | 0x0F: 255
0xFF ~ 0x0F: 240
~0x0F: -16

Bit shifts:
1 << 4: 16
0x10 >> 4: 1

Bit manipulation functions:
getBits(0x12345678, 4, 8): 0x37
setBits(0x12345678, 0xFF, 16, 8): 0x12FF5678
```

The Package Library

The package library manages modules and packages:

```lua
-- Package library demonstration
print("Package library:")

-- Display current module search paths
print("\nPackage search paths:")
print("Lua paths (package.path):")
for path in package.path:gmatch("[^;]+") do
    print("  " .. path)
end

print("\nC library paths (package.cpath):")
for path in package.cpath:gmatch("[^;]+") do
    print("  " .. path)
end

-- List loaded modules
print("\nLoaded modules (package.loaded):")
local count = 0
for name, _ in pairs(package.loaded) do
    count = count + 1
    if count <= 5 then
```

```
        print("  " .. name)
    end
end
print("  ... and " .. (count - 5) .. " more")

-- Package.preload demonstration
package.preload["demo_module"] = function()
    return {
        name = "Demo Module",
        version = "1.0",
        greeting = function() return "Hello from demo module!" end
    }
end

print("\nLoading a preloaded module:")
local demo = require("demo_module")
print("Module name:", demo.name)
print("Module version:", demo.version)
print("Module greeting:", demo.greeting())

-- Package.searchers
print("\nPackage searchers:")
for i, searcher in ipairs(package.searchers or package.loaders) do
    print("  Searcher " .. i .. ": " .. tostring(searcher))
end

-- Adding to package.path
print("\nAdding to package.path:")
local originalPath = package.path
package.path = "./?.lua;" .. package.path
print("New first entry:", package.path:match("^([^;]+)"))

-- Restore original path
package.path = originalPath
```

Output (will vary by system):

```
Package library:

Package search paths:
Lua paths (package.path):
  ./?.lua
  /usr/local/share/lua/5.3/?.lua
  /usr/local/share/lua/5.3/?/init.lua
  /usr/local/lib/lua/5.3/?.lua
  /usr/local/lib/lua/5.3/?/init.lua
```

```
    /usr/share/lua/5.3/?.lua
    /usr/share/lua/5.3/?/init.lua

C library paths (package.cpath):
  ./?.so
  /usr/local/lib/lua/5.3/?.so
  /usr/lib/lua/5.3/?.so
  /usr/local/lib/lua/5.3/loadall.so
  /usr/lib/lua/5.3/loadall.so

Loaded modules (package.loaded):
  string
  _G
  table
  io
  os
  ... and 12 more

Loading a preloaded module:
Module name: Demo Module
Module version: 1.0
Module greeting: Hello from demo module!

Package searchers:
  Searcher 1: function: 0x556b0c58c8f0
  Searcher 2: function: 0x556b0c58c920
  Searcher 3: function: 0x556b0c58c950
  Searcher 4: function: 0x556b0c58c980

Adding to package.path:
New first entry: ./?.lua
```

Creating Custom Libraries

You can extend Lua with your own libraries. Here's an example of creating a custom utility library:

```
-- Creating a custom library
local utils = {}

-- String utilities
utils.string = {}

function utils.string.trim(s)
    return s:match("^%s*(.-)%s*$")
```

```lua
end

function utils.string.split(s, delimiter)
    delimiter = delimiter or "%s"
    local result = {}
    for match in (s..delimiter):gmatch("(.-)"..delimiter) do
        table.insert(result, match)
    end
    return result
end

function utils.string.startsWith(s, prefix)
    return s:sub(1, #prefix) == prefix
end

function utils.string.endsWith(s, suffix)
    return s:sub(-#suffix) == suffix
end

-- Table utilities
utils.table = {}

function utils.table.copy(t)
    local result = {}
    for k, v in pairs(t) do
        result[k] = v
    end
    return result
end

function utils.table.deepCopy(t)
    if type(t) ~= "table" then return t end
    local result = {}
    for k, v in pairs(t) do
        if type(v) == "table" then
            result[k] = utils.table.deepCopy(v)
        else
            result[k] = v
        end
    end
    return result
end

function utils.table.keys(t)
    local keys = {}
    for k, _ in pairs(t) do
        table.insert(keys, k)
```

```lua
        end
        return keys
    end

    function utils.table.values(t)
        local values = {}
        for _, v in pairs(t) do
            table.insert(values, v)
        end
        return values
    end

    function utils.table.find(t, value)
        for k, v in pairs(t) do
            if v == value then
                return k
            end
        end
        return nil
    end

    function utils.table.filter(t, predicate)
        local result = {}
        for k, v in pairs(t) do
            if predicate(v, k, t) then
                result[k] = v
            end
        end
        return result
    end

    function utils.table.map(t, mapper)
        local result = {}
        for k, v in pairs(t) do
            result[k] = mapper(v, k, t)
        end
        return result
    end

    -- Math utilities
    utils.math = {}

    function utils.math.round(num, decimal)
        local mult = 10^(decimal or 0)
        return math.floor(num * mult + 0.5) / mult
    end
```

```lua
function utils.math.clamp(value, min, max)
    return math.min(math.max(value, min), max)
end

function utils.math.lerp(a, b, t)
    return a + (b - a) * t
end

-- Test the custom library
print("Custom utility library test:")

print("\nString utilities:")
print("trim(' hello '):", utils.string.trim(" hello "))
print("split('apple,banana,cherry', ','):",
table.concat(utils.string.split("apple,banana,cherry", ","), " | "))
print("startsWith('Hello', 'He'):", utils.string.startsWith("Hello", "He"))
print("endsWith('Hello', 'lo'):", utils.string.endsWith("Hello", "lo"))

print("\nTable utilities:")
local original = {a = 1, b = 2, c = {d = 3}}
local copied = utils.table.copy(original)
local deepCopied = utils.table.deepCopy(original)

original.c.d = 4
print("Original table c.d:", original.c.d)
print("Shallow copied table c.d:", copied.c.d)
print("Deep copied table c.d:", deepCopied.c.d)

local numbers = {10, 20, 30, 40, 50}
print("table.keys:", table.concat(utils.table.keys(original), ", "))
print("table.values of numbers:", table.concat(utils.table.values(numbers), ",
"))
print("table.find(numbers, 30):", utils.table.find(numbers, 30))

local even = utils.table.filter(numbers, function(v) return v % 2 == 0 end)
print("Filtered even numbers:", table.concat(even, ", "))

local doubled = utils.table.map(numbers, function(v) return v * 2 end)
print("Mapped (doubled) numbers:", table.concat(doubled, ", "))

print("\nMath utilities:")
print("round(3.14159, 2):", utils.math.round(3.14159, 2))
print("clamp(15, 0, 10):", utils.math.clamp(15, 0, 10))
print("lerp(0, 100, 0.25):", utils.math.lerp(0, 100, 0.25))

-- Example of converting to a proper module
-- This would typically be in a separate file
```

```
--[[
-- utils.lua
local utils = {
    string = { ... },
    table = { ... },
    math = { ... }
}
return utils

-- Then in another file:
local utils = require("utils")
]]
```

Output:

```
Custom utility library test:

String utilities:
trim('  hello  '): hello
split('apple,banana,cherry', ','): apple | banana | cherry
startsWith('Hello', 'He'): true
endsWith('Hello', 'lo'): true

Table utilities:
Original table c.d: 4
Shallow copied table c.d: 4
Deep copied table c.d: 3
table.keys: a, b, c
table.values of numbers: 10, 20, 30, 40, 50
table.find(numbers, 30): 3
Filtered even numbers: 10, 20, 30, 40, 50
Mapped (doubled) numbers: 20, 40, 60, 80, 100

Math utilities:
round(3.14159, 2): 3.14
clamp(15, 0, 10): 10
lerp(0, 100, 0.25): 25
```

Best Practices for Using the Standard Library

Here are some best practices for effectively using Lua's standard library:

1. **Know what's available**: Familiarize yourself with the functions in each library to avoid reinventing the wheel.

2. **Use the most efficient approach**: For example, use `table.concat` instead of string concatenation in loops, and `ipairs` for array-like tables.

3. **Handle version differences**: Be aware of differences between Lua versions and provide fallbacks when necessary.

4. **Extend rather than modify**: Create your own libraries that extend Lua's functionality rather than modifying the standard libraries.

5. **Organize your code**: Group related functions into namespaces (tables) for better organization and to avoid polluting the global namespace.

```lua
-- Example of handling version differences
local function getBit(n, pos)
    -- Check if we have Lua 5.3+ bitwise operators
    if _VERSION >= "Lua 5.3" then
        return (n >> pos) & 1
    elseif bit32 then
        -- Lua 5.2 bit32 library
        return bit32.extract(n, pos, 1)
    else
        -- Fallback for older versions
        return math.floor(n / 2^pos) % 2
    end
end

print("Version-safe bit extraction:")
print("Bit 3 of 42:", getBit(42, 3))

-- Example of organizing related functions
local StringUtils = {}

function StringUtils.trim(s)
    return s:match("^%s*(.-)%s*$")
end

function StringUtils.capitalize(s)
    return s:sub(1,1):upper() .. s:sub(2)
end

-- Usage
print("\nOrganized utility functions:")
print("Trimmed:", StringUtils.trim("  hello  "))
print("Capitalized:", StringUtils.capitalize("hello"))
```

Output:

```
Version-safe bit extraction:
Bit 3 of 42: 1

Organized utility functions:
Trimmed: hello
Capitalized: Hello
```

Chapter Summary

In this chapter, we've explored Lua's standard library, a compact but powerful collection of functions and utilities that form the core of Lua programming. We've covered the basic global functions, as well as the specialized libraries for strings, tables, mathematics, input/output, operating system interaction, debugging, and cooperative multitasking.

We've also seen how to extend Lua with custom libraries, handle version differences, and organize code effectively. Despite its minimalist approach, Lua's standard library provides most of the functionality needed for common programming tasks, from text processing and mathematical calculations to file I/O and process management.

Understanding the standard library is essential for effective Lua programming, as it allows you to leverage built-in functionality rather than implementing everything from scratch. The libraries are designed to work together seamlessly, providing a consistent and coherent programming experience.

In the next chapter, we'll explore how to integrate Lua with C/C++, which allows you to extend Lua's capabilities even further by adding custom functions and types implemented in a lower-level language.

Chapter 14: Integrating Lua with C/C++

Introduction to Lua/C Integration

One of Lua's greatest strengths is its ability to integrate with C and C++. This integration allows Lua scripts to call C functions and for C programs to interact with Lua code. This feature makes Lua an excellent choice for embedding in applications, where it can serve as a scripting layer on top of high-performance C/C++ code.

In this chapter, we'll explore the Lua C API, which provides the interface between Lua and C. We'll learn how to:

- Embed a Lua interpreter in a C/C++ application
- Call Lua functions from C
- Call C functions from Lua
- Share data between Lua and C
- Create Lua modules in C
- Handle errors across the language boundary

While this chapter assumes some familiarity with C programming, we'll focus on explaining the concepts clearly, with plenty of examples.

The Lua C API

The Lua C API is centered around a virtual stack that serves as the interface between Lua and C. This stack is used to pass values between the two languages, manage function calls, and handle errors.

The Lua Virtual Stack

Here's a simplified view of how the Lua virtual stack works:

1. Values are pushed onto the stack from C
2. Lua operations consume values from the stack and push results back
3. C code can retrieve values from the stack
4. The stack is automatically managed during function calls

Let's look at a simple example that demonstrates using the stack:

```c
#include <stdio.h>
#include <lua.h>
#include <lauxlib.h>
#include <lualib.h>

int main(void) {
    // Create a new Lua state
    lua_State *L = luaL_newstate();

    // Open the standard libraries
    luaL_openlibs(L);

    printf("Working with the Lua stack:\n");

    // Push values onto the stack
    lua_pushnil(L);                // stack: nil
    lua_pushboolean(L, 1);         // stack: nil, true
    lua_pushnumber(L, 42.5);       // stack: nil, true, 42.5
    lua_pushinteger(L, 123);       // stack: nil, true, 42.5, 123
    lua_pushstring(L, "Hello");    // stack: nil, true, 42.5, 123, "Hello"

    // Display the stack size
    printf("Stack size: %d\n", lua_gettop(L));

    // Access values from the stack (indices can be positive or negative)
    printf("Value at index 1 (bottom): %s\n", lua_typename(L, lua_type(L, 1)));
    printf("Value at index -1 (top): %s\n", lua_tostring(L, -1));
    printf("Value at index 3: %f\n", lua_tonumber(L, 3));

    // Manipulate the stack
    lua_pop(L, 2);                 // stack: nil, true, 42.5
    printf("After pop(2), stack size: %d\n", lua_gettop(L));

    lua_pushvalue(L, -2);          // stack: nil, true, 42.5, true
    printf("After pushvalue(-2), stack size: %d\n", lua_gettop(L));

    lua_remove(L, 2);              // stack: nil, 42.5, true
    printf("After remove(2), stack size: %d\n", lua_gettop(L));

    lua_insert(L, 1);              // stack: true, nil, 42.5
```

```
    printf("After insert(1), type at index 1: %s\n", lua_typename(L, lua_type(L,
1)));

    lua_replace(L, 2);              // stack: true, true
    printf("After replace(2), stack size: %d\n", lua_gettop(L));

    // Clean up
    lua_close(L);
    return 0;
}
```

When compiled and run, this program demonstrates basic operations on the Lua stack, showing how to push values, retrieve them, and manipulate the stack.

Key C API Functions

The Lua C API provides numerous functions for working with the Lua state. Here are some of the most important categories:

1. **State Management**

    - `lua_State *luaL_newstate()`: Creates a new Lua state
    - `void lua_close(lua_State *L)`: Closes a Lua state
    - `void luaL_openlibs(lua_State *L)`: Opens the standard libraries

2. **Stack Manipulation**

    - `int lua_gettop(lua_State *L)`: Gets the stack size
    - `void lua_settop(lua_State *L, int index)`: Sets the stack size
    - `void lua_pushvalue(lua_State *L, int index)`: Pushes a copy of a value
    - `void lua_remove(lua_State *L, int index)`: Removes a value
    - `void lua_insert(lua_State *L, int index)`: Inserts a value
    - `void lua_replace(lua_State *L, int index)`: Replaces a value

3. **Pushing Values**

    - `void lua_pushnil(lua_State *L)`: Pushes nil
    - `void lua_pushboolean(lua_State *L, int b)`: Pushes a boolean
    - `void lua_pushinteger(lua_State *L, lua_Integer n)`: Pushes an integer
    - `void lua_pushnumber(lua_State *L, lua_Number n)`: Pushes a number
    - `void lua_pushstring(lua_State *L, const char *s)`: Pushes a string

```
```

4. **Retrieving Values**

- `int lua_isnil(lua_State *L, int index)`: Checks if a value is nil
- `int lua_isboolean(lua_State *L, int index)`: Checks if a value is boolean
- `int lua_isnumber(lua_State *L, int index)`: Checks if a value is a number
- `int lua_isstring(lua_State *L, int index)`: Checks if a value is a string
- `int lua_istable(lua_State *L, int index)`: Checks if a value is a table
- `int lua_type(lua_State *L, int index)`: Gets a value's type
- `lua_Integer lua_tointeger(lua_State *L, int index)`: Gets an integer value
- `lua_Number lua_tonumber(lua_State *L, int index)`: Gets a number value
- `const char *lua_tostring(lua_State *L, int index)`: Gets a string value

5. **Function Calls**

- `void lua_call(lua_State *L, int nargs, int nresults)`: Calls a function
- `int lua_pcall(lua_State *L, int nargs, int nresults, int errfunc)`: Protected call

Embedding Lua in C Applications

One of the most common uses of the Lua C API is to embed a Lua interpreter in a C/C++ application. This allows the application to use Lua for configuration, scripting, or other tasks.

Basic Embedding

Here's a simple example of embedding Lua in a C program:

```
#include <stdio.h>
#include <lua.h>
#include <lauxlib.h>
#include <lualib.h>

int main(void) {
```

```c
// Create a new Lua state
lua_State *L = luaL_newstate();

// Open the standard libraries
luaL_openlibs(L);

printf("Embedded Lua interpreter example:\n");

// Execute a simple Lua chunk
if (luaL_dostring(L, "print('Hello from Lua!')")) {
    fprintf(stderr, "Error: %s\n", lua_tostring(L, -1));
    lua_pop(L, 1);  // Remove the error message
}

// Define a Lua variable
luaL_dostring(L, "answer = 42");

// Retrieve the variable from Lua
lua_getglobal(L, "answer");
if (lua_isnumber(L, -1)) {
    int answer = (int)lua_tonumber(L, -1);
    printf("Answer from Lua: %d\n", answer);
}
lua_pop(L, 1);  // Remove the answer

// Execute a Lua file
printf("\nExecuting a Lua file:\n");

// Create a test Lua file
FILE *f = fopen("test_embedded.lua", "w");
fprintf(f, "print('This is from a Lua file')\n");
fprintf(f, "return 'File executed successfully'\n");
fclose(f);

// Execute the file
if (luaL_dofile(L, "test_embedded.lua")) {
    fprintf(stderr, "Error: %s\n", lua_tostring(L, -1));
    lua_pop(L, 1);
} else if (lua_isstring(L, -1)) {
    // Get the return value
    printf("Return value: %s\n", lua_tostring(L, -1));
    lua_pop(L, 1);
}

// Clean up
lua_close(L);
remove("test_embedded.lua");  // Delete the test file
```

```
        return 0;
}
```

This program demonstrates how to create a Lua state, execute Lua code, and exchange data between C and Lua.

Handling Errors

When executing Lua code from C, it's important to handle errors properly. The lua_pcall function provides a way to execute Lua code in a protected environment, catching any errors that occur:

```c
#include <stdio.h>
#include <lua.h>
#include <lauxlib.h>
#include <lualib.h>

// Custom error handler
static int error_handler(lua_State *L) {
    const char *msg = lua_tostring(L, 1);
    if (msg == NULL) {
        if (luaL_callmeta(L, 1, "__tostring") &&
            lua_type(L, -1) == LUA_TSTRING)
            return 1;   // Use the result of __tostring metamethod
        else
            msg = lua_pushfstring(L, "(error object is a %s value)",
                                  luaL_typename(L, 1));
    }

    // Add stack trace information
    luaL_traceback(L, L, msg, 1);
    return 1;
}

int main(void) {
    // Create a new Lua state
    lua_State *L = luaL_newstate();

    // Open the standard libraries
    luaL_openlibs(L);

    printf("Error handling example:\n");

    // Execute Lua code that will succeed
    printf("\nExecuting valid code:\n");
```

```c
// Push the error handler
lua_pushcfunction(L, error_handler);
int errfunc = lua_gettop(L);

// Load the string (pushes the compiled chunk onto the stack)
if (luaL_loadstring(L, "print('This code is valid')")) {
    printf("Error loading code: %s\n", lua_tostring(L, -1));
    lua_pop(L, 1);  // Remove the error message
} else {
    // Execute the chunk with error handling
    if (lua_pcall(L, 0, 0, errfunc)) {
        printf("Error executing code: %s\n", lua_tostring(L, -1));
        lua_pop(L, 1);  // Remove the error message
    }
}

// Execute Lua code that will fail
printf("\nExecuting invalid code:\n");

// The error handler is already on the stack (at errfunc)

// Load the string (pushes the compiled chunk onto the stack)
if (luaL_loadstring(L, "error('This code will fail')")) {
    printf("Error loading code: %s\n", lua_tostring(L, -1));
    lua_pop(L, 1);  // Remove the error message
} else {
    // Execute the chunk with error handling
    if (lua_pcall(L, 0, 0, errfunc)) {
        printf("Error executing code: %s\n", lua_tostring(L, -1));
        lua_pop(L, 1);  // Remove the error message
    }
}

// Execute Lua code with a syntax error
printf("\nExecuting code with syntax error:\n");

// Load the string (note the missing closing bracket)
if (luaL_loadstring(L, "function invalid(x print(x) end")) {
    printf("Error loading code: %s\n", lua_tostring(L, -1));
    lua_pop(L, 1);  // Remove the error message
} else {
    // This won't be reached due to the syntax error
    if (lua_pcall(L, 0, 0, errfunc)) {
        printf("Error executing code: %s\n", lua_tostring(L, -1));
        lua_pop(L, 1);  // Remove the error message
    }
```

```
    }

    // Remove the error handler
    lua_pop(L, 1);

    // Clean up
    lua_close(L);
    return 0;
}
```

This example demonstrates how to handle different types of errors that can occur when executing Lua code from C.

Calling Lua Functions from C

One of the key aspects of Lua/C integration is the ability to call Lua functions from C code. This allows C code to use functionality implemented in Lua.

Basic Function Calls

Here's an example of calling a Lua function from C:

```
#include <stdio.h>
#include <lua.h>
#include <lauxlib.h>
#include <lualib.h>

int main(void) {
    // Create a new Lua state
    lua_State *L = luaL_newstate();

    // Open the standard libraries
    luaL_openlibs(L);

    printf("Calling Lua functions from C:\n");

    // Define a Lua function
    const char *lua_code =
        "function add(a, b)\n"
        "    return a + b\n"
        "end\n"
        "\n"
        "function greeting(name)\n"
        "    return 'Hello, ' .. name .. '!'\n"
        "end\n"
```

```c
            "\n"
            "function get_table()\n"
            "    return {name = 'Lua', year = 1993, features = {'lightweight',
'embeddable'}}\n"
            "end\n"
            "\n"
            "function multi_return()\n"
            "    return 'first', 'second', 'third'\n"
            "end";

    // Execute the code to define the functions
    if (luaL_dostring(L, lua_code)) {
        fprintf(stderr, "Error: %s\n", lua_tostring(L, -1));
        lua_pop(L, 1);
        lua_close(L);
        return 1;
    }

    // Call the add function
    printf("\nCalling add(10, 20):\n");

    // Push the function onto the stack
    lua_getglobal(L, "add");

    // Check if it's actually a function
    if (!lua_isfunction(L, -1)) {
        fprintf(stderr, "add is not a function\n");
        lua_pop(L, 1);
        lua_close(L);
        return 1;
    }

    // Push the arguments
    lua_pushinteger(L, 10);
    lua_pushinteger(L, 20);

    // Call the function with 2 arguments and 1 result
    if (lua_pcall(L, 2, 1, 0)) {
        fprintf(stderr, "Error: %s\n", lua_tostring(L, -1));
        lua_pop(L, 1);
        lua_close(L);
        return 1;
    }

    // Get the result
    if (!lua_isnumber(L, -1)) {
        fprintf(stderr, "Result is not a number\n");
```

```c
        lua_pop(L, 1);
        lua_close(L);
        return 1;
    }

    int result = (int)lua_tonumber(L, -1);
    printf("Result: %d\n", result);

    // Pop the result
    lua_pop(L, 1);

    // Call the greeting function
    printf("\nCalling greeting('John'):\n");

    lua_getglobal(L, "greeting");
    lua_pushstring(L, "John");
    if (lua_pcall(L, 1, 1, 0)) {
        fprintf(stderr, "Error: %s\n", lua_tostring(L, -1));
        lua_pop(L, 1);
        lua_close(L);
        return 1;
    }

    printf("Result: %s\n", lua_tostring(L, -1));
    lua_pop(L, 1);

    // Call the function that returns a table
    printf("\nCalling get_table():\n");

    lua_getglobal(L, "get_table");
    if (lua_pcall(L, 0, 1, 0)) {
        fprintf(stderr, "Error: %s\n", lua_tostring(L, -1));
        lua_pop(L, 1);
        lua_close(L);
        return 1;
    }

    if (!lua_istable(L, -1)) {
        fprintf(stderr, "Result is not a table\n");
        lua_pop(L, 1);
        lua_close(L);
        return 1;
    }

    // Access table fields
    printf("Table contents:\n");
```

```c
    lua_getfield(L, -1, "name");
    printf("  name: %s\n", lua_tostring(L, -1));
    lua_pop(L, 1);

    lua_getfield(L, -1, "year");
    printf("  year: %d\n", (int)lua_tonumber(L, -1));
    lua_pop(L, 1);

    lua_getfield(L, -1, "features");
    if (lua_istable(L, -1)) {
        printf("  features: [");
        lua_len(L, -1);  // Get the length of the features array
        int len = (int)lua_tonumber(L, -1);
        lua_pop(L, 1);  // Pop the length

        for (int i = 1; i <= len; i++) {
            lua_rawgeti(L, -1, i);  // Get features[i]
            printf("%s%s", lua_tostring(L, -1), i < len ? ", " : "");
            lua_pop(L, 1);  // Pop the feature
        }
        printf("]\n");
    }
    lua_pop(L, 1);  // Pop the features table

    // Pop the result table
    lua_pop(L, 1);

    // Call the function that returns multiple values
    printf("\nCalling multi_return():\n");

    lua_getglobal(L, "multi_return");
    if (lua_pcall(L, 0, 3, 0)) {  // Expect 3 results
        fprintf(stderr, "Error: %s\n", lua_tostring(L, -1));
        lua_pop(L, 1);
        lua_close(L);
        return 1;
    }

    // Process the results (stack has them in reverse order)
    printf("Result 3: %s\n", lua_tostring(L, -1));
    printf("Result 2: %s\n", lua_tostring(L, -2));
    printf("Result 1: %s\n", lua_tostring(L, -3));

    // Pop all results
    lua_pop(L, 3);

    // Clean up
```

```c
        lua_close(L);
        return 0;
}
```

This example shows how to call Lua functions of varying complexity, including functions that return tables and multiple values.

Using the Auxiliary Library

The Lua auxiliary library (lauxlib.h) provides higher-level functions that simplify
common tasks. Here's an example using these functions:

```c
#include <stdio.h>
#include <lua.h>
#include <lauxlib.h>
#include <lualib.h>

int main(void) {
    // Create a new Lua state
    lua_State *L = luaL_newstate();

    // Open the standard libraries
    luaL_openlibs(L);

    printf("Using the Lua auxiliary library:\n");

    // Define a Lua function
    luaL_dostring(L,
        "function calculate(a, b, operation)\n"
        "    if operation == 'add' then\n"
        "        return a + b\n"
        "    elseif operation == 'subtract' then\n"
        "        return a - b\n"
        "    elseif operation == 'multiply' then\n"
        "        return a * b\n"
        "    elseif operation == 'divide' then\n"
        "        if b == 0 then error('Division by zero') end\n"
        "        return a / b\n"
        "    else\n"
        "        error('Unknown operation: ' .. operation)\n"
        "    end\n"
        "end");

    // Helper function to call calculate with different operations
    void calculate(lua_State *L, const char *operation, double a, double b) {
        // Using auxiliary functions for a cleaner implementation
```

```
        lua_getglobal(L, "calculate");

        // Check if function exists
        if (!lua_isfunction(L, -1)) {
            luaL_error(L, "calculate is not a function");
            return;
        }

        // Push arguments
        lua_pushnumber(L, a);
        lua_pushnumber(L, b);
        lua_pushstring(L, operation);

        // Call the function (3 arguments, 1 result)
        if (lua_pcall(L, 3, 1, 0) != LUA_OK) {
            printf("Error: %s\n", lua_tostring(L, -1));
            lua_pop(L, 1);
            return;
        }

        // Get the result using luaL_checknumber (safer than lua_tonumber)
        double result = luaL_checknumber(L, -1);
        printf("%g %s %g = %g\n", a, operation, b, result);

        // Pop the result
        lua_pop(L, 1);
    }

    // Test with different operations
    calculate(L, "add", 10, 20);
    calculate(L, "subtract", 50, 30);
    calculate(L, "multiply", 6, 7);
    calculate(L, "divide", 100, 4);

    // Test error handling
    printf("\nTesting error handling:\n");

    lua_getglobal(L, "calculate");
    lua_pushnumber(L, 10);
    lua_pushnumber(L, 0);
    lua_pushstring(L, "divide");

    if (lua_pcall(L, 3, 1, 0) != LUA_OK) {
        printf("Expected error: %s\n", lua_tostring(L, -1));
        lua_pop(L, 1);
    } else {
        printf("Result: %g\n", lua_tonumber(L, -1));
```

```
        lua_pop(L, 1);
    }

    // Clean up
    lua_close(L);
    return 0;
}
```

The auxiliary library functions like `luaL_checknumber` provide additional type checking and error handling, making the C code more robust.

Registering C Functions in Lua

One of the most powerful features of the Lua/C API is the ability to register C functions that can be called from Lua code. This allows you to extend Lua with custom functionality implemented in C.

Creating C Functions for Lua

To create a C function that can be called from Lua, you need to follow the `lua_CFunction` prototype:

```c
#include <stdio.h>
#include <math.h>
#include <lua.h>
#include <lauxlib.h>
#include <lualib.h>

// A C function that will be callable from Lua
static int c_add(lua_State *L) {
    // Check and get the first argument
    double a = luaL_checknumber(L, 1);

    // Check and get the second argument
    double b = luaL_checknumber(L, 2);

    // Perform the operation
    double result = a + b;

    // Push the result onto the stack
    lua_pushnumber(L, result);

    // Return the number of results (1 in this case)
    return 1;
```

```c
}

// A more complex C function that returns multiple values
static int c_stats(lua_State *L) {
    // Check that the argument is a table
    luaL_checktype(L, 1, LUA_TTABLE);

    int count = 0;
    double sum = 0.0;
    double min = INFINITY;
    double max = -INFINITY;

    // Iterate through the table
    lua_pushnil(L);  // Push nil to start iteration
    while (lua_next(L, 1) != 0) {
        // Value is at index -1, key at index -2
        if (lua_isnumber(L, -1)) {
            double value = lua_tonumber(L, -1);
            sum += value;
            count++;

            if (value < min) min = value;
            if (value > max) max = value;
        }

        // Remove the value, keep the key for the next iteration
        lua_pop(L, 1);
    }

    // Calculate average
    double avg = count > 0 ? sum / count : 0.0;

    // Push the results onto the stack
    lua_pushnumber(L, count);
    lua_pushnumber(L, sum);
    lua_pushnumber(L, avg);
    lua_pushnumber(L, min == INFINITY ? 0 : min);
    lua_pushnumber(L, max == -INFINITY ? 0 : max);

    // Return the number of results
    return 5;
}

// A C function that uses Lua's error handling
static int c_divide(lua_State *L) {
    double a = luaL_checknumber(L, 1);
    double b = luaL_checknumber(L, 2);
```

```c
    if (b == 0) {
        // Raise a Lua error
        return luaL_error(L, "Division by zero");
    }

    lua_pushnumber(L, a / b);
    return 1;
}

int main(void) {
    // Create a new Lua state
    lua_State *L = luaL_newstate();

    // Open the standard libraries
    luaL_openlibs(L);

    printf("Registering C functions in Lua:\n");

    // Register the C functions in Lua
    lua_pushcfunction(L, c_add);
    lua_setglobal(L, "c_add");

    lua_pushcfunction(L, c_stats);
    lua_setglobal(L, "c_stats");

    lua_pushcfunction(L, c_divide);
    lua_setglobal(L, "c_divide");

    // Test the C functions from Lua
    printf("\nCalling C functions from Lua:\n");

    luaL_dostring(L,
        "-- Test c_add\n"
        "local result = c_add(10, 20)\n"
        "print('c_add(10, 20) =', result)\n"
        "\n"
        "-- Test c_stats\n"
        "local numbers = {1, 5, 2, 8, 3, 9, 4, 7, 6}\n"
        "local count, sum, avg, min, max = c_stats(numbers)\n"
        "print('Stats for', table.concat(numbers, ', '))\n"
        "print('  Count:', count)\n"
        "print('  Sum:', sum)\n"
        "print('  Average:', avg)\n"
        "print('  Min:', min)\n"
        "print('  Max:', max)\n"
        "\n"
```

```
                "-- Test c_divide\n"
                "print('c_divide(100, 5) =', c_divide(100, 5))\n"
                "\n"
                "-- Test error handling\n"
                "local success, error_msg = pcall(function() return c_divide(10, 0)
end)\n"
                "if not success then\n"
                "    print('Expected error:', error_msg)\n"
                "end");

        // Clean up
        lua_close(L);
        return 0;
}
```

This example demonstrates how to create C functions that can be called from Lua, including functions that return multiple values and handle errors.

Creating Lua Modules in C

For more complex extensions, it's common to create Lua modules in C. A module is a table containing related functions and values. Here's an example:

```c
#include <stdio.h>
#include <string.h>
#include <math.h>
#include <lua.h>
#include <lauxlib.h>
#include <lualib.h>

// Module functions

// Calculate the Euclidean distance between two points
static int vector_distance(lua_State *L) {
    // Check for the correct number of arguments
    if (lua_gettop(L) != 4) {
        return luaL_error(L, "Expected 4 arguments (x1, y1, x2, y2)");
    }

    // Get the coordinates
    double x1 = luaL_checknumber(L, 1);
    double y1 = luaL_checknumber(L, 2);
    double x2 = luaL_checknumber(L, 3);
    double y2 = luaL_checknumber(L, 4);

    // Calculate the distance
```

```c
    double dx = x2 - x1;
    double dy = y2 - y1;
    double distance = sqrt(dx*dx + dy*dy);

    // Return the result
    lua_pushnumber(L, distance);
    return 1;
}

// Normalize a vector
static int vector_normalize(lua_State *L) {
    double x = luaL_checknumber(L, 1);
    double y = luaL_checknumber(L, 2);

    double length = sqrt(x*x + y*y);

    if (length < 1e-10) {
        // Avoid division by near-zero
        lua_pushnumber(L, 0);
        lua_pushnumber(L, 0);
    } else {
        lua_pushnumber(L, x / length);
        lua_pushnumber(L, y / length);
    }

    return 2;
}

// Calculate the dot product of two vectors
static int vector_dot(lua_State *L) {
    double x1 = luaL_checknumber(L, 1);
    double y1 = luaL_checknumber(L, 2);
    double x2 = luaL_checknumber(L, 3);
    double y2 = luaL_checknumber(L, 4);

    double dot = x1*x2 + y1*y2;

    lua_pushnumber(L, dot);
    return 1;
}

// Module registration function
int luaopen_vector(lua_State *L) {
    // Create the module table
    lua_newtable(L);

    // Register functions
```

```c
    lua_pushcfunction(L, vector_distance);
    lua_setfield(L, -2, "distance");

    lua_pushcfunction(L, vector_normalize);
    lua_setfield(L, -2, "normalize");

    lua_pushcfunction(L, vector_dot);
    lua_setfield(L, -2, "dot");

    // Add a constant
    lua_pushnumber(L, M_PI);
    lua_setfield(L, -2, "PI");

    // Add version information
    lua_pushstring(L, "1.0.0");
    lua_setfield(L, -2, "VERSION");

    // Return the module table
    return 1;
}

// For testing within this example
int main(void) {
    // Create a new Lua state
    lua_State *L = luaL_newstate();

    // Open the standard libraries
    luaL_openlibs(L);

    printf("Creating a Lua module in C:\n");

    // Register our module
    luaopen_vector(L);
    lua_setglobal(L, "vector");  // Make the module available globally

    // Test the module
    printf("\nTesting the vector module:\n");

    luaL_dostring(L,
        "-- Print module information\n"
        "print('Vector module version:', vector.VERSION)\n"
        "print('PI constant:', vector.PI)\n"
        "\n"
        "-- Test distance function\n"
        "local dist = vector.distance(0, 0, 3, 4)\n"
        "print('Distance from (0,0) to (3,4):', dist)\n"
        "\n"
```

```
            "-- Test normalize function\n"
            "local nx, ny = vector.normalize(3, 4)\n"
            "print('Normalized (3,4):', nx, ny)\n"
            "\n"
            "-- Test dot product\n"
            "local dot = vector.dot(1, 0, 0, 1)\n"
            "print('Dot product of (1,0) and (0,1):', dot)\n"
            "\n"
            "-- Create a helper function using the module\n"
            "function vector.angle(x1, y1, x2, y2)\n"
            "    local dot = vector.dot(x1, y1, x2, y2)\n"
            "    local len1 = vector.distance(0, 0, x1, y1)\n"
            "    local len2 = vector.distance(0, 0, x2, y2)\n"
            "    return math.acos(dot / (len1 * len2)) * 180 / vector.PI\n"
            "end\n"
            "\n"
            "-- Test the helper function\n"
            "local angle = vector.angle(1, 0, 0, 1)\n"
            "print('Angle between (1,0) and (0,1):', angle, 'degrees')");

    // Clean up
    lua_close(L);
    return 0;
}
```

This example creates a vector module with functions for vector operations, showing how to organize C functions into a cohesive Lua module.

Working with Userdata

Userdata allows you to store C data structures in Lua variables. This is useful for implementing complex data types or wrapping C libraries.

Basic Userdata Example

Here's a simple example of using light userdata:

```
#include <stdio.h>
#include <stdlib.h>
#include <lua.h>
#include <lauxlib.h>
#include <lualib.h>

int main(void) {
    // Create a new Lua state
```

```c
    lua_State *L = luaL_newstate();

    // Open the standard libraries
    luaL_openlibs(L);

    printf("Basic userdata example:\n");

    // Create a pointer in C
    int *data = (int*)malloc(sizeof(int));
    *data = 42;

    // Push the pointer as light userdata
    lua_pushlightuserdata(L, data);

    // Store it in a global variable
    lua_setglobal(L, "c_data");

    // Define a function to access the data
    luaL_dostring(L,
        "function get_c_data()\n"
        "    return c_data\n"
        "end");

    // Retrieve the data from Lua
    lua_getglobal(L, "get_c_data");
    if (lua_pcall(L, 0, 1, 0) != LUA_OK) {
        fprintf(stderr, "Error: %s\n", lua_tostring(L, -1));
        lua_pop(L, 1);
    } else {
        if (lua_islightuserdata(L, -1)) {
            int *retrieved = (int*)lua_touserdata(L, -1);
            printf("Retrieved data: %d\n", *retrieved);
        } else {
            printf("Not userdata\n");
        }
        lua_pop(L, 1);
    }

    // Clean up
    free(data);
    lua_close(L);
    return 0;
}
```

Light userdata is simple but limited—it's just a pointer without type information or garbage collection.

Full Userdata with Metatables

For more complex scenarios, you can use full userdata with metatables to implement custom types:

```c
#include <stdio.h>
#include <stdlib.h>
#include <string.h>
#include <lua.h>
#include <lauxlib.h>
#include <lualib.h>

// Define a simple point structure
typedef struct {
    double x;
    double y;
} Point;

// Userdata methods

// Create a new point
static int point_new(lua_State *L) {
    double x = luaL_optnumber(L, 1, 0.0);
    double y = luaL_optnumber(L, 2, 0.0);

    // Allocate memory for the point
    Point *point = (Point*)lua_newuserdata(L, sizeof(Point));
    point->x = x;
    point->y = y;

    // Set the metatable for the userdata
    luaL_getmetatable(L, "Point");
    lua_setmetatable(L, -2);

    return 1;  // Return the userdata
}

// Get the coordinates of a point
static int point_get(lua_State *L) {
    Point *point = (Point*)luaL_checkudata(L, 1, "Point");

    lua_pushnumber(L, point->x);
    lua_pushnumber(L, point->y);

    return 2;  // Return two values
}

// Set the coordinates of a point
```

```c
static int point_set(lua_State *L) {
    Point *point = (Point*)luaL_checkudata(L, 1, "Point");

    point->x = luaL_checknumber(L, 2);
    point->y = luaL_checknumber(L, 3);

    return 0;  // Return nothing
}

// Calculate the distance between two points
static int point_distance(lua_State *L) {
    Point *p1 = (Point*)luaL_checkudata(L, 1, "Point");
    Point *p2 = (Point*)luaL_checkudata(L, 2, "Point");

    double dx = p2->x - p1->x;
    double dy = p2->y - p1->y;
    double distance = sqrt(dx*dx + dy*dy);

    lua_pushnumber(L, distance);
    return 1;
}

// String representation of a point
static int point_tostring(lua_State *L) {
    Point *point = (Point*)luaL_checkudata(L, 1, "Point");

    char buffer[64];
    snprintf(buffer, sizeof(buffer), "Point(%.2f, %.2f)", point->x, point->y);

    lua_pushstring(L, buffer);
    return 1;
}

// Garbage collection function
static int point_gc(lua_State *L) {
    // The memory for the Point structure was allocated with lua_newuserdata,
    // so Lua will free it automatically. We don't need to free it ourselves.
    // This function is just for demonstration purposes.

    Point *point = (Point*)luaL_checkudata(L, 1, "Point");
    printf("Collecting Point(%.2f, %.2f)\n", point->x, point->y);

    return 0;
}

// Register the Point type
int luaopen_point(lua_State *L) {
```

```c
    // Create metatable for Point userdata
    luaL_newmetatable(L, "Point");

    // Metatable.__index = metatable
    lua_pushvalue(L, -1);  // Duplicate metatable
    lua_setfield(L, -2, "__index");  // metatable.__index = metatable

    // Register metamethods
    lua_pushcfunction(L, point_tostring);
    lua_setfield(L, -2, "__tostring");

    lua_pushcfunction(L, point_gc);
    lua_setfield(L, -2, "__gc");

    // Register methods
    lua_pushcfunction(L, point_get);
    lua_setfield(L, -2, "get");

    lua_pushcfunction(L, point_set);
    lua_setfield(L, -2, "set");

    lua_pushcfunction(L, point_distance);
    lua_setfield(L, -2, "distance");

    // Create a library table
    luaL_newlib(L, (luaL_Reg[]){
        {"new", point_new},
        {NULL, NULL}
    });

    return 1;
}

int main(void) {
    // Create a new Lua state
    lua_State *L = luaL_newstate();

    // Open the standard libraries
    luaL_openlibs(L);

    printf("Full userdata example with metatable:\n");

    // Register the Point type
    luaopen_point(L);
    lua_setglobal(L, "Point");

    // Test the Point type
```

```
    printf("\nTesting Point userdata:\n");

    luaL_dostring(L,
        "-- Create Points\n"
        "local p1 = Point.new(3, 4)\n"
        "local p2 = Point.new(6, 8)\n"
        "\n"
        "-- Test tostring metamethod\n"
        "print('p1 =', p1)\n"
        "print('p2 =', p2)\n"
        "\n"
        "-- Test get method\n"
        "local x, y = p1:get()\n"
        "print('p1 coordinates:', x, y)\n"
        "\n"
        "-- Test set method\n"
        "p1:set(10, 20)\n"
        "print('After setting: p1 =', p1)\n"
        "\n"
        "-- Test distance method\n"
        "local dist = p1:distance(p2)\n"
        "print('Distance between p1 and p2:', dist)\n"
        "\n"
        "-- Test garbage collection\n"
        "local function test_gc()\n"
        "    local p = Point.new(1, 1)\n"
        "    print('Created temporary point:', p)\n"
        "end\n"
        "\n"
        "test_gc()\n"
        "collectgarbage()");

    // Clean up
    lua_close(L);
    return 0;
}
```

This example demonstrates a more complex userdata implementation with metatables, methods, and garbage collection.

Memory Management and Resource Handling

When integrating Lua with C, proper memory management is crucial to avoid leaks and crashes.

Garbage Collection and References

Lua uses automatic garbage collection, but when C code holds references to Lua values, you need to manage those references explicitly:

```c
#include <stdio.h>
#include <lua.h>
#include <lauxlib.h>
#include <lualib.h>

int main(void) {
    // Create a new Lua state
    lua_State *L = luaL_newstate();

    // Open the standard libraries
    luaL_openlibs(L);

    printf("Memory management and references:\n");

    // Create a Lua table
    lua_newtable(L);
    lua_pushstring(L, "This table is stored in the registry");
    lua_setfield(L, -2, "message");

    // Store the table in the registry using a reference
    int ref = luaL_ref(L, LUA_REGISTRYINDEX);
    printf("Created reference: %d\n", ref);

    // The table is now in the registry and no longer on the stack

    // Later, we can retrieve the table using the reference
    printf("\nRetrieving table from reference:\n");
    lua_rawgeti(L, LUA_REGISTRYINDEX, ref);

    // Check if we got a table
    if (lua_istable(L, -1)) {
        printf("Retrieved table successfully\n");

        // Access a field in the table
        lua_getfield(L, -1, "message");
        printf("Message: %s\n", lua_tostring(L, -1));
        lua_pop(L, 1);  // Pop the message
    } else {
        printf("Failed to retrieve table\n");
    }

    // When we're done with the reference, release it
    luaL_unref(L, LUA_REGISTRYINDEX, ref);
```

```
    printf("\nReleased reference %d\n", ref);

    // Try to retrieve the table again (should fail)
    lua_rawgeti(L, LUA_REGISTRYINDEX, ref);
    printf("After releasing, got type: %s\n", lua_typename(L, lua_type(L, -1)));
    lua_pop(L, 1);  // Pop the nil value

    // Clean up
    lua_close(L);
    return 0;
}
```

This example demonstrates how to store and retrieve Lua values using the registry and references, which is essential for managing long-lived references in C code.

Managing Resources with Userdata

When userdata wraps external resources (like file handles or database connections), proper cleanup is essential:

```
#include <stdio.h>
#include <stdlib.h>
#include <string.h>
#include <lua.h>
#include <lauxlib.h>
#include <lualib.h>

// Define a resource structure
typedef struct {
    FILE *file;
    char *filename;
    int closed;
} FileResource;

// Create a new file resource
static int file_open(lua_State *L) {
    const char *filename = luaL_checkstring(L, 1);
    const char *mode = luaL_optstring(L, 2, "r");

    // Allocate memory for the resource
    FileResource *fr = (FileResource*)lua_newuserdata(L, sizeof(FileResource));
    fr->file = NULL;
    fr->filename = NULL;
    fr->closed = 0;

    // Try to open the file
```

```
        fr->file = fopen(filename, mode);
        if (!fr->file) {
            return luaL_error(L, "Cannot open file '%s': %s", filename,
strerror(errno));
        }

        // Copy the filename
        fr->filename = strdup(filename);
        if (!fr->filename) {
            fclose(fr->file);
            return luaL_error(L, "Out of memory");
        }

        // Set the metatable for the userdata
        luaL_getmetatable(L, "FileResource");
        lua_setmetatable(L, -2);

        return 1;  // Return the userdata
}

// Read a line from the file
static int file_readline(lua_State *L) {
    FileResource *fr = (FileResource*)luaL_checkudata(L, 1, "FileResource");

    // Check if the file is closed
    if (fr->closed) {
        return luaL_error(L, "Attempt to use a closed file");
    }

    // Read a line
    char buffer[1024];
    if (fgets(buffer, sizeof(buffer), fr->file)) {
        // Remove trailing newline
        size_t len = strlen(buffer);
        if (len > 0 && buffer[len-1] == '\n') {
            buffer[len-1] = '\0';
        }

        lua_pushstring(L, buffer);
        return 1;
    } else {
        // End of file or error
        return 0;  // Return no values
    }
}

// Write to the file
```

```c
static int file_write(lua_State *L) {
    FileResource *fr = (FileResource*)luaL_checkudata(L, 1, "FileResource");
    const char *text = luaL_checkstring(L, 2);

    // Check if the file is closed
    if (fr->closed) {
        return luaL_error(L, "Attempt to use a closed file");
    }

    // Write to the file
    fprintf(fr->file, "%s", text);

    return 0;   // Return no values
}

// Close the file
static int file_close(lua_State *L) {
    FileResource *fr = (FileResource*)luaL_checkudata(L, 1, "FileResource");

    // Check if the file is already closed
    if (fr->closed) {
        return 0;   // Already closed
    }

    // Close the file
    fclose(fr->file);
    free(fr->filename);
    fr->file = NULL;
    fr->filename = NULL;
    fr->closed = 1;

    return 0;   // Return no values
}

// Garbage collection function
static int file_gc(lua_State *L) {
    FileResource *fr = (FileResource*)luaL_checkudata(L, 1, "FileResource");

    // Only close if not already closed
    if (!fr->closed) {
        printf("GC closing file: %s\n", fr->filename);
        fclose(fr->file);
        free(fr->filename);
        fr->file = NULL;
        fr->filename = NULL;
        fr->closed = 1;
    }
```

```c
    return 0;
}

// String representation of file resource
static int file_tostring(lua_State *L) {
    FileResource *fr = (FileResource*)luaL_checkudata(L, 1, "FileResource");

    lua_pushfstring(L, "File(%s, %s)",
                    fr->filename ? fr->filename : "nil",
                    fr->closed ? "closed" : "open");

    return 1;
}

// Register the FileResource type
int luaopen_fileresource(lua_State *L) {
    // Create metatable for FileResource userdata
    luaL_newmetatable(L, "FileResource");

    // Metatable.__index = metatable
    lua_pushvalue(L, -1);  // Duplicate metatable
    lua_setfield(L, -2, "__index");  // metatable.__index = metatable

    // Register metamethods
    lua_pushcfunction(L, file_tostring);
    lua_setfield(L, -2, "__tostring");

    lua_pushcfunction(L, file_gc);
    lua_setfield(L, -2, "__gc");

    // Register methods
    lua_pushcfunction(L, file_readline);
    lua_setfield(L, -2, "readline");

    lua_pushcfunction(L, file_write);
    lua_setfield(L, -2, "write");

    lua_pushcfunction(L, file_close);
    lua_setfield(L, -2, "close");

    // Create a library table
    luaL_newlib(L, (luaL_Reg[]){
        {"open", file_open},
        {NULL, NULL}
    });
```

```c
        return 1;
}

int main(void) {
    // Create a new Lua state
    lua_State *L = luaL_newstate();

    // Open the standard libraries
    luaL_openlibs(L);

    printf("Resource management with userdata:\n");

    // Register the FileResource type
    luaopen_fileresource(L);
    lua_setglobal(L, "File");

    // Create a test file
    FILE *f = fopen("test_file.txt", "w");
    fprintf(f, "Line 1: This is a test file.\n");
    fprintf(f, "Line 2: It contains multiple lines.\n");
    fprintf(f, "Line 3: For testing file operations.\n");
    fclose(f);

    // Test the FileResource
    printf("\nTesting FileResource:\n");

    luaL_dostring(L,
        "-- Open a file\n"
        "local f = File.open('test_file.txt', 'r')\n"
        "print('Opened file:', f)\n"
        "\n"
        "-- Read from the file\n"
        "print('Reading lines:')\n"
        "local line = f:readline()\n"
        "while line do\n"
        "    print('  ' .. line)\n"
        "    line = f:readline()\n"
        "end\n"
        "\n"
        "-- Explicitly close the file\n"
        "f:close()\n"
        "print('After closing:', f)\n"
        "\n"
        "-- Open a file for writing\n"
        "local f2 = File.open('test_file_output.txt', 'w')\n"
        "print('Opened file for writing:', f2)\n"
        "\n"
```

322

```
        "-- Write to the file\n"
        "f2:write('This line was written by Lua.\\n')\n"
        "f2:write('Another line from Lua.\\n')\n"
        "\n"
        "-- Let the garbage collector close the file\n"
        "print('Letting GC close the file')\n"
        "f2 = nil  -- Remove reference to the file\n"
        "collectgarbage()  -- Force garbage collection");

    // Clean up
    lua_close(L);

    // Display the contents of the output file
    printf("\nContents of output file:\n");
    f = fopen("test_file_output.txt", "r");
    if (f) {
        char buffer[1024];
        while (fgets(buffer, sizeof(buffer), f)) {
            printf("%s", buffer);
        }
        fclose(f);
    }

    // Remove test files
    remove("test_file.txt");
    remove("test_file_output.txt");

    return 0;
}
```

This example demonstrates proper resource management for userdata that wraps external resources like file handles.

Advanced Topics and Best Practices

Let's explore some advanced topics and best practices for integrating Lua with C.

Error Handling Across Language Boundaries

Proper error handling is crucial when calling between Lua and C:

```
#include <stdio.h>
#include <lua.h>
#include <lauxlib.h>
#include <lualib.h>
```

```c
// A C function that might raise a Lua error
static int might_error(lua_State *L) {
    int n = luaL_checkinteger(L, 1);

    if (n < 0) {
        return luaL_error(L, "Negative values not allowed");
    }

    if (n == 0) {
        // Create a detailed error with traceback
        luaL_traceback(L, L, "Division by zero", 1);
        lua_error(L);  // Raise the error
        return 0;  // Never reached
    }

    lua_pushinteger(L, 100 / n);
    return 1;
}

// A C function that safely calls Lua code
static int call_lua_safely(lua_State *L) {
    // Push the error handler
    lua_pushcfunction(L, luaL_traceback);
    int errfunc = lua_gettop(L);

    // Get the function to call
    luaL_checktype(L, 1, LUA_TFUNCTION);
    lua_pushvalue(L, 1);  // Copy the function

    // Copy the remaining arguments (if any)
    int nargs = lua_gettop(L) - 2;  // -2 for errfunc and function copy
    for (int i = 1; i <= nargs; i++) {
        lua_pushvalue(L, i + 1);
    }

    // Make the protected call
    int status = lua_pcall(L, nargs, LUA_MULTRET, errfunc);

    if (status != LUA_OK) {
        // An error occurred, error message is on top of the stack
        lua_pushboolean(L, 0);  // false (error indicator)
        lua_insert(L, -2);  // Move false before error message
        return 2;  // Return false + error message
    } else {
        // Call succeeded, all return values are on the stack
        int nresults = lua_gettop(L) - errfunc;
```

```c
            lua_pushboolean(L, 1);  // true (success indicator)
            lua_insert(L, errfunc + 1);  // Insert true before results
            lua_remove(L, errfunc);  // Remove the error handler
            return nresults + 1;  // Return true + all results
        }
    }

    int main(void) {
        // Create a new Lua state
        lua_State *L = luaL_newstate();

        // Open the standard libraries
        luaL_openlibs(L);

        printf("Error handling across language boundaries:\n");

        // Register the C functions
        lua_pushcfunction(L, might_error);
        lua_setglobal(L, "might_error");

        lua_pushcfunction(L, call_lua_safely);
        lua_setglobal(L, "call_lua_safely");

        // Test the functions
        printf("\nTesting error handling:\n");

        luaL_dostring(L,
            "-- Test might_error with valid input\n"
            "print('calling might_error(4):')\n"
            "local result = might_error(4)\n"
            "print('Result:', result)\n"
            "\n"
            "-- Test might_error with error\n"
            "print('\\ncalling might_error(-1):')\n"
            "local success, err = pcall(might_error, -1)\n"
            "print('Success:', success)\n"
            "print('Error:', err)\n"
            "\n"
            "-- Define a Lua function that might error\n"
            "local function lua_function(x)\n"
            "    if x < 0 then\n"
            "        error('Negative input: ' .. x)\n"
            "    end\n"
            "    return x * 2\n"
            "end\n"
            "\n"
            "-- Test call_lua_safely with success\n"
```

```
        "print('\\ncalling lua_function safely with valid input:')\n"
        "local success, result = call_lua_safely(lua_function, 5)\n"
        "print('Success:', success)\n"
        "print('Result:', result)\n"
        "\n"
        "-- Test call_lua_safely with error\n"
        "print('\\ncalling lua_function safely with error:')\n"
        "local success, err = call_lua_safely(lua_function, -10)\n"
        "print('Success:', success)\n"
        "print('Error:', err)");

    // Clean up
    lua_close(L);
    return 0;
}
```

This example demonstrates techniques for handling errors across the Lua/C boundary, including using the error handler parameter in `lua_pcall`.

Thread Safety and Multiple States

When using Lua in a multi-threaded environment, it's important to ensure thread safety:

```
#include <stdio.h>
#include <pthread.h>
#include <lua.h>
#include <lauxlib.h>
#include <lualib.h>

// Structure to pass data to threads
typedef struct {
    int thread_id;
    const char *script;
} ThreadData;

// Thread function
void* run_lua_script(void *arg) {
    ThreadData *data = (ThreadData*)arg;

    printf("Thread %d starting\n", data->thread_id);

    // Create a new Lua state for this thread
    lua_State *L = luaL_newstate();
    luaL_openlibs(L);
```

```c
        // Set a global with the thread ID
        lua_pushinteger(L, data->thread_id);
        lua_setglobal(L, "THREAD_ID");

        // Execute the script
        if (luaL_dostring(L, data->script)) {
            fprintf(stderr, "Thread %d error: %s\n",
                    data->thread_id, lua_tostring(L, -1));
            lua_pop(L, 1);
        }

        // Clean up
        lua_close(L);

        printf("Thread %d finished\n", data->thread_id);
        return NULL;
}

int main(void) {
    printf("Thread safety and multiple Lua states:\n");

    // Define scripts for each thread
    const char *scripts[] = {
        // Script for thread 1
        "print('Thread ' .. THREAD_ID .. ' running')\n"
        "for i = 1, 3 do\n"
        "    print('Thread ' .. THREAD_ID .. ': step ' .. i)\n"
        "    -- Simulate work\n"
        "    for j = 1, 1000000 do end\n"
        "end\n"
        "print('Thread ' .. THREAD_ID .. ' done')",

        // Script for thread 2
        "print('Thread ' .. THREAD_ID .. ' running')\n"
        "local t = {}\n"
        "for i = 1, 5 do\n"
        "    t[i] = i * THREAD_ID\n"
        "end\n"
        "print('Thread ' .. THREAD_ID .. ' result: ' .. table.concat(t, ', '))"
    };

    // Create thread data
    ThreadData thread_data[2];
    for (int i = 0; i < 2; i++) {
        thread_data[i].thread_id = i + 1;
        thread_data[i].script = scripts[i];
    }
```

```
    // Create threads
    pthread_t threads[2];
    for (int i = 0; i < 2; i++) {
        pthread_create(&threads[i], NULL, run_lua_script, &thread_data[i]);
    }

    // Wait for threads to finish
    for (int i = 0; i < 2; i++) {
        pthread_join(threads[i], NULL);
    }

    printf("\nAll threads finished\n");
    return 0;
}
```

This example demonstrates using multiple Lua states for thread safety. Each thread has its own Lua state, avoiding conflicts.

Performance Considerations

When integrating Lua with C, performance can be a concern. Here are some techniques to optimize performance:

```
#include <stdio.h>
#include <time.h>
#include <lua.h>
#include <lauxlib.h>
#include <lualib.h>

// Helper function for timing operations
double time_operation(void (*operation)(lua_State *L), lua_State *L, const char
*name) {
    clock_t start = clock();
    operation(L);
    clock_t end = clock();

    double elapsed = (double)(end - start) / CLOCKS_PER_SEC;
    printf("%-30s: %.6f seconds\n", name, elapsed);

    return elapsed;
}

// Test functions

// Repeated table access without caching values
```

```c
void test_uncached_table_access(lua_State *L) {
    luaL_dostring(L,
        "local t = {value = 42}\n"
        "local sum = 0\n"
        "for i = 1, 1000000 do\n"
        "    sum = sum + t.value\n"
        "end\n"
        "return sum");
    lua_pop(L, 1);  // Pop result
}

// Repeated table access with cached value
void test_cached_table_access(lua_State *L) {
    luaL_dostring(L,
        "local t = {value = 42}\n"
        "local sum = 0\n"
        "local value = t.value\n"
        "for i = 1, 1000000 do\n"
        "    sum = sum + value\n"
        "end\n"
        "return sum");
    lua_pop(L, 1);  // Pop result
}

// Function call overhead
void test_function_calls(lua_State *L) {
    luaL_dostring(L,
        "local function f(x) return x end\n"
        "local result\n"
        "for i = 1, 1000000 do\n"
        "    result = f(i)\n"
        "end\n"
        "return result");
    lua_pop(L, 1);  // Pop result
}

// Direct calculation without function calls
void test_direct_calculation(lua_State *L) {
    luaL_dostring(L,
        "local result\n"
        "for i = 1, 1000000 do\n"
        "    result = i\n"
        "end\n"
        "return result");
    lua_pop(L, 1);  // Pop result
}
```

```c
// String concatenation with ..
void test_string_concat_operator(lua_State *L) {
    luaL_dostring(L,
        "local s = ''\n"
        "for i = 1, 10000 do\n"
        "    s = s .. 'a'\n"
        "end\n"
        "return #s");
    lua_pop(L, 1);  // Pop result
}

// String concatenation with table.concat
void test_string_concat_table(lua_State *L) {
    luaL_dostring(L,
        "local t = {}\n"
        "for i = 1, 10000 do\n"
        "    t[i] = 'a'\n"
        "end\n"
        "local s = table.concat(t)\n"
        "return #s");
    lua_pop(L, 1);  // Pop result
}

// C implementation of a function
static int c_iterate(lua_State *L) {
    lua_Integer n = luaL_checkinteger(L, 1);
    lua_Integer sum = 0;

    for (lua_Integer i = 1; i <= n; i++) {
        sum += i;
    }

    lua_pushinteger(L, sum);
    return 1;
}

// Test Lua implementation vs C implementation
void test_lua_implementation(lua_State *L) {
    luaL_dostring(L,
        "local function sum(n)\n"
        "    local result = 0\n"
        "    for i = 1, n do\n"
        "        result = result + i\n"
        "    end\n"
        "    return result\n"
        "end\n"
        "return sum(1000000)");
```

```
        lua_pop(L, 1);  // Pop result
    }

    void test_c_implementation(lua_State *L) {
        lua_pushcfunction(L, c_iterate);
        lua_pushinteger(L, 1000000);
        lua_call(L, 1, 1);
        lua_pop(L, 1);  // Pop result
    }

    int main(void) {
        // Create a new Lua state
        lua_State *L = luaL_newstate();

        // Open the standard libraries
        luaL_openlibs(L);

        printf("Performance considerations:\n\n");

        // Register the C function
        lua_pushcfunction(L, c_iterate);
        lua_setglobal(L, "c_iterate");

        // Run the tests
        printf("Testing table access:\n");
        time_operation(test_uncached_table_access, L, "Uncached table access");
        time_operation(test_cached_table_access, L, "Cached table access");

        printf("\nTesting function call overhead:\n");
        time_operation(test_function_calls, L, "Function calls");
        time_operation(test_direct_calculation, L, "Direct calculation");

        printf("\nTesting string concatenation:\n");
        time_operation(test_string_concat_operator, L, "String concat with ..");
        time_operation(test_string_concat_table, L, "String concat with table");

        printf("\nTesting Lua vs C implementation:\n");
        time_operation(test_lua_implementation, L, "Lua implementation");
        time_operation(test_c_implementation, L, "C implementation");

        // Clean up
        lua_close(L);
        return 0;
    }
```

This example demonstrates several performance optimization techniques, including caching table values, minimizing function calls, efficient string concatenation, and implementing performance-critical functions in C.

Best Practices for Lua/C Integration

Based on the examples we've seen, here are some best practices for integrating Lua with C:

1. **Use the Lua stack carefully**: Always maintain the stack correctly, pushing and popping items as needed.

2. **Handle errors gracefully**: Use lua_pcall with an error handler to catch and handle Lua errors.

3. **Manage memory and resources**: Clean up resources properly, especially when working with userdata.

4. **Check function arguments**: Use luaL_check* functions to validate arguments and provide clear error messages.

5. **Use the registry for long-lived references**: Store Lua values that need to persist in the registry with proper reference management.

6. **Implement userdata with metatables**: For complex data types, use full userdata with metatables to provide a clean interface.

7. **Ensure thread safety**: Use separate Lua states for each thread, or implement proper locking if sharing a state.

8. **Optimize for performance**: Implement performance-critical code in C, and use techniques like caching to minimize overhead.

9. **Follow Lua idioms**: Make C functions and userdata behave like native Lua objects for a consistent API.

10. **Document your API**: Clearly document the interface between Lua and C, including function signatures, error handling, and memory management expectations.

Chapter Summary

In this chapter, we've explored the integration of Lua with C/C++, one of Lua's most powerful features. We've learned how to embed Lua in C applications, call Lua functions from C, call C functions from Lua, work with userdata to represent C structures, and manage memory and resources across the language boundary.

We've also examined advanced topics like error handling, thread safety, and performance optimization, and we've established best practices for Lua/C integration.

The ability to seamlessly integrate Lua with C allows for powerful and flexible application architectures, where performance-critical code can be implemented in C while high-level logic can be written in Lua. This integration has made Lua a popular choice for embedding in applications across various domains, from game development to embedded systems.